EcoGothic

MANCHESTER
1824

Manchester University Press

INTERNATIONAL
GOTHiC

Each volume in this series contains new essays on the many forms assumed by – as well as the most important themes and topics in – the ever-expanding range of international 'Gothic' fictions from the eighteenth to the twenty-first century. Launched by leading members of the International Gothic Association (IGA) and some editors and advisory board members of its journal, *Gothic Studies*, this Series thus offers cutting-edge analyses of the great many variations in the Gothic mode over time and all over the world, whether these have occurred in literature, film, theatre, art, several forms of cybernetic media, or other manifestations ranging from 'Goth' group identities to *avant garde* displays of aesthetic and even political critique.

The 'Gothic Story' began in earnest in 1760s England, both in fiction and drama, with Horace Walpole's efforts to combine the 'ancient' or supernatural and the 'modern' or realistic romance. This blend of anomalous tendencies has proved itself remarkably flexible in playing out the cultural conflicts of the late Enlightenment and of more recent periods. Antiquated settings with haunting ghosts or monsters and deep, dark secrets that are the mysteries behind them, albeit in many different incarnations, continue to intimate what audiences most fear in both the personal subconscious and the most pervasive tensions underlying Western culture. But this always unsettling interplay of conflicting tendencies has expanded out of its original potentials as well, especially in the hands of its greatest innovators, to appear in an astounding variety of expressive, aesthetic, and public manifestations over time. The results have transported this inherently boundary-breaking mode across geographical and cultural borders into 'Gothics' that now appear throughout the world, in the settler communities of Canada, New Zealand, and Australia; in such post-colonial areas as India and Africa; in the Americas and the Caribbean; and in East Asia and several of the islands within the entire Pacific Rim.

These volumes consequently reveal and explain the 'globalization' of the Gothic as it has proliferated across two-and-a-half centuries. The General Editors of this series and the editors of every volume, of course, bring special expertise to this expanding development, as well as the underlying dynamics, of the Gothic. Each resulting collection, plus the occasional monograph, therefore draws together important new studies about particular examples of the international Gothic – past, present, or emerging – and these contributions can come from both established scholars in the field and the newest 'rising stars' of Gothic studies. These scholars, moreover, are and must be just as international in their locations and orientations as this Series is. Interested experts from throughout the globe, in fact, are invited to propose collections and topics for this series to Manchester University Press. These will be evaluated, as appropriate, by the General Editors, members of the Editorial Advisory Board, and/or other scholars with the requisite expertise so that every published volume is professionally put together and properly refereed within the highest academic standards. Only in this way can the International Gothic series be what its creators intend: a premiere world-wide venue for examining and understanding the shape-shifting 'strangeness' of a Gothic mode that is now as multi-cultural and multi-faceted as it has ever been in its long, continuing, and profoundly haunted history.

EcoGothic

Edited by Andrew Smith and William Hughes

Manchester University Press

Published by Manchester University Press
Altrincham Street, Manchester M1 7JA, UK
www.manchesteruniversitypress.co.uk

British Library Cataloguing-in-Publication Data is available

Library of Congress Cataloging-in-Publication Data is available

ISBN 978 1 5261 0689 6 *paperback*

First published by Manchester University Press in hardback 2013

This edition first published 2016

Printed by TJ International Ltd, Padstow

Ian Coppack,
Stanley Kaufman

In memoriam

Contents

Acknowledgements

This book began with a panel on 'EcoGothic' at the International Gothic Association's 2009 conference held at the University of Lancaster. On that panel were the editors and David Punter (whose expanded paper is included here) and we would like to thank our auditors for their many helpful and insightful comments and questions which inspired us to take the project forward as an edited collection. It was also at that conference that Matthew Frost from Manchester University Press first indicated an interest in establishing a new series, 'International Gothic', consisting of edited collections, and this volume takes its place within that series. We are very grateful to Matthew for his support and to the series editors for their enthusiasm for this project.

Andrew Smith delivered a paper on research for his chapter at the American Literature Association annual conference in San Francisco in 2010 and would like to thank delegates for their constructive comments and Ben Fisher for inviting him to speak on the panel. We would like to thank our colleagues at the University of Glamorgan and Bath Spa University.

Finally, we would like to thank Joanne Benson and Gillian Wheeler for their love, tolerance and support throughout the editing of this project.

Notes on contributors

Alanna F. Bondar is Associate Professor of English and Creative Writing at Algoma University in Sault Ste Marie, Ontario. She has published articles in *Studies in Canadian Literature, Canadian Poetry* and *Teaching North American Environmental Literature* (MLA). Her prose-poetry manuscript, *There are many ways to die while travelling in Peru*, was launched in 2012 by Your Scrivener Press. While she has strong interests in ecological Canadian literature, she also explores contemporary Gothic, magical realism and minority voice writing.

Emily Carr has published two books of poetry: *Directions For Flying* (Furniture Press, 2010) and *13 ways of happily: books 1 & 2* (Parlor Press, 2010). Excerpts from her Tarot novel, *Name Your Bird Without A Gun*, are widely available online and in print. Some strands of her work in ecofeminist literacy forage into happiness, identity and ecology. She teaches at the University of California, Santa Cruz.

Kevin Corstorphine is Lecturer in English at the University of Hull. His most recent publication was a chapter on the short stories of Robert Bloch in *It Came from the 1950s: Popular Culture, Popular Anxieties* (2011). He has also published articles on H. P. Lovecraft, Stephen King and John Ajvide Lindqvist. He is currently working on a monograph on space and fear in American horror fiction.

Sharae Deckard is a Lecturer in World Literature at University College Dublin. Her monograph, *Paradise Discourse, Imperialism and*

Globalization: Exploiting Eden, appeared with Routledge in 2010. She is the editor of a special issue of *Green Letters* (16) on 'Global and Postcolonial Ecologies', and co-editor of an issue of the *Journal of Postcolonial Literature* on 'Spectres of World Literature' (December 2012). She has published articles on Sri Lankan eco-literature (*Postcolonial Green*), Roberto Bolano and millennial capitalism, and has multiple articles forthcoming on environmental literature. Her current book project is provisionally titled *Fictions of the World-Ecology: Neoliberalism, Crisis and the Novel.*

Shoshannah Ganz is an Assistant Professor of English at Grenfell Campus, Memorial University, Newfoundland and Labrador, Canada. Her areas of particular interest are in Canadian literature, religious influence on Canadian writing, travel writing and women's writing. Shoshannah has published on a number of Canadian authors and co-edited *The Ivory Thought: Essays on Al Purdy* with the University of Ottawa Press in 2008. Her monograph on Canadian Literary Pilgrimage is under peer review with Wilfred Laurier University Press. Shoshannah's current book project examines the influence of Eastern thought on Canadian women travellers writing about South East Asia from 1850 to 1940.

Tom J. Hillard is an Assistant Professor of English at Boise State University, where he teaches courses on early American literature, literature and the environment and the literary Gothic. His recent scholarly research focuses on intersections between Gothic literature and early American nature writing. He is Book Review Editor for the journal *ISLE: Interdisciplinary Studies in Literature and Environment.*

William Hughes is Professor of Gothic Studies at Bath Spa University, and the editor of *Gothic Studies,* the refereed journal of the International Gothic Association. The author, editor and co-editor of 15 books to date, his most recent publications include *Victorian Gothic: An Edinburgh Companion* (2012), edited with Andrew Smith, and *The Encyclopedia of the Gothic* (2013), edited with Andrew Smith and David Punter. He lives on the pagan processional axis that connects the sacred sites of Avebury, Stonehenge and Glastonbury.

Lisa Kröger teaches academic writing to graduate students at Mississippi State University. Her research interests include everything from Ann Radcliffe to Shirley Jackson. She has worked with Udolpho Press, annotating a new edition of Mary Charlton's *Phedora; or, The Forest of Minksi*. Her current project is an essay collection called *Spectral Identities*, exploring social ghosting in literature and film.

Catherine Lanone is a Professor of English Literature at the University of Paris 3. She has written a book on E. M. Forster, *E. M. Forster: Odyssée d'une écriture* (1998) and a book on Emily Brontë, *Emily Brontë, 'Wuthering Heights': Un vent de sorcière* (1999) and has published papers on Victorian literature and modernism (Woolf and Forster). She is currently working on representations of the Arctic.

David Punter is Professor of English at the University of Bristol. He is the author of many books, including *The Literature of Terror: A History of Gothic Fictions from 1765 to the Present Day* (1980, revised 1996); his most recent publications include *Metaphor, Modernity* (2007) and *Rapture: Literature, Addiction, Secrecy* (2009). He is currently working on a new monograph under the title *The Literature of Pity*.

Andrew Smith is Reader in Nineteenth-Century English Literature at the University of Sheffield. Published books include *The Ghost Story 1840–1920: A Cultural History* (2010) *Gothic Literature* (2007; revised second edition 2013), *Victorian Demons* (2004) and *Gothic Radicalism* (2000). He is currently researching a monograph on *Gothic Death 1740–1920*. He is co-president of the International Gothic Association with William Hughes.

Susan J. Tyburski is a recovering lawyer who teaches law and literature courses at the University of Denver. Her publications include 'The History of Crime and Punishment in America: 2001 to 2012', in *The Social History of Crime & Punishment in America* (forthcoming from Sage Publications) and '"The Lingering Scent of Divinity" in Cormac McCarthy's *The Sunset Limited* and *The Road*', in *The Cormac McCarthy Society Journal*. She is currently working on a series of articles exploring Cormac McCarthy's jurisprudential vision.

Andrew Smith and William Hughes

Introduction: defining the ecoGothic

This volume is the first to explore the Gothic through theories of eco-criticism; its appearance might seem timely given current concerns about climate change which have helped shape an ecological aware-ness, but in fact the belated presence of this volume should be sur-prising when we consider the history of criticism on the Romantic Gothic. That the ecological has been hitherto overlooked in accounts of the Romantic Gothic is strange given the critical synergies that exist between accounts of Romanticism and the Gothic that go back to Mario Praz's *The Romantic Agony* (1933). This is not to suggest that the Gothic exists only as an offshoot of Romanticism, but to acknowledge that shared critical languages exist between the two. To that degree Jonathan Bate's seminal *Romantic Ecology: Wordsworth and the Environmental Tradition* (1991) seems an odd omission from Gothic consideration and one which this Introduction will address by briefly sketching a point of origin for an ecologically aware Gothic that has its roots within the Romantic, and not just within recent environmental concerns.

Bate argues that a 'green reading of Wordsworth' moves the critic into a Romantic vision because:

> if one historicizes the idea of an ecological viewpoint – a respect for the earth and a scepticism as to the orthodoxy that economic growth and material production are the be-all and end-all of human society – one finds oneself squarely in the Romantic tradition.[1]

This, however, raises the question of whether the Gothic vision is a more troubling one. In part this is because of that key Gothic term:

ambivalence. The type of questioning posed by the Gothic has traditionally raised concerns about its political orientations. How the
Gothic's representation of 'evil' can be used for radical or reaction-
ary ends becomes an important consideration within this context.
Certainly it poses a different order of problem than that encountered
by Bate, who argues that Wordsworth's pastoral extols a life free from
the dictates of capitalism which means (*pace* Coleridge) that 'pastoral
life begets republicanism', due to its comparative political and economic freedoms.[2] The problem with the Gothic is that, at one level,
'nature' is a more contested term as it is one which (at least in its
post-Radcliffean guise) appears to participate in a language of estrange-
ment rather than belonging. For Bate, it is Ruskin (the inheritor of
Wordsworth's model of nature) who identifies this problem of alienation as one which reflects the fragmented subject who is forced to work
within the divided labour system of industrial capitalism. In his chapter
'The Nature of Gothic' from *The Stones of Venice* (1851–53), Ruskin
argues that 'It is not, truly speaking, the labour that is divided, but the
men: – Divided into segments of men – broken into small fragments
and crumbs of life.'[3] This contrasts with the more holistic approach to
nature taken by the Romantics. However, it is the image of fragments
which seems to persist in the Gothic and it meets its clearest expression
in Victor Frankenstein's horror at his first sight of the patchwork creation that is his creature:

> His limbs were in proportion, and I had selected his features as beautiful.
> Beautiful! – Great God! His yellow skin scarcely covered the work of muscles
> and arteries beneath; his hair was of a lustrous black, and flowing; his teeth of a
> pearly whiteness; but these luxuriances only formed a more horrid contrast with
> his watery eyes, that seemed almost of the same colour as the dun white sockets
> in which they were set, his shrivelled complexion and straight black lips.[4]

This disjunction between the utopian idealism of the project and its
dystopian aftermath is intended as a critique of a Romantic idealism
which asserts that nature can be apprehended as natural rather than
cultural. The creature's function is to challenge what is meant by nature
and to erode Victor's sense that nature represents a transcendent category of experience. To that degree *Frankenstein* (1818; revised 1831)
can be read as the dark shadow that critiques a Wordsworthian model
of nature. This is also manifested in how the novel ends (and indeed
begins), in the ecological dead zone of the polar ice cap. Nature fails
to signify as anything other than a type of blankness which also demonstrates a crisis of representation. This means that the environment

is established as a semiotic problem, one which is addressed in this volume by Catherine Lanone in a chapter centring on Arctic voyages that have been shaped by Shelley's novel.

Bate addresses the issue of naming as one which is rooted in the Bible and in *Paradise Lost* (1667). Bate sees Wordsworth's 'Poems on the Naming of Places' (1800) as a reworking of Adam's responsibility to name the animals in Milton's version of the biblical injunction in *Paradise Lost*. This gives Adam control over nature, but also symbolically represents Wordsworth's poetic mastery over nature. This means that for Bate, while images of rustic life might constitute 'idealizations' in Wordsworth, they are 'worth making in order to bring writer and reader back to nature'.[5] Writing thus serves to make present a meaningful sense of the ecological by inserting both reader and writer into a realm in which meaning can be generated in an unmediated way. This leads Bate to argue that the sequence of poems in the *Lyrical Ballads* (1798) begins with Schiller's conception of the Sentimental (in which the poet is self-conscious about their reflections) and progressively embraces the Naive (in which one confronts experience in a seemingly unmediated fashion).[6] *Lyrical Ballads* thus represents an attempt to get back to nature and this is a journey which is, as this volume testifies, more problematically constructed in the Gothic. Victor Frankenstein's creature, an auditor of *Paradise Lost*, repeatedly refers to himself as a potential Adam (as a type of first man – one who sees Victor as his God), but his language is second-hand and he has no authority to name and so claim ownership over nature. Instead he is unable to discriminate between fact and fiction and he is excluded from the utopian vision of the De Lacey family and their warm cottage-life and propelled towards the dystopian cold blankness of the polar ice cap. *Frankenstein* thus reverses the tendency of the *Lyrical Ballads* as it heads towards death, alienation and emptiness. The Romantic Gothic, in other words, does the ecological in a different way to the Romantics, but its presumptive dystopianism (certainly in Mary Shelley's case) illustrates how nature becomes constituted in the Gothic as a space of crisis which conceptually creates a point of contact with the ecological. As in the creature's problem in *Frankenstein*, the key issue is how to find a language which 'owns' the ecological and so anchor it as a site of coherent meaning.

This very brief sketch of how *Frankenstein* can be read as repositioning the ecological beyond a Wordsworthian tradition is intended to give a flavour of how the Gothic approaches environmental factors.

This issue of meaning touched on above is central to the Gothic (at least in its more radical guises) as it variously questions, compromises and challenges the way in which the world has been understood. The Romantic context sketched here is one addressed in the opening chapter of this book by Lisa Kröger. However, debates about the environment are also nationally inflected and Bate acknowledges an alternative North American strand of ecological writing that was inaugurated by Thoreau's *Walden* (1854). The role of the wilderness and the frontier is a recurring motif in American fiction. Melville's *Moby-Dick* (1851) provides an interesting counterpoint to *Frankenstein*; it, too, is a voyage narrative and centres on a monomaniacal attempt to tame nature. The whiteness of the whale constitutes a blankness which cannot be read by 'unlettered Ishmael', and which echoes the whiteness of the polar cap.[7] In some ways this appears to be a gloss on Poe's *The Narrative of Arthur Gordon Pym of Nantucket* (1838) which concludes on a mysterious white figure that brings the voyage to an end, where Pym notes 'there arose in our pathway a shrouded human figure, very far larger in its proportions than any dweller among men. And the hue of the skin of the figure was of the perfect whiteness of the snow.'[8] However, these images are surrounded by an aura of menace, whereas in *Frankenstein* there is a contrary feeling of fatigued, and so failed, revenge.[9] The landscape in the North American context seems to invite mastery through images of the frontier and this dynamic is explored in a number of essays in this volume which address changing representations of the wilderness in American and Canadian Gothic writings and films. Such issues have been shaped by ecocriticism and this volume explores how current ideas about ecocriticism can be applied to Gothic narratives in order to help draw out their often dystopian ecological visions. Ecocriticism also acknowledges a number of theoretical paradigms that help to critically reinvigorate debate about the class, gender and national identities that inhere within representations of the landscape. To that end this volume also makes explicit these links in a chapter by Emily Carr which explores how ecocritical issues can be aligned with feminist praxis, illuminated by an analysis of Gothic texts by Joy Williams.

There are national variations in what might be termed the ecological. The British Romantic Gothic can be contrasted to a post-Thoreauvian North American tradition, for example. However, Sharae Deckard, in an innovative concluding essay on Rana Dasgupta, explores how far it might be possible to establish a global geopolitical context for an ecocritical engagement with the Gothic and images of the ecological. This volume thus begins a debate on how we might examine the cultural and national diversity of the environment through a number of critical prisms that are linked to the ecocritical.

Debates about climate change and environmental damage have been key issues on most industrialized countries' political agendas for some time. These issues have helped shape the direction and application of ecocritical languages. The Gothic seems to be the form which is well placed to capture these anxieties and provides a culturally significant point of contact between literary criticism, ecocritical theory and political process. While the origins of this ecoGothic can be traced back to Romanticism the growth in environmental awareness has become a significant development. The political urgency of ecological issues is often self-consciously elaborated in many of the contemporary novels and films which are discussed here.

The structure of the volume broadly follows national trends, beginning with a British tradition, moving through a Canadian context, and then through a specifically American model of the ecoGothic, before concluding with Deckard's discussion of a possible global context which could overcome national variations.

Lisa Kröger, in 'Panic, paranoia and pathos: ecocriticism in the eighteenth-century Gothic novel', argues that an overview of Gothic criticism would seem to suggest that the castle and the convent are the only spaces which the Gothic inhabits because critics often overlook the third space: the forest. Kröger's examination of these forested spaces reveals that the early Gothic novel foreshadows an ecologically aware society, one in which the heroines are often depicted as sympathetic to their surroundings. One example is Ann Radcliffe's *The Mysteries of Udolpho* (1794). Emily St Aubert is connected to nature – so much so that she is ignorant of any other way of life. Emily's experience of nature is feral, almost primitive, as she gleans both solace and inspiration from the natural world. The forest is not, however, an entirely idyllic space. The benevolent nature of the pastoral lands eventually gives way to a darker, more sublime environment. During his visit to the St Auberts, Monsieur Quesnel indicates that he wants to chop down the chestnut trees, an idea that horrifies Emily and her father. In most of these novels, the desecration of the natural world is met with psychological trauma and can usually be traced to an oppressive ruling power (a structure which mirrors modern conceptions of a feminized nature attacked by a patriarchy – technology, industry or even society itself). As the attack on nature progresses in these novels, the environments become more frightening. Using the works of Ann Radcliffe, Matthew Lewis and the Marquis de Sade, Kröger's chapter explores the dual nature of the Gothic environment and how it foreshadows modern ecocriticism, particularly an awareness of wilderness preservation and the fear of an impending environmental catastrophe.

In 'Monsters on the ice and global warming: from Mary Shelley and Sir John Franklin to Margaret Atwood and Dan Simmons', Catherine Lanone argues that, from chilling Victorian panoramas to films such as *Frankenstein* or *The Thing* (1951) the Arctic looms large as a blank screen on which fantasies of Gothic entrapment may be projected. At a time when global warming turns the sheltering ice and starving bears into the victims of hubris rather than the monsters of yore, Lanone considers the evolving versions of ice monsters, beginning with Mary Shelley's paradigmatic hideous creature, drawing Victor farther and farther north and emblematizing Shelley's uneasiness about colonial conquest. Lanone argues that the fate of the 1845 Franklin expedition located the monster within the self, as the myth of British technological progress was inverted into a tale of disaster complete with rumours of cannibalism among the crew. The Franklin story haunts the twentieth century, from Margaret Atwood's 1991 short story 'The Age of Lead' (in which Franklin's spectacular disaster portrayed on TV becomes a metaphor for waste, pollution and the mysterious diseases both trigger) to Dan Simmons's loose, baggy monster of a novel, *The Terror* (2007). Rewriting the 1845 Franklin expedition, *The Terror* gives a Gothic twist to the tale, adding to the frozen ships a gigantic mysterious white Thing that plagues the crew, cunningly maiming, killing and wreaking havoc. Lanone thus explores how Gothic motifs are transposed and used to raise complex, urgent environmental issues, addressing global warming through the metaphor of the lost expedition.

David Punter, in 'Algernon Blackwood: nature and spirit', explores selected tales of Algernon Blackwood (1869–1951), who was regarded in his time as one of the great masters of the supernatural short story. The particular stories under discussion are 'The Man whom the Trees Loved' (1912), 'The Willows' (1907) and 'The Lost Valley' (1910). Punter's principal concern is to show some of the ways in which Blackwood blurs the distinctions between the human world and a wider natural and spiritual ecology. In his stories human beings are constantly shown as being at the mercy of larger forces of nature, such that, for example, Bittacy, the forest-ranger protagonist of 'The Man whom the Trees Loved', eventually becomes 'one with the trees', being subsumed into a different life which is only barely comprehensible to the fellow humans whom he has left behind. In the course of the discussion, Punter examines the relations between nature and spirit in relation to similar concerns found in Hegel, principally in *The Phenomenology of Mind* (1807) and *Lectures on the Philosophy of Religion* (1821–31). Punter draws attention to the possibilities which might be contained within this fiction of 'writing like the forest', or 'writing as the forest'. These are an extension – before the fact – of the considerations offered by Deleuze and Guattari in their conceptualization of 'becoming': 'becoming-animal' or 'becoming-woman', for example, which are relevant to Blackwood's version of 'becoming-forest', which he underpins with an eclectic mix of theology, philosophy and mythopoeia.[10] Punter argues that, while it would be obviously terminologically incorrect to think of Blackwood directly in 'ecological' terms, the kinds of consciousness he is attempting to describe are eminently suited to responding to an ecological criticism, which enables the stories to yield a new life that places the concept of the 'supernatural' itself in a different light.

William Hughes, in '"A strange kind of evil": superficial paganism and false ecology in *The Wicker Man*', argues that *The Wicker Man* (1973) has not yet attracted a significant body of criticism from a specifically Gothic perspective. This is surprising, given the film's extensive depiction of pagan spirituality, rampant sexuality and blood sacrifice. These, though, are intimate to a plot explicitly related to both a looming environmental crisis and a consequent economic collapse. Bearing these latter in mind, it is equally surprising that *The Wicker Man* has been overlooked by ecocriticism. Hughes considers how the man-made ecology which supports the island community of *The Wicker Man* interfaces with a meticulously detailed – and equally artificial – neo-pagan earth religion. Far from being a utopian alternative to the spiritually orthodox and rule-bound world represented by Police Sergeant Howie, Lord Summerisle's ostensibly feudal domain retains at its heart a capitalist ruthlessness ironically more akin to the secular mainland from which the Christian policeman travels. The violence that concludes the film represents a clash of cultures – secular and spiritual, modern and feudal, metropolitan and provincial – although the boundaries between these, as Howie discovers, are by no means clear or even consistent. Hughes demonstrates how the Gothic script of *The Wicker Man* embraces the classic preoccupations of the Gothic while rescheduling them in a manner wholly appropriate to the troubled years that succeeded the idealism of the 1960s. *The Wicker Man* is a film that anticipates many aspects of current ecocritical and green concern – and it embodies, equally, a chilling reminder that idealistic alternatives may carry, occluded within them, traces of the repressive orthodoxies that they claim to resist.

In 'Bodies on earth: exploring sites of the Canadian ecoGothic', Alanna F. Bondar examines a Canadian post-pastoral or ecological literature which is currently emerging through and in response to the ecofeminist movement of the 1980s and 1990s, which suggests ways in which the human–nature paradigm might be redirected through positive identifications with the body in nature and the natural body. Through the contemporary and cultural lens of postmodern pastiche which includes elements of Gothic and magical realism, literary texts respond to a Canadian cultural fear of nature and a 'garrison mentality' as a means of exploring ecological shifts in spiritual and intellectual consciousness. Authors such as Camilla Gibb (*Sweetness in the Belly*, 2006), Michael Ondaatje (*Anil's Ghost*, 2000), Nancy Huston (*Instruments of Darkness*, 1997) and Lola Lemire Tostevin (*Frog Moon*, 1994) embrace ideologies in their writings that seek resolution of the geopsyche (as defined by Gregory Cajete and explored by American ecocritic Patrick Murphy); this 'geopsyche' is that which moves past the 'us *versus* them' or 'human *versus* wilderness' paradigm into a more encompassing 'anotherness' which reconsiders binary oppositions that remain contained and conditioned within gender differences, the individual body, community and culture.[11] These authors explore how the body as site of Gothic fear – sexual, injured, dismembered and celebrated – can be seen and positively re-membered in a literary landscape. This chapter explores this process of 'informed recentring' of ecological literature and examines and recognizes the articulate responsibility of the biotic community.

Shoshannah Ganz, in 'Margaret Atwood's monsters in the Canadian ecoGothic', argues that Margaret Atwood has created a sub-genre of Gothic and Canadian fiction known as Southern Ontario Gothic. The Atwood *oeuvre* of Gothic works includes most famously *The Handmaid's Tale* (1986), *Surfacing* (1972) and *Lady Oracle* (1976). To these can be added *Oryx and Crake* (2003) and *The Year of the Flood* (2009). Ever a timely writer, Atwood's most recent fiction explores what she terms in the final pages of *Oryx and Crake* the 'end game' for the human race. Ganz explores the possibility of Gothic literature serving as a form to critique environmental destruction and advocate restoration.

The chapter explores in particular the monsters in the texts – Jimmy/ Snowman, the monstrous human survivor who cares for the Crakers; the humanoid Crakers, manufactured by the real Frankenstein of the text, Crake, who deliberately and sadistically attempts to destroy all human life forms (except one); the various monstrous manufactured and mutated creatures that prey on the surviving humans; and the sexual predators, among others. Atwood plays with all the stock characteristics of the Gothic genre, but with an eye to a world ravaged by climate change – empty warehouses become the decrepit mansions of survivors hiding from manufactured animals and crazed monsters; incestuous love triangles play across and between the two books, and between monsters and humans. Atwood clearly uses the markers of the Gothic genre to advocate environmental awareness and change before the crazed monsters at the centre of the text destroy all life forms. Ganz also argues that *Oryx and Crake* and *The Year of the Flood* help to demarcate the characteristics of the ecoGothic, and she demonstrates how other Canadian environmental works, and the monsters therein, can be usefully explored as part of the emergent Canadian ecoGothic genre.

Tom J. Hillard, in 'From Salem witch to *Blair Witch*: the Puritan influence on American Gothic nature', examines the seventeenth-century New England Puritan influence on later Gothic representations of the natural world in North America. Hillard argues that a 'pre-Gothic' symbolic structure can be found in experiences with 'wilderness' described by New England Puritan settlers throughout the 1600s. This Gothic symbolism, while at first rooted deeply in Puritan theology, has changed and evolved over the centuries, but its basic characteristics can still be located in nearly all Gothicized representations of nature. Hillard examines texts by several Puritan writers – including William Bradford and Cotton Mather – in order to reveal their typological reading of the natural world (and 'wilderness' in particular) as a fallen one, made so when Adam and Eve were expelled from Eden. For many of the New England saints, entering the wilderness of Massachusetts was tantamount to confronting the nightmarish landscape of Original Sin. Images of a desolate wilderness function as a precursor to the dark dungeon or haunted castle of later Gothic fictions – a fearful space inhabited by threatening characters (or creatures) and marked by deep-seated secrets or past transgressions that threaten the status quo. This concept of nature as haunted house (to borrow a phrase from Emily Dickinson) has persisted in American culture, and Hillard frames the chapter with an analysis of the 1999 film *The Blair Witch Project*, looking specifically at its (anti-)environmental subtexts. There has been recent ecocritical interest in 'ecophobia', and Hillard argues that *The Blair Witch Project* stands as just one manifestation of a widespread contemporary cultural anxiety about nature.

In '"The blank darkness outside": Ambrose Bierce and wilderness Gothic at the end of the frontier', Kevin Corstorphine provides an overview of recent studies on the American Gothic which have drawn attention to the notion of the wilderness as an ideological lens through which early settlers viewed the strange and vast landscape they found themselves in. This chapter examines the importance of the wilderness in the American social and political imagination, focusing on the late nineteenth-century end of the frontier as described by Frederick Jackson Turner in his 1893 lecture.[12] It identifies an ambivalent relationship with the environment and situates this in the context of the legacy of Puritanism as well as Emersonian transcendentalism. The first part of the chapter discusses the development of these ideas in relation to authors such as Charles Brockden Brown, Robert Montgomery Bird and Nathaniel Hawthorne, and offers an overview of critical perspectives, arguing that the Gothic tradition in the United States is predicated on a flawed appeal to a utopian origin myth. The second part is a close examination of Ambrose Bierce's short stories 'The Damned Thing' (1893), 'The Eyes of the Panther' (1897) and 'The Boarded Window' (1891), all contemporary with the twilight of the frontier period. They are examined in their historical context which includes the development of photography, the sentimentalization of the Native American and the mass extermination of the buffalo. Corstorphine also reads them in the light of recent developments in ecocriticism and examines to what extent these theories and Bierce's writing can comment on each other and make sense of the contentious relationship between human and nature that is expressed in each. He argues that the concept of nature gains importance only through human perspective, and that a critical examination of the representation of nature in fiction is crucial to an understanding of our relationship with it.

In 'Locating the self in the post-apocalypse: the American Gothic journeys of Jack Kerouac, Cormac McCarthy and Jim Crace', Andrew Smith takes as his starting point a moment from Jack Kerouac's *On the Road* (1957) when the narrator recalls an incident when he awoke in a motel room and conceived of himself as a ghost. The scene suggests that this was not because he had forgotten where he was but because he had forgotten *who* he was. This troubling moment of self-assessment is later reflected in characters that similarly see themselves as ghosts during their pursuit of post-war pleasures revolving around music, drink, sex and the freedom of physical movement that America could ostensibly provide. The book's superficial suggestion that the way out is also the way in (an inner life and its desires now met) is compromised in these moments which suggest that in reality they involve the *loss* of self. The journey across America underpins this sense of loss as America appears as a Gothic space of potential danger. How to maintain a sense of self in explicitly post-apocalyptic terrains is the subject matter of later, more obviously Gothic texts such as Cormac McCarthy's *The Road* (2006) and Jim Crace's *The Pesthouse* (2007). Like *On the Road* they too are focused on how to maintain the self when the environment which produced that self no longer exists. McCarthy's and Crace's texts thus directly explore how environmental issues underpin models of subjectivity which have their roots in Kerouac's model of being on the road, as a journey about an eroded sense of self. How these ideas relate to a Gothic ecology and theories of ecocriticism and notions of the home are the principal issues addressed in this chapter.

  Susan J. Tyburski, in 'A Gothic apocalypse: encountering the monstrous in American cinema', discusses a growing number of apocalyptic films from the United States, such as Larry Fessenden's *The Last Winter* (2007), M. Night Shyamalan's *The Happening* (2008), Roland Emmerich's *2012* (2009) and John Hillcoat's *The Road* (2009), which depict humans encountering monstrous versions of nature. Nature becomes an avenging force – or, even more monstrous, an alien entity utterly indifferent to the fate of humanity. Just as our modern societies have appeared to disavow any necessary connection to nature, the natural world seems to reject humanity as expendable. Humans are cast adrift in an alien, hostile environment, encountering monsters unleashed by the destructive force of a consumerist, solipsistic society. Tyburski argues that these recent films reflect a growing trend in 'eco-horror' cinema which taps into this growing current of eco-anxiety, creating monstrous visions mirroring our fears about the fate of our civilization and the planet we call home. The various depictions of the monstrous in these films, and the way such monstrosity is encountered by the characters, determine whether or not these cinematic narratives qualify as 'Gothic'. Tyburski explores the following questions: How have traditional Gothic tropes been transformed to explore modern crises and fears in recent apocalyptic films? And what can we learn about the Gothic, and about our relationship with the natural world by exploring these modern apocalyptic narratives?

In 'The riddle was the angel in the house: towards an American ecofeminist Gothic', Emily Carr argues that, from its origins, women's Gothic fiction has undermined fictions of the human and the nonhuman, the natural and the unnatural by creating worlds in which the everyday is collapsed with the nightmarish. Distortion, dislocation and disruption become the norm, and the domestic and the grotesque, the alluring and the terrible coexist. Because of its obsession with the role of place in subject formation and in the destabilization of the 'home' as a foundation of myths of domesticity, the Gothic is a particularly appropriate genre in which to explore new possibilities for ecofeminism. The very useful intersections of the genre of the Gothic and the theory of the ecofeminist teach strategies for dislocating our anthropocentric assumptions about, for example, who speaks and for whom; what it means to suffer; the logical fallacies and cultural blind spots that lead to the supremacy of the 'sentient'; the linguistic sleight of hand that turns bodies into commodities; and the deep-rooted (however we might try to deny it) assumption that our obligations to our home, the earth, and the creatures that inhabit it are economic rather than ecological. Carr explores five strands of the contemporary ecofeminist Gothic: beauty (as agency) versus the beautiful (as thing), desire (how it looks) versus love (what it means), the problem of becoming a person you did not intend to become, the myth of marriage, and the links between questions of autonomy and of living well. Through a close reading of Joy Williams's *The Changeling* (1978), Carr carves out a distinctly American space for the ecofeminist Gothic that is maverick, alarming, animalized, sexualized, without mediation or exception, with a propensity for exaggeration, for the fabulous, for the colloquial, for the melancholy, the obscene, the forbidden and the unspeakable. It is in this space, Carr argues, that we can begin again – ethically and ecoethically – to celebrate the often terrifying consequences of re-articulating what should have gone unsaid, the mysterious and sometimes sinister underbelly behind the clean white porch of normal American life.

Sharae Deckard, in '"Uncanny states": global ecoGothic and the world-ecology in Rana Dasgupta's *Tokyo Cancelled*', argues that the world-system is a thoroughly differentiated physical environment divided between zones of production, in which peripheral environments suffer heightened resource extraction and environmental degradation in an age of accelerating climate crisis. This means that developing a methodology attentive to the systemic nature of combined and uneven development across the world-ecology is an urgent task for environmental literary studies. Adapting Fredric Jameson's theory of the political unconscious, film critic Adrian Ivakhiv has called for a 'global-meteorological reading practice' of the 'geopolitical unconscious' in order to reverse 'ecological unconscionization', the ideological mystification of ecological destruction.[13] Ivakhiv argues that the Cartesian project has 'repressed the entire network of biological interdependencies and corporeal confraternities that shape and structure our material existence'.[14] Environmental historian Jason Moore has developed a world-systems-inflected theory of the capitalist world-ecology as comprised of ecological regimes and revolutions, in which financialization has produced new forms of social–nature relations.[15] Deckard draws on Moore and Ivakhiv to elaborate a praxis for reading the capitalist world-ecology in Gothic literature, exploring how literary form can embed the social–ecological contradictions of capitalism. Deckard offers a case study of 'global ecoGothic', reading the viral excrescences and monstrous transformations of human bodies into vegetable matter in Rana Dasgupta's *Tokyo Cancelled* (2005) as Gothic apparitions that register the world-ecology, particularly the ecological regimes corresponding to neoliberalism and financialization. In British-Asian Dasgupta's thirteen-story cycle, the process of ecological unconscionization is deliberately reversed through stagings of uncanny states that dramatize the traumatic impact of abstract economic systems on local ecologies and subjects in multiple world cities from Delhi, to Paris, to Istanbul.

All of the chapters in this book have been specially commissioned for it. They represent a new way of thinking about the Gothic because they indicate the way in which it engages with a major pressing political issue that confronts the world today. We hope that it provides a starting point for future discussion on these points of contact.

Notes

1 Jonathan Bate, *Romantic Ecology: Wordsworth and the Environment Tradition* (London: Routledge, 1991), p. 9.
2 Bate, *Romantic Ecology*, p. 25.
3 John Ruskin, 'The Nature of Gothic', in *The Stones of Venice*, Vol. I, xvi in *The Complete Works of John Ruskin*, ed. E. T. Cook and Alexander Wedderburn (London: Library Edition, 1903–12), cited in Bate, *Romantic Ecology*, p. 58.

4 Mary Shelley, *Frankenstein: The 1818 Text*, ed. Marilyn Butler (Oxford: Oxford University Press, 1993), p. 39.
5 Bate, *Romantic Ecology*, p. 105.
6 Friedrich Schiller, *On the Sublime & Naïve and Sentimental Poetry*, trans. J. A. Elias (New York: Ungar, 1975).
7 Herman Melville, *Moby-Dick* (London: Collector's Library, 2004), p. 474.
8 Edgar Allan Poe, *The Narrative of Arthur Gordon Pym of Nantucket* in *The Complete Tales and Poems of Edgar Allan Poe* (Harmondsworth: Penguin, 1982), pp. 748–883, at p. 882.
9 Ahab's descent into 'madness' also represents a failed act of revenge, but the novel as a whole is also about how other characters feel about the nature of the quest and so is arguably more interrogative about such matters than *Frankenstein*.
10 See Gilles Deleuze and Félix Guattari, *A Thousand Plateaus: Capitalism and Schizophrenia*, trans. Brian Massumi (Minneapolis: University of Minnesota Press, 1987).
11 Patrick D. Murphy, *Literature, Nature and Other: Ecofeminist Critiques* (New York: State University of New York Press, 1995), pp. 4–5.
12 Frederick Jackson Turner, *The Frontier in American History* (New York: Henry Holt, 1947).
13 Adrian Ivakhiv, 'Stirring the Geopolitical Unconscious', *New Formations: Earthographies: Ecocriticism and Culture* 64 (2008): 98–109.
14 Ivakhiv, 'Stirring the Geopolitical Unconscious', p. 107.
15 See Jason Moore, 'Wall Street is a Way of Organizing Nature', *Upping the Anti: A Journal of Theory and Action* 12 (2011): 39–53, and his 'The End of the Road? Agricultural Revolutions in the Capitalist World-Ecology, 1450–2010', *Journal of Agrarian Change* 10/3 (2010): 389–413.

2

Lisa Kröger

Panic, paranoia and pathos: ecocriticism in the eighteenth-century Gothic novel

Ecology began as a scientific study some time around the 1860s, when German zoologist Ernst Haeckel coined the term *oecology* in response to the theories of Charles Darwin. The science of ecology as we know it today began with a group of American botanists in the 1890s.[1] Literature, though, indicates that the roots of ecology were taking hold even earlier, reaching back into the eighteenth century, perhaps even beyond. Jonathan Bate cites Oliver Goldsmith's *Deserted Village* (1770) as an example. In Bate's *The Song of the Earth* (2000), he sees a clear link between Goldsmith's theme – one of 'blaming modern consumerism for the desolation of the land'[2] – and what contemporary ecologists are fighting against today. Bate suggests that what appears to be a problem unique to today's world is merely, for lack of a better word, recycled from a few hundred years ago, years filled with both industrial progress and the inevitable destruction of the land that follows.

Bate's studies have focused primarily on the Romantics, particularly the poetics of Wordsworth and Blake, though he does include such writers as Jane Austen and Thomas Hardy in his theory of literary ecology. Bate in *Romantic Ecology* (1991) developed a new way to read those Romantic writers, whose prose and poetry he regards as a natural way of defining ecology:

> The 'Romantic ecology' reverences the green earth because it recognizes that neither physically nor psychologically can we live without green things; it proclaims that there is 'one life' within us and abroad, that the earth is a single vast ecosystem which we destabilize at our peril. In sharp contrast to the so-called

'Romantic Ideology', the Romantic ecology has nothing to do with flight from the material world, from society – it is in fact an attempt to enable mankind the better to live in the material world by entering into harmony with the environment.[3]

This same model of thought could be applied to the Gothic novel, particularly that of the latter half of the eighteenth century. While much is made about the Gothic edifices, such as the ancient estate or the crumbling castle, the environment, most often seen in the Gothic forest, plays just as integral a role in these novels. These outdoor spaces help to create a Gothic ecology, to borrow from Bate's thesis, which demonstrates a convergence of the human world and the natural world. Beginning with Horace Walpole's seminal novel of the genre, *The Castle of Otranto* (1764), the framework for a Gothic ecology emerges. Despite the title, the action of *The Castle of Otranto* is not restricted only to the castle walls. Walpole spreads his novel over three main settings: the castle, the abbey and the forest. *The Castle of Otranto*'s plot hinges on the fact that Manfred is not the true heir to Otranto; this conflict must be resolved for the novel to reach its conclusion. Interestingly, Walpole stages the revelation of the true identity of the prince outside the castle walls. While the castle is certainly central to the ancestral curse which is the subject of the novel, the forest sees some of the pivotal action, as it witnesses the clues that will reveal the true heir to Otranto.

Theodore first introduces the space of the forest as he seeks refuge from Manfred. Matilda pleads with Theodore to go to the church of Saint Nicholas, via the underground passage, where Isabella had hidden earlier. Theodore rejects her idea, however:

—To sanctuary! said Theodore: No princess; sanctuaries are for helpless damsels, or for criminals. Theodore's soul is free from guilt, nor will wear the appearance of it. Give me a sword, lady, and thy father shall learn that Theodore scorns an ignominious flight.[4]

For Theodore, the convent is not a proper place for escape, and because of Manfred's rage, he cannot stay in the castle as he wishes. The forest is, therefore, the only true world for a man like him. Theodore's dilemma presents an interesting point for this study: the forest is a unique space in the Gothic as it represents neither the Church-dominated convent nor the aristocratic power struggle found within the castle.

Theodore is in a cavern in the forest when he meets 'an armed knight' (110), who later reveals himself to be Isabella's father, Frederic. As Frederic is telling his story, he relates an incident that occurred in a

forest. While a 'prisoner to the infidels' (113), Frederic has a dream that
tells him to go 'to a wood near Joppa' (114), where he meets a hermit,
who tells the knight of a buried treasure, 'an enormous sabre – the very
weapon yonder in the court!' (114). The sabre, of course, is the sword
which prophesies that 'Alphoso's blood alone can save the maid' (115).
Significantly, the two pieces of information that will resolve the mystery of the true heir of Otranto, the sword and Theodore's true lineage,
are revealed at different times in outdoor spaces – though the latter is
first revealed, admittedly, in the courtyard of the castle. Because the
forest is free of the social power struggles at work in the castle/convent,
Frederic and Theodore can find the sanctuary and solace needed to
solve the mystery of the true prince of Otranto. The liminal quality of
the forest plays an important role as the Gothic genre gains in popular-
ity throughout the latter half of the eighteenth century. Walpole's use
of the forest sets up the paradigm of Gothic ecology that would be
popular in the Gothic novels that came in the 1790s. Outdoor spaces
have a specific purpose for the characters: solace, renewal, protection.
These characters and writers, as Bate writes, are the true ecologists as
they delve into, 'not a disengaged thinking about [the environment],
but an experiencing of it'.[5]

This 'ecoGothic' theory is most often seen in the works of Ann
Radcliffe. In its many descriptions of the landscape, *The Mysteries
of Udolpho* (1794) best illustrates the effect of the environment on
Radcliffe's characters. After Madame Cheron tells Emily that she must
leave La Vallée, Emily seeks solace in nature:

> she silently passed into the garden, and hastening towards the distant groves, was
> glad to breathe once more the air of liberty, and to sigh unobserved. The deep
> repose of the scene, the rich scents that floated on the breeze, the grandeur of
> the wide horizon and of the clear blue arch, soothed and gradually elevated her
> mind to that sublime complacency, which renders the vexations of this world so
> insignificant and mean in our eyes, that we wonder they have had the power for
> a moment to disturb us.[6]

The allure of nature is in the 'air of liberty' – the freedom to be 'unob-
served'. The solitude nature provides is dependent upon one thing:
the absence of civilization. By placing nature and civilization in binary
opposition to each other, Radcliffe opens an interesting thesis on the
relationship between the city and the country. In Radcliffe's estimation, the city is far removed from nature and, therefore, the urban
corrupts. The forest, on the other hand, has only one law: that of God.
Radcliffe begins chapter three of *The Romance of the Forest* (1791) with

an epitaph from Shakespeare's *As You Like It* (1660: II. i. 3–7): 'Are not these woods / More free from peril than the envious court? / Here feel we but the penalty of Adam, / The season's difference, as the icy fang / And churlish chiding of the winter's wind.'[7] Man's idea of lawfulness (and lawlessness) is much harsher than God's, whose law provides for an easy life for the virtuous.

This sentiment is repeated by La Motte's reaction to living in the forest of Fontainville: 'His mornings were usually spent in shooting, or fishing, and the dinner, thus provided by his industry, he relished with a keener appetite than had ever attended him at the luxurious tables of Paris' (33). Awakened within La Motte is a greater connection to the world around him, something he never experienced in the numbing influence of Paris. Here we see the ecological idea that the city, with its rich artifice and rampant consumerism, can almost dehumanize in its ability not only to blur the lines of morality but also to dull Radcliffe's characters' experience of the world. Only immersion in nature can bring these people back to their true selves. In other words, a connection to the natural world, an experience of the untouched environment, makes human beings better than they would be in the city. Awareness of the natural world is not the end result for Radcliffe, however. Echoing the Graveyard poets, Radcliffe's characters seek union with nature in order to find a relationship with the creator of that nature. Above all else, nature brings about worship, as in Robert Blair's 'The Grave' (1743), in which a vision of the natural world (in Blair's case, a country graveyard) prompts spontaneous worship of God. For Radcliffe's characters, it is impossible to look upon scenes of natural beauty without considering their creator, as Emily experiences in *The Mysteries of Udolpho*:

> From the consideration of His works her mind arose to the adoration of the Deity, in His goodness and power; whenever she turned her view, whether on the sleeping earth, or to the vast regions of space, glowing with worlds beyond the reach of human thought, the sublimity of God, and the majesty of his presence appeared. (47–8)

As if to intensify the act of veneration, Radcliffe stages this scene in a monastery, as monks are chanting prayers and hymns in the background. Adoration of the Divine appears to be the ultimate reason for Radcliffe's vision of nature.

At La Vallée, we also see characters who share no sense of community with nature – a sign, we learn quickly, of evil intentions. During his visit to the St Auberts, Monsieur Quesnel indicates that he wants to chop down the chestnut trees (13), an idea that horrifies Emily and her father. This episode is a good example of the Gothic ecology as it demonstrates a direct connection between the destruction of the land and the whims of the people (after all, Quesnel only wants to cut down the trees to replace them with Lombardy poplars, which he views as more beautiful and fashionable than the old chestnuts). The chopping of the trees proves to be an omen; Quesnel is the connecting factor between Emily and her kidnapper, Montoni. Emily actually meets Montoni and Cavigni at Quesnel's dinner party, which sets the primary plot of the novel in action. At the dinner party, besides the talk of cutting down the chestnuts, there seems to be a complete rejection of the natural world. Everything is in praise of artifice, from 'the heavy walls' and 'frivolous ornaments' to the 'false taste and corrupted sentiments' (23). Similarly, villainy is established through connection with an urban setting. Montoni and Morano are associated with the decadence of Venice rather than the quiet simplicity of the countryside. In the same way, the hero, Valancourt, almost forgets Emily while amid the 'fashionable circles of Paris' (295). Paris has corrupted Valancourt; he is described as 'unworthy' (503) and 'fallen' (514) when he returns from the city, again evoking Radcliffe's Edenic themes. Accompanying his corruption is a loss of connection to the land, as Emily notes:

> 'Observe those moonlight woods, and the towers, which appear obscurely in the perspective. You used to be a great admirer of landscape, and I have heard you say, that the faculty of deriving consolation, under misfortune, from the sublime prospects, which neither oppression, or poverty with-hold from us was the peculiar blessing of the innocent.' Valancourt was deeply affected. 'Yes,' replied he, 'I had once a taste for innocent and elegant delights – I once had an uncorrupted heart.' (503)

Valancourt's travels into the city have distanced him from nature and, therefore, from God. His fallen status has thus made him 'unworthy' of Emily's pure and chaste love.

The environment, at least for the characters of Radcliffe, acts as a kind of conduit of emotions, a way to experience feelings and sometimes to purge them. Whether it is a feeling of creativity and renewal or even an indication of the potential evil in someone, the environment is alive as it responds to these characters who reside within its boundaries. Not all Gothic writers, however, share Radcliffe's God-centred view of ecology, most notably Matthew Lewis. The battle lines separating Radcliffe and Lewis are widely documented, and were so even in the writers' own day, when Radcliffe made clear her distinction between her own brand of terror and Lewis's predilection for horror.[8] In their definitions of the Gothic, these two novelists have always occupied opposite ends of the spectrum, and the same holds true of their views regarding ecology. Lewis is representative of those writers who viewed nature as a force entirely separate from humanity. It is a feral and wild place best left untouched. Unlike Radcliffe, whose characters benefit from – and become better by – their connection to nature, Lewis wrote a brand of nature that was not at all kind towards its human invaders. Where Radcliffe does not seem to consider the unattainable nature of her heroine's environment, Lewis challenges it by allowing vice to corrupt virtue. He accomplishes this by staging scenes of violence in the pastoral wilderness. One prominent example in *The Monk* (1796) centres on the forest surrounding Lindenberg castle, where Raymond meets his lover, Agnes.

Raymond tells the reader he has 'turned from the Inhabitants of Paris with disgust', desiring an escape from the empty life in the city.[9] Travelling under the name 'Don Alphonso', Raymond finds himself in 'a thick Forest' (97) when his chaise breaks down. The forest space here echoes Ambrosio's words regarding the nature of seclusion. Ambrosio tells the novice Rosario that only weariness and a dulling of the senses can come from too much time alone in nature. Through Ambrosio's words and Raymond's experiences within the forest, Lewis reinforces the idea that mankind cannot find solace by withdrawing from society. While in the forest, Raymond and the Baroness Lindenberg go to a woodman's cottage to seek help. The home of Marguerite and Baptiste appears to be like those ubiquitous peasant homes found throughout the forests in Radcliffe's novels. Raymond is even told that Baptiste is 'a very honest Fellow' who 'will shelter you for the night with pleasure' (98). The scene that follows is, however, not reminiscent of Radcliffe's dancing peasants. Instead, Raymond and the Baroness encounter a bloody and violent scene, as Baptiste turns out to be the leader of a group of banditti and his wife is only a prisoner in his house. Raymond does escape, only to encounter another bloody house – the Castle of Lindenberg and the murderous history of the Bleeding Nun. Through the story of Raymond, Lewis emphasizes that the forest is no place for either innocence or solace. However, Lewis does not completely revise Radcliffe's ideas of innocence and the environment on his own; his ideas are greatly influenced by the writings of the Marquis de Sade, particularly the novel *Justine, Or Good Conduct Well Chastised* (1791).

In the essay 'Must We Burn de Sade?' (1952), Simone de Beauvoir offers an elucidation of de Sade's use of familiar Gothic settings: 'Caves, underground passageways, mysterious castles, all the props of the Gothic novel take on a particular meaning in his work. They symbolize the isolation of the image.'[10] De Sade seems to understand the true terror of the wilderness as it is presented in the Gothic novel in which isolation leaves humanity to its own devices. Radcliffe recognized this too, but refused to explore it. After all, she stages her villains' plots and plans in the most remote regions (as in Montoni's taking of Emily to Udolpho). The isolated locales are ideal because there is nothing to interfere with the villains' schemes. These conspiracies are never brought to fruition in Radcliffe, however. Both de Sade and Lewis use these remote environments to prove the Hobbesian idea that, to borrow from Beauvoir's essay, 'man is a wolf to man'.[11] If man's nature is to be evil, then Edenic scenes of virtuous bliss are nothing more than fiction. In this view of Gothic ecology, the nature of humanity is to corrupt, and that force carries over into mankind's environment. Whereas Radcliffe's corrupt characters sought only to cut down a few trees, the characters of de Sade and Lewis want to take down the entire realm of the natural world. Evil would thrive if given the opportunity to feast on innocence isolated. This perhaps explains why de Sade moves his novel further from the city as he increases the violence inflicted upon Justine. The most vicious scene occurs in the remote Sainte-Marie-de-Bois ('Saint Mary-in-the-Wood') monastery.

According to de Sade, virtue is what makes a heroine vulnerable – something Lewis applies to his own characters. Upon arriving at the Sainte-Marie-de-Bois monastery, Justine (Thérèse, as she is known at this point in the novel) is told that her innocence is what made her the perfect victim for the four lecherous monks, echoing Ambrosio's lust for the virgin Antonia: '[T]hey would send away any girl who was to come here voluntarily; ... had they not recognized a veritable fund of virtue in you, and, consequently, the possibility of crime, they would not have kept you twenty-four hours.'[12] In Radcliffe's novels, wars waged by the villains upon the heroines are usually done verbally. Montoni repeatedly asks Emily to turn over her estate, even resorting to threats in order to intimidate her. Why then does he need to isolate Emily in Udolpho? Perhaps the seclusion of the location could help Montoni coerce his victim and gain him riches, but this deed could have been accomplished just as well in Venice, a city foreign to Emily. After all, Emily has proven that running away goes against her virtue by refusing to elope with Valancourt. Radcliffe recognizes that the forest is frightening, especially for the innocent. De

Sade sees this too – and stages his novel accordingly. However, where Emily could draw strength from the natural world, even during her kidnapping, Justine is allowed no comfort in her surroundings.

An interesting point is that *Justine*'s most violent episode takes place in one of the most pastoral settings of the novel. The scene leading up to Justine's kidnapping and subsequent rape and torture by the corrupt monks is as close as de Sade comes to nature as it is presented in Radcliffe: 'I was absorbed in these thoughts when a girl of my age, keeper of a flock of sheep grazing upon the plateau, suddenly appeared before my eyes; … she tells me what I see is a Benedictine monastery' (559). Justine is lulled into a sense of safety by the young shepherdess and the grazing sheep. Yet the scenes that follow of sexual violence and both physical and mental torture call into question Radcliffe's binary assumption that the country equals virtue and the city equals vice. This point is further supported by the fact that every pastoral scene Justine encounters somehow brings her misery (for example, the kindly country doctor Rodin, who takes in Justine, is guilty of child abuse, torture and incest, and the woods hide Saint-Florent, a brutal rapist). It is by this version of nature that Lewis is inspired.

Every element of *The Monk*, while certainly honouring the stylistic devices employed by Radcliffe, corroborates de Sade's theories regarding Radcliffe's 'cloistered virtue'. As with the character of Antonia, true virtue does not last long in Lewis's Gothic universe. Innocence is almost always destroyed, if it exists at all. At times, the professed virtue is just an act, feigned for effect. An example is Antonia's aunt Leonella, a superannuated coquette who uses false modesty to ensnare a husband. In a letter to Lorenzo, Leonella professes a virgin demureness while, at the same time, audaciously making her desire for the young Condé d'Ossorio known (202). Leonella's letter is emblematic of an important trend in Lewis's work. None of the women in *The Monk*, with the exception of Antonia, exhibit the modesty and propriety that characterize the Radcliffean women. For Lewis's women, virtue has its limits. They all eventually leave their Eden in the forest when they discover, like Justine, that their virtue is not rewarded. By leaving the forest for the city, the 'Gothic's supposed sexual innocence' falls under investigation.[13]

In Radcliffe's estimation of the world, the wilderness, devoid of sinful man, is the desired state of being. As stated earlier in this chapter, Lewis's urban setting is a likely reaction to the Radcliffean ideal of another Eden on earth. *The Monk*'s Madrid setting does not, however, dismiss every wilderness backdrop. Lewis does stage some important scenes in what could best be described as 'wilderness'. The best example is the Abbey-Garden. The language Lewis uses to describe this space could be considered Edenic:

> The choicest flowers adorned it in the height of luxuriance, and though artfully arranged, seemed only planted by the hand of Nature: Fountains, springing from basons [sic] of white Marble, were entirely covered by Jessamine, vines, and Honey-suckles. ... The full Moon ranging through a blue and cloudless sky, shed upon the trees a trembling luster, and the waters of the fountains sparkled in the silver beam: A gentle breeze breathed the fragrance of Orange-blossoms along the Alleys; and the Nightingale poured forth her melodious murmur from the shelter of an artificial wilderness. (50)

The last two words of this passage hold the key to understanding it: 'artificial wilderness'. The garden is described here as one which was created to look as if it was 'planted by the hands of Nature'. Emma McEvoy makes the point that the garden 'is not the secluded formal garden that might be expected, but instead is laid out in late eighteenth-century taste'.[14] Late eighteenth-century taste dictated that gardens should strive for what McEvoy calls 'picturesque disorder';[15] landscaping should never appear too geometric, for fear of looking over-planned. Gardens should appear as though simply sprung up from the ground. Lewis is surely writing this scene in reaction to the pastorals that are prevalent in Radcliffe's writings, but an interesting facet of Gothic ecology emerges as well. Lewis's Abbey-Garden reminds readers of the extent of the destruction of the natural world. The theme may not be as evident as in Goldsmith's *The Deserted Village*, but it exists nonetheless. Humanity's greed and focus on progress (as seen in the building of a city like Madrid) has compromised the natural environment, so much so that mankind has to resort to building false natures to take its place.

The Abbey-Garden, in the hands of someone like Radcliffe, would have been a place of familial bliss, untouched by evil. In the hands of Lewis, though, the garden is the setting for the most lurid and sexual events – the first of which is the secret rendezvous of the lovers Agnes and Raymond. Agnes, essentially a prisoner behind the convent walls, can only meet her lover by night, under the cover of the gardens of St Clare's. What should be a place for quiet meditation upon God's creation becomes a place of sexual union, resulting in a pregnancy, violating Radcliffe's ideas that a cloistered life equals a virtuous one. The garden becomes a perverse Garden of Eden. Whereas Radcliffe's nature is meant to bring the participant closer to a holy state of being, Lewis's nature is purely meant to inspire the five senses; its 'sensuousness'[16] is evident throughout the descriptions of the outdoor spaces in *The Monk*. Instead of meditation and prayer, this land inspires 'voluptuous tranquility' (50).

The perversion of Eden continues as the relationship between Ambrosio and Matilda unfolds. The garden offers a perfect backdrop for Ambrosio's meeting of the young novice Rosario, who later reveals herself to be Matilda in disguise. Lewis's nature appears complicit in Rosario's/Matilda's revelation:

> She had torn open her habit, and her bosom was half-exposed. The weapon's point rested upon her left breast: And Oh! That was such a breast! The Moon-beams darting full upon it, enabled the Monk to observe its dazzling whiteness. His eye dwelt with insatiable avidity upon the beauteous Orb. A sensation till then unknown filled his heart with a mixture of anxiety and delight: A raging fire shot through every limb; The blood boiled in his veins, and a thousand wild wishes bewildered his imagination. (65)

Rosario's revelation as Matilda may have come as a surprise to the first-time reader. Lewis no doubt meant to shock his readers by having Matilda bare her breast to a monk. But the setting foreshadowed the act. The Abbey-Garden has already been discussed as an artificial wilderness in the model of an eighteenth-century garden. The focus then is on the space's artifice. A true wilderness, at least in the hands of Radcliffe or even the Graveyard poets, would lead to God's glory; this wilderness centres on sensuousness. Everything, from the 'white Marble' to the 'Jessamine, vines, and Honey-suckle' (50), is meant to appeal to and awaken the five senses through its 'luxuriance' (50). Lewis creates a garden to represent society, which he views 'as imploding because of its hypocrisies'.[17]

In this sense, Lewis and Radcliffe are not that far apart, at least in their views of ecology. For Lewis, the only nature that can be seen in the city is an artificial one, representative of how far humanity has drifted from the natural world. This artifice, a product of destruction and corruption, seems to represent the ultimate downfall of man. The revelation of the woman Matilda, which again occurs in the space of the Abbey-Garden, begins Ambrosio's transformation from pious monk to villain. It is difficult to read this scene of Ambrosio's downfall in the Abbey-Garden without considering the allusion to the Garden of Eden. Lewis is not blind to this similarity either. Shortly after Rosario's revelation as Matilda, Ambrosio is bitten by a venomous snake, what

McEvoy terms a 'crude allusion' to the biblical story of the Fall of Man.[18] The snake bite is certainly a metaphor for Ambrosio's sinful relationship with Matilda and the events that will occur as a result of the monk's awakened lust. But the snake bite can also be read as a literal interpretation of Ambrosio's former critique of the cloistered lifestyle. Even in the 'wilderness' – removed from man's society – sin still lurks. Syndy Conger also reads Lewis's view of nature in direct opposition to Radcliffe's Edenic one:

> Lewis's natural landscape, with its seductive, demonic quality, draws people down to egoistic thoughts of physical gratification, not only Ambrosio but Raymond and Agnes in their monastic garden. His nature is quite literally in league with the devil – serpent, insect, eagle, all participate in Ambrosio's spiritual destruction – a fact that has led more than one Lewis critic to speak of his Manichean world view, his 'dark heresy.' Radcliffe's nature, the obverse of his, draws people away from themselves upward to pious reflections.[19]

Conger here speaks of the essential difference between Radcliffe and Lewis. They both employ the same tropes, essentially the Gothic setting of the forest, but where Radcliffe's woods are haunted by banditti who never seem to surface, Lewis's natural environment encompasses the full range of good and evil.

As Matilda and Ambrosio delve deeper into their evil plans, the garden becomes more and more intrinsic to their plotting. They use the cover of the garden to perform their magic in solitude. A piece of the garden betrays Antonia, as Matilda uses it for her black magic:

> Receive this constellated Myrtle: While you bear this in your hand, every door will fly open to you. It will procure you access tomorrow night to Antonia's chamber: Then breathe upon it thrice, pronounce her name, and place it upon her pillow. A death-like slumber will immediately seize upon her, and deprive her the power of resisting your attempts. (278)

McEvoy makes the note that the myrtle referred to here is an

> evergreen shrub or tree. It has a long connection with physical love. It is supposed to symbolize the eyes, and acts as an atonement for lust in Judaic tradition. In Greek medicine, it was sacred to Aphrodite, goddess of love.[20]

The myrtle could also be the fruit in the Garden of Eden, where a piece of the land was literally a cause of the downfall, an agent for the sin of man.

Nature plays an interesting role in the conclusion of Lewis's novel. *The Monk* does not end with a reclaimed pastoral scene as Radcliffe's works often do. He does leave the city to conclude the story of

Ambrosio, but the environment presented is much darker: 'The caves and mountains rang with Ambrosio's shrieks. The Dæmon continued to soar aloft, till reaching a dreadful height, He released the sufferer' (441). Nature is complicit with Ambrosio's sentence of death – the insects, the animals, the river, even the storm all help to act as judge, jury and executioner:

> The Sun now rose above the horizon; Its scorching beams darted full upon the head of the expiring Sinner. Myriads of insects were called forth by the warmth; They drank the blood which trickled from Ambrosio's wounds; ... The Eagles of the rock tore his flesh piecemeal, and dug out his eye-balls with their crooked beaks. A burning thirst tormented him; He heard the river's murmur as it rolled beside him, but strove in vain to drag himself towards the sound. (442)

Following this torment, a storm arises, causing the river to overflow and carrying Ambrosio to his death. Conger sees this last scene as a 'spectacular ironical reversal' of Ambrosio's initial experience with nature in the Abbey-Garden: 'Ambrosio's sensory organs, which have feasted so voraciously on life, now become a virtual feast for other predators'.[21] The image of Ambrosio's eyes in the beaks of the birds is a haunting one. Lewis's natural world is triumphant; the birds enact justice by taking the part of the body most connected to the monk's lust for Antonia. Lewis's version of the Gothic environment is triumphant as well, appearing in future Gothic novels of the 1790s and following decades. The Gothic ecology, then, seems to be one that suggests it is best for humanity and nature to live harmoniously with one another, though it may be the human counterpart that suffers most if that relationship is severed. Just as nature is always reclaiming its space, as seen in the crumbling ruins so prevalent in the Gothic, it will always be victorious in the end.

Notes

1 S. E. Kingsland, 'Foundational Papers: Defining Ecology as a Science', in L. A. Real and J. H. Brown (eds), *Foundations of Ecology: Classic Papers with Commentaries* (Chicago: University of Chicago Press, 1991), pp. 1–2.

2 Jonathan Bate, *The Song of the Earth* (Cambridge, MA: Harvard University Press, 2000), p. 25.

3 Jonathan Bate, *Romantic Ecology: Wordsworth and the Environmental Tradition* (London: Routledge, 1991), p. 40.

4 Horace Walpole, *The Castle of Otranto*, in *Three Gothic Novels*, ed. P. Fairclough (Harmondsworth: Penguin Books, 1968), pp. 37–148. Subsequent references are to this edition and are given in parentheses in the text.

5 Bate, *Romantic Ecology*, p. 42.

6 Ann Radcliffe, *The Mysteries of Udolpho*, ed. Bonamy Dobrée (Oxford: Oxford University Press, 1998), pp. 113–14. Subsequent references are to this edition and are given in parentheses in the text.

7 Quoted in Ann Radcliffe, *The Romance of the Forest*, ed. Chloe Chard (Oxford: Oxford University Press, 1999), p. 33.

8 The 'fight' between Radcliffe and Lewis is documented in Radcliffe's 1826 article in *New Monthly Magazine*. See also Robert Hume's article which outlines the two versions, though Hume highly favours Lewis's 'horror' Gothic. Robert D. Hume, 'Gothic versus Romantic: A Revaluation of the Gothic Novel', *PMLA* 84/2 (1969): 282–90.

9 Matthew Lewis, *The Monk*, ed. Howard Anderson (Oxford: Oxford University Press, 1998), p. 97. Subsequent references are to this edition and are given in parentheses in the text.

10 Simone de Beauvoir, 'Must We Burn de Sade?', trans. Annette Michelson, in A. Wainhouse and R. Seaver (eds), *The Marquis de Sade: The 120 Days of Sodom and Other Writings* (New York: Grove Press, 1966), p. 37.

11 De Beauvoir, 'Must We Burn de Sade?', p. 43.

12 Marquis de Sade, *Justine, Or Good Conduct Well Chastised*, in Wainhouse and Seaver (eds), *The Marquis de Sade: The 120 Days of Sodom and Other Writings*, p. 587. Subsequent references are to this edition and are given in parentheses in the text.

13 Emma McEvoy, 'Introduction', in Lewis, *The Monk*, pp. i–xi, p. xix.

14 Emma McEvoy, 'Explanatory Notes', in Lewis, *The Monk*, p. 446.

15 Ibid.

16 S. M. Conger, 'Sensibility Restored: Radcliffe's Answer to Lewis's *The Monk*', in K. W. Graham (ed.), *Gothic Fictions: Prohibition/Transgression* (New York: AMS Press, 1989), pp. 113–49, p. 122.

17 Andrew Smith, *Gothic Literature* (Edinburgh: Edinburgh University Press, 2007), p. 33.

18 McEvoy, 'Explanatory Notes', p. 447.

19 Conger, 'Sensibility Restored', p. 133.

20 McEvoy, 'Explanatory Notes', p. 453.

21 Conger, 'Sensibility Restored', p. 120.

3

Catherine Lanone

Monsters on the ice and global warming: from Mary Shelley and Sir John Franklin to Margaret Atwood and Dan Simmons

> Environmentalists frequently feel that time is running out. They feel panic in the face of the world's indifference ... This is the ecological disaster as warning: the shock we needed, the lesson administered by providence to open our eyes just in time.[1]

Richard Kerridge argues that part of the problem with environmental concerns is the need for what Barbara Adams calls a 'timescape perspective',[2] a perspective transcending the time span of individual existence in order to grasp the concealed impact of industrial mutations. For Kerridge, 'ecothrillers' seek to dramatize events connected with climate change and global risk on a different scale, but run the risk of unleashing catastrophe to replace it with a pattern of 'ordeal and redemption' as normality returns after the crisis. Though they may not entirely escape the paradox Kerridge sees in apocalyptic fantasies and ecothrillers, ecoGothic narratives turn to the ghosts of the past in order to shock capitalist logic into changing while there may still be time. The lessons of the past come to haunt the present, suggesting that man should acknowledge technological hubris and, like Victor Frankenstein, learn to recoil from the sweet poison of progress. Thus, instead of using projections into the future to mimic the temporal scale needed to turn 'matters of fact' into 'matters of concern', to use Latour's concepts, the past surfaces as the spectral event warning and demands change without further ado.[3] This may be the reason why so many reconstructions of the Franklin expedition (the quest with no survivors) are now being published, at a time when what is at stake in the fast-melting, coveted areas of the North seems of far greater urgency than the fate of long-gone Victorian explorers.

A seasoned explorer, John Franklin had led two expeditions by land mapping the coast of the Arctic Sea; when he left in 1845 with his two ships, the *Erebus* and the *Terror*, his name was considered a 'national guarantee', as the president of the Geographical Society put it. Yet he was getting too old to play a leader's part and his second-in-command, Francis Crozier, wrote home that he feared that they would blunder into the ice. And so they did: when they reached King William's Island, which was thought at the time to be King William's Land, Franklin went the wrong way and his ships were trapped in ice that would not melt for years. The glorious expedition turned into a national disaster, as rescue expeditions could find no trace of survivors; little remained of the crew but a few relics and disquieting rumours, prompting many a writer to provide imaginary accounts of the tragedy. We shall see how the lost Franklin expedition has been repeatedly turned into a topos of textual haunting, casting a disturbing light less on the past than on present decay, pollution and global warming. Evolving from a cliché and a myth, the Franklin story has turned into an ecoGothic paradigm.

Arctic exploration as a monstrous venture

The representation of the Arctic was linked to the Gothic by Mary Shelley's archetypal novel, *Frankenstein*. In a way, it might be argued that the disastrous 1845 Franklin expedition only came to confirm the forebodings of Shelley, who had used the Arctic as the narrative and geographic frame of her key Gothic tale; as early as 1818, when Arctic exploration was just being resumed after the end of the Napoleonic wars, Shelley seems to have sensed that the Holy Grail of the Northwest Passage was just one more invention of armchair explorers. Her enthusiastic Walton is a great believer in the Open Sea theory, a dreamer who knows more about Coleridge's visions than about the shifting nature of ice, and whose ship is soon hopelessly beset. It is no wonder that Victor should accuse him of sharing his madness, as if Walton's imperial dream answered Victor's scientific and medical hubris. Inspired by galvanism and contemporary medical experimentation, Shelley's tale about resurrecting a dead body composed of sewn-together body parts creates a new composite genre, blending intertextual allusions and philosophical meditation with early science fiction. But the novel might also be read, like Coleridge's 'The Rime of the Ancient Mariner' of 1798 (where the unmotivated death of the albatross is read as a crime against the One Life, and where the crew fail to respond to the deed in terms of right and wrong, only paying attention to the wind and their own interest) as a proto-ecocritical text. Recent studies stress as a key influence upon Shelley's writing the gloomy atmosphere created by the distant eruption of Mount Tambora, so that 1816 came to be known as the year without a summer. Disturbing climate change was responsible for the long evenings at the Villa Diodati, where Byron, Shelley and Polidori discussed science and ghost stories, and when Mary's story was conceived to respond to the men's bet. Mary's monster remains impervious to cold; he defies his creator in the sublime Alps and draws him farther and farther north; he ultimately vanishes in the ice, promising to light a funeral pyre and cast himself on to it, while Walton is persuaded to give up the quest and sail for Europe. This cautionary Gothic tale suggests that Arctic regions are best left alone, lest they might prove home to mankind's most monstrous progeny rather than a haven for conquerors. Though Mary Shelley could have had no inkling of the impact of early industrialization on polar ice (the layers of polar ice register global pollution and clearly reveal the changes brought by nineteenth-century technology), she expresses an uneasiness before colonial conquest which extends the debate on scientific responsibility to geography.

Against all expectations, the fate of the 1845 Franklin expedition came to confirm that technological progress can lead to dehumanizing regression; the expedition was the epitome of Victorian progress, complete with iron-plated ships, steam engines and canned food, the latest technological wonder designed to prevent starvation. Yet the ships vanished without a trace, shattering the Victorian construction of the Arctic, as Jen Hill points out:

> framed in this heroic context, Franklin's disappearance reads as a form of cultural aporia, an incident of literal 'lost passage' that revealed the important symbolic role of the Arctic in imagining national and imperial masculinity, and forced on the Victorians a reluctant recognition that these models were much less stable than had been understood.[4]

Worse than that, in 1854 a surveyor for the Hudson's Bay Company, John Rae, brought back artefacts and Inuit reports of kettles containing human flesh.[5] The obsessional response of Charles Dickens, for instance, who challenged John Rae's discovery with a vengeance in his *Household Words* articles, then prompted Wilkie Collins to write a play, *The Frozen Deep* (1857),[6] which he supervised and performed, is a case in point that shows how hard it was for Victorians to accept that monstrous cannibalism might have plagued the finest expedition of the British Navy. Panoramas, dioramas, newspaper articles, books and ballads continued to dramatize the search for Franklin.[7] Lady Jane, Franklin's wife, financed several expeditions to prove Rae wrong; she sought to restore an official version of events, and was responsible for several monuments erected to the memory of Franklin, including one in Westminster Abbey. But Franklin's memory continued to haunt the Victorians, if only because the clues that were being found – whether skulls and bones, buttons and relics, Inuit stories or the one document left by the expedition in a cairn (an official form in several languages, with its first handwritten message bearing Franklin's name and concluding 'all well', and its second message scribbled in the margins, stating that nine officers and fifteen men had already died, and that the survivors were abandoning the ships) – remained tantalizingly inconclusive fragments in a truly Gothic maze.

Forensic analysis and 'The Age of Lead'

In 1984 forensic analysis added a twist to the Franklin variation on the Frankenstein scenario. Scientists exhumed three bodies buried on Beechey Island, where the *Erebus* and the *Terror* had wintered during their first year, before venturing into more perilous uncharted waters. Analysis detected an unusually high level of lead in the bodies, which would have weakened and disoriented the men, if not killed them; lead poisoning was blamed on the badly soldered food cans. The excavation of the bodies and the widely circulated pictures, books and film footage brought a fresh 'iconography of horror', which led to a new rush of Franklin tales, as if there were as compelling an interest in the story today as in Victorian England.

Margaret Atwood was perhaps the first writer to be fascinated by the new evidence and by the different light such discoveries cast on the Franklin legacy. Atwood has always considered the Franklin story as a key component of the saga of the North; she devotes a chapter to the Franklin myth in her ground-breaking *Strange Things: The Malevolent North in Canadian Literature* (1995), where she compares the *Erebus* and the *Terror* to the legendary *Titanic*, 'a sort of twentieth-century Frankenstein creation – notice it has a heart and lungs – composed of equal parts technology and hubris'.[8] In her preface to *Frozen in Time* (1987), the account of Geiger's and Beattie's exhumation of the Beechey

Island bodies, she traces the mutations of the Franklin myth, from hero to colonial blunderer. She opposes demystification to what she sees as 'exoneration', a process of restoration of Franklin's mythical status which does include, for her, Geiger's and Beattie's dramatic excavation, experimentation and lead-poisoning theory.[9] Her own short story entitled 'The Age of Lead' revisits the Franklin story from an ecoGothic perspective to offer an ironic reading of this process of exoneration.

In 'The Age of Lead', the return of the dead occurs at one remove: Jane, the protagonist, is watching a television programme depicting the excavation of the Beechey Island bodies, which leads to the scientists' investigation and conclusions. Snippets of the programme pace the story. As the layers of ice are melted to reveal John Torrington's body, Jane remembers her friend Vincent, who has recently died of an unknown virus; the men's search seems to cast a light not simply on Torrington's death, but also on that of Vincent, since layers of denial thaw in Jane's mind as she remembers Vincent and seeks to put together the pieces of their lives. The Franklin expedition thus turns into a catalyst and a recipe for disaster, acting as a metaphor for Jane's loneliness, but also in a wider sense for the late twentieth-century's perverse relationship with the environment.

For Guy Debord, the spectacular character of modern society 'has nothing fortuitous or superficial about it; on the contrary, this society is based upon the spectacle in the most fundamental way'.[10] The spectacle is part of the logic of the ruling economic order and it is meant to alienate though it pretends to connect: 'Spectators are linked by a one-way relationship to the very center that maintains their isolation from one another.'[11] In Atwood's story, Jane watches TV sporadically, and food imagery harps on the theme of automatic consumption: Torrington's body is compared to iced cocktail cherries, his eyes are the colour of milky tea, 'he's a beige colour, like a gravy stain on linen'.[12] Defrosting the body recalls the memory of Vincent, only to leave Jane in a world of echoing emptiness: her 'all white' kitchen looks impersonal, with its technological apparatus, the microwave oven, the espresso maker, the flotsam and jetsam of modernity: 'They might well be the pieces of an exploded spaceship orbiting the moon' (169). In the white desert of her flat, Jane can find no purpose for her life.

The image of the spaceship travesties the tale of the lost *Erebus* and *Terror*, while Jane's name vaguely parodies the part played by Lady Jane Franklin, arguably the most famous Victorian widow after Queen Victoria. Jane mourns the loss of Vincent, the scattering of his possessions, paralleled by the bones and buttons found here and there on King William Island, the relics of the lost expedition. The story thus creates pathos (the lost young sailor, the emptiness of Jane's and Vincent's lives) but denies the satisfaction of sentimentality. The story remains cold, mocking the enthusiasm of the scientists: 'The scientists are back on the screen. They are excited, their earnest mouths are twitching, you could almost call them joyful' (168). Atwood's story refuses the comfort of exoneration, suggesting that the tragedy is made more absurd, rather than less, by the scientists' discovery: 'A finger points: it was the tin cans that did it, a new invention back then, a new technology, the ultimate defence against starvation and scurvy' (168). Atwood undermines the *narrative* of disaster, with the dramatic close-ups on the cans; finding a villain (Goldner, the maker of the cans) may account for madness and disorientation, may have added to the horror, but it cannot turn the story of disaster back into an epic myth. What it does is re-enact the paradigm of technological hubris: the expedition has been destroyed by a monster of its own creation. The story offers a variation on the Frankenstein motif, both because the scientists, by digging up the frozen body, seek to revive the past, to quicken it into a kind of monstrous rebirth so that it may tell its own story, and because lead poison is the invisible monster, the unforeseen consequence of technological design, which will devour what it was meant to save.

But the story can only retain a touch of *Frankenstein* if the image of the cans may be used as a paradigm for the present and the future. For Jane, the cans look like an exploded shell, suggesting that technology is a time bomb. The Franklin disaster is used as a metaphor for Vincent's and Jane's barren lives; seeking to be free, to escape from the constraints of their mothers' bickering words, they have eschewed commitment and failed to truly live. Atwood heaps up images that identify the dying Vincent with Torrington's mummified body: Vincent is lying on a white hospital bed, wrapped in a white sheet with his feet poking out, ice packed around him to ease the pain. Even when Vincent is dying, he refuses to take the situation seriously, making brave but ludicrous little jokes about aliens, or claiming that it must have been something that he ate. The Franklin expedition becomes a metaphor for blindness, the blindness of Vincent's and Jane's unorthodox longings, which turn out to be the product of their alienating, consumerist, pseudo-artistic professional background rather than an original gift. Their personal blindness is inseparable from a greater, more insidious and perverse blindness, that of society at large. Vincent's joke, that it must have

been something that he ate, rings ominously in a story where men
are poisoned by invisible lead absorbed from the cans. Jane becomes
suddenly aware that the world she lives in is indeed poisoned, full of
invisible lethal substances. The ghost of Franklin's past only comes to
illuminate the present predicament, a cold, perverse, polluted world.
Jane becomes aware of pesticides, acid rain, the corruption of beef and
fish; she opts for bottled water, only to realize that poison has spread
into the air and the earth, and therefore seeped into any kind of water.
She thinks of moving into the countryside, but the pastoral ideal has
vanished too; it only remains as the theatrical backdrop masking the
lethal forces at work: 'toxic dumps, radioactive waste, concealed here
and there in the countryside and masked by the lush, deceitful green
of waving trees' (166–7). People around her seem to just collapse and
die, of AIDS, cancer, heart failure or any other cause: 'It was as if they
had been weakened by some mysterious agent, a thing like a colourless
gas, scentless and invisible, so that any germ that happened along could
invade their bodies, take them over' (166).

The story ends with the refuse left outside Jane's window, plastic cups
and broken cans, which she picks up but which reappear 'overnight, like
a trail left by an army on the march ... discarding the objects which were
once thought essential but which are now too heavy to carry' (169).
The trail of rubbish recalls the relics left by the Franklin expedition, as
if urban consumer society were marching forward towards inevitable
destruction. The plight of the last survivors of the Franklin crew foreshadows the rout of modern civilization, blind to the consequences
of its way of life upon both the environment and human bodies, and
though haunted by the past, utterly unable to decipher the message.

The masque of the white death

Whereas British retellings of the Franklin expedition tend to revive
the Franklin myth (see Andrew Lambert's 2009 biography[13] or
McGregor's *The Ice Child* [2001]),[14] Canadian texts move from eulogy
(Gwendolen McEwen's radio play)[15] to postcolonial deconstruction
(Wiebe's *A Discovery of Strangers* [1995],[16] Mordecai Richler's *Solomon
Gursky Was Here* [1989][17] or Atwood's *Strange Things* and 'The Age of
Lead'). But after *Frozen in Time*, American writers also began to offer
creative versions of the story. *The Rifles* (1995), by William Vollmann,[18]
creates a chilling parallelism between the displacement of the British
crew stranded in the Arctic, and the Canadian relocation policy in the

1950s that forced Inuit families to move north in order to underline Canadian ownership of the northern territories during the Cold War. Vollmann recreates the three expeditions led by Franklin, but disturbs the Gothic frame: the modern focalizer, Captain Subzero (Vollmann's alter ego) may be obsessed with the lost Franklin expedition, but the nineteenth-century Franklin is equally haunted by the twentieth-century Subzero. The text creates uncanny passages between the centuries, blurring boundaries in a radically unsettling way. The novel depicts environmental imbalance, portraying the dissemination of weapons in the Arctic (a whole chapter is devoted to the eponymous rifles, an ironic inversion of Melville's chapter on the whales in *Moby-Dick* [1851]) and gratuitous shooting (emblematized by a raven and a fox found on a heap of refuse) but also the plight of the Inuit, cut off from their culture as traditional hunters and the victims of cheap American television, cigarettes and alcohol. The suicide of Reepah, Subzero's Inuk mistress, is emblematic of the destruction of the Inuit territories by so-called progress. Reepah is also associated with Sedna, the Inuit goddess of animals, stressing the impact of cultural destruction. With its anachronistic shifts from century to century, *The Rifles* makes reading challenging and erratic, forcing the reader to face a disorientation which is meant to reproduce the disorientation faced by Arctic travellers in the maze of ice.

Since the logic of Vollmann's novel, for all its dazzling and disturbing feats, concerns the plight of the Inuit more than the environment per se, it might be best to end this brief survey of the use of the Franklin expedition as an ecoGothic paradigm with Dan Simmons's bestseller *The Terror* (2007),[19] which suggests that, in the twentieth century as much as in the nineteenth, the Franklin motif pervades popular culture. For Fred Botting, Gothic is the literature of excess, but in Dan Simmons's case, there is an excess of excess.[20] Indeed, just as his Franklin tries 'every trick in his Arctic inventory' (84) to free his boats, hacking and sawing at the ice, using steam, spreading soot, 'hauling the ships forward a sweating, cursing, shouting, spirit-killing, gut-wrenching, backbreaking inch at a time' (84), Simmons uses every trick in the Arctic repertoire, playing both on realistic reconstruction and fantastic apparitions. Not only do the crew of the *Terror* and the *Erebus* find themselves lost in the Arctic maze, with its passages that open and close into a deadly trap, facing scurvy, extreme cold, darkness and starvation, but they are stalked by a mysterious creature, a predator more powerful and uncanny than any living Arctic bear. This Thing kills and maims relentlessly, and at one point leaves on deck a sickening body composed of the top of one sailor and the lower half of another. Simmons's text is equally composite, sewing together different genres, playing with pieces to compose his own version of the story.

The gripping reconstruction of the story of the doomed expedition is bent and recast to fit in with a scenario which recalls Howard Hawks's 1951 movie *The Thing From Another World*;[21] indeed, Simmons dedicates his novel, 'with love and many thanks for the indelible Arctic memories', to the film crew and cast of *The Thing*. In the film, the inhabitants of an Arctic polar station are attacked by an alien which they find frozen in a flying saucer which crashed on the ice; for the scientist, the alien is vastly superior to the human race, because it has no feelings, a metaphor, as Kendall R. Phillips points out, for both rampant communism and ruthless capitalism.[22] Simmons's novel hovers between realism and fantasy, blending historical recreation with science fiction visual effects. The text is a patchwork of log entries and extracts from the diaries of members of the expedition, creating an intricate temporal structure; each chapter (except towards the end, when geographic and temporal landmarks are lost) begins with a date, a latitude and a longitude, and a name, so that we know whose viewpoint we are about to share. The familiar story unfolds, as Simmons recreates the swift, joyful journey down Peel Sound, the 'Stygian cold and gloom' (32) of winter after winter, the sounds of the ice slowly crushing the hulls of the ships, the burning fingers and frosted breath of the men, the symptoms of alcohol withdrawal (as far as Crozier is concerned) and spreading scurvy, the signs of lead poisoning and the growing mistrust of Goldner's canned meals, the gradual loss of food and hope and the last desperate venture to abandon ship and try the impossible march to Back's Great Fish River. Simmons portrays Crozier reading from Hobbes's 1651 'book of Leviathan' as if it were part of the Bible, and the men baptize the boats they drag across the ice 'solitary, poor, nasty, brutish and short' accordingly.

Though he creates verisimilitude with undeniable skill, Simmons also seems to steer the tale of disaster towards the tradition of the grand adventure story. Good characters like Lieutenant Irving or Doctor Goodsir are pitted against a villain, Cornelius Hickey, who dances like a naked leprechaun before killing and disembowelling Irving, and who bears the responsibility, with his very small party of men, for the scenes of cannibalism, which are thus strictly limited, as if Simmons wished to relocate the scandal elsewhere. And, just in case the human monster were not enough, Simmons also adds his supernatural creature, a white shape with two emotionless black holes for eyes: 'Then ... the ice just rose up, Captain' (151). With its carrion stench and inhuman strength, the 'Thing' is all malevolent intelligence. Two very striking purple passages dramatize the confrontation between the Thing and the men: the escape of Blanky, the ice master, on the one hand, and the carnival scene on the other. In a breathless set piece, we witness Blanky climbing masts, swinging from iced rope to iced rope, throwing himself to clutch the rigging instinctively in the dark, feeling himself and tons of rigging impossibly drawn upwards, ripped by claws; Blanky lurches madly, falls and runs to the shelter of a small ice tunnel. However, Blanky's feats do not simply update swashbuckling antics on ships in the manner of Errol Flynn: he only survives for a while, until he is attacked again, surviving again only to hobble on the snow on rough wooden prostheses which keep breaking, until he gives up and waits for the monster to come and get him. Spectacular pathos, for all its efficiency, seems pointless. Heroism remains rather vain, in the repetitive scenario which seems to harp on the absence of survivors with a vengeance. Similarly, Goodsir's progress from nondescript little doctor to the undaunted last man to stand up to Hickey seems to be of little use – Hickey and Manson are starving anyway.

The second set piece begins to dispel the impression that we are reading nothing but a latter-day version of Jules Verne's *Hatteras* (1866),[23] and of his celebration of the ordeal of Arctic explorers beset by monsters, in the guise of extremely cunning malevolent Arctic bears in Verne's case, and a Thing from the ice in Simmons's. For the scene of the carnival parodies the tradition of Arctic theatrical performances (so dear to Parry and his crew, for instance). The scene anchors the text firmly within the tradition of American Gothic, and starts to shift the meaning of the tale. To celebrate the New Year, the men manage to kill a bear and her cub, prepare a feast and build a maze of dyed sails and elaborate rigging tied to a towering iceberg, with torches and braziers burning bright, creating seven tents with a specific colour code: the tent on the east is dyed blue, like the invisible absent sky; a purple 'room' contains rugs and casks painted purple; there is punch in the orange room, men dressed as exotic birds in the green room, music in the white room, thanks to the *Terror*'s mechanical music player; and the violet room leads to 'the ebony gloom of this final, terrible compartment' (314), a tent dyed black, with soot spread over the ice to create a dark floor; a gloomy ebony clock, the late Sir John

Franklin's clock, is ticking like a heartbeat, while a huge white bear's head is nailed above the clock. The costumes of the men (Napoleon, gladiators, fairies) are as lavish as they are inappropriate for an Arctic expedition. This spectacular scene (and the dyeing of cloth in the dead of Arctic winter) stretches the reader's ability to suspend disbelief, but intertextual energy gives the passage momentum. The maze of tents is explicitly designed after Poe's classic story, 'The Masque of the Red Death', which was published in 1842 and which one of the men remembers having read in America.

Poe's short story describes the outbreak of a mysterious plague, which the rich Prospero wishes to defeat by retiring into the 'deep seclusion of his castellated abbey' with a thousand friends whom he has carefully selected: 'The external world could take care of itself.'[24] Regardless of the pestilence outside, Prospero designs a series of coloured rooms (the rainbow colours may connote the seven ages of man, or the seven deadly sins) and entertains his friends with a magnificent masked ball. But on the last stroke of midnight, a gaunt figure with a 'corpse-like mask' (273) appears. The more secure Prospero has sought to be, the more exposed he is in the end. The tale is an ironic allegory of disease and death; it plays on the tension between inside and outside, as the spectral intruder (the Red Death itself) turns the shelter, the sealed place of pleasure, into a place of 'darkness and decay': 'And one by one died the revellers in the blood-bedewed halls of their revel, and died each in the despairing posture of his fall. And the life of the ebony clock went out with the last of the gay' (273).

In Simmons's novel, the performance of Poe's story challenges power and order, turning the mock Venetian carnival into a grotesque display which recalls Bakhtin's definition of the carnival, that is to say a time of inversion and cross-dressing where the world is turned upside down and hierarchy suspended.[25] While everyone chants the talismanic refrain of 'Rule Britannia', promising that Britons never never shall be slaves (a refrain which is printed in increasingly large capital letters to denote drunken loudness), British rule is challenged by a 'travesty of a lampoon' (325), an absurdly large figure with huge epaulettes carrying its papier-mâché head under its arm, followed by a white monster, a parody both of the intrusion of the Red Death (in this case the White Thing, perhaps echoing the shrouded figure 'of the perfect whiteness of the snow' whose apparition abruptly ends *The Narrative of Arthur Gordon Pym of Nantucket* [1838])[26] and of Franklin's inglorious demise, slain by the Thing which ripped off his head, a fitting punishment, presumably, for a thoughtless leader who failed to find the way. The mutinous Hickey rallies the men around the iconoclastic spectacle, defying both the memory of Franklin and the new leader, the rough Crozier.

However, as if on cue, the mysterious Mask of the White Death materializes in the ebony tent, and the supernatural Thing wreaks havoc – the men flee and the tents catch fire, an oxymoronic pyre on ice. The scene is a parable of hubris; Hickey mocks Franklin and colonial order, but his own thirst for power is insatiable and mad; Hickey is a sadistic tyrant who kills, maims and feeds on human flesh, only to encounter the White Beast at the moment of his death. In a wider sense, Poe's tale functions as a metaphor for the Franklin expedition: the boats are a deceptive shelter, tombs rather than wombs. Poe's hideous red death with blood as its 'Avatar and its seal' (269) may recall consumption or a plague: 'There were sharp pains, and sudden dizziness, and then profuse bleeding at the pores, with dissolution' (260). But this also eerily evokes the symptoms of scurvy, the 'crown of thorns' worn by Franklin's men as blood begins to 'weep' from hair, not just on the head but all over the body.[27] Like Poe's revellers, Franklin's men will die one by one in the following months, 'each in the despairing posture of his fall'. And just as in Poe's tale the battlements prove no barrier to a death that can materialize inside, the red death seeps into the ships and inside the bodies through Goldner's badly soldered cans of food, an insidious, invisible and inescapable poison of lead. The grotesque display is proleptic, exposing the failure of the expedition and prophesying doom. Above all, the Gothic vignette is meant to hold up a mirror darkly, suggesting that we are all Franklins or Prosperos, seeking a vain Grail and believing in our technological fortresses, regardless of the Grim Death that will always seep inside and await us where we least expect it, in a final conflagration of our own designing.

In an interview, Simmons admits that he uses the frame of the grand American adventure novel not only to reflect on British colonial hubris, but on the US:

> there is an American sense to it, but we've sort of traded places with the British, haven't we. We're – we're now the imperial power that dominates the earth and thinks we can do anything we want and we're the ones with the technology that gives us the hubris to think that we can set up bases on the moon and travel to Mars.

The Americans share the British blindness and inability to learn: 'We've been rapped on the nose a few times by both political realities and Nature recently ... so in a sense it is a great American adventure novel because we're the ones with that mindset now.'[28] Like Atwood and Geiger before him,[29] Simmons uses the image of the canary in the mine: writers of fantasy and science fiction may never predict the future, but they may warn against Frankensteinian hubris, like canaries in a mine; and the main issue is now global warming.

The final chapters achieve a spectacular shift in viewpoint. Crozier is shot by Hickey, crawls on the ice, falls into icy water and is presumed dead; yet the final chapters take us back within Crozier's consciousness, as he struggles to make sense of his surroundings, awakening in a fur tent with Lady Silence watching over him. The mock epic turns into a revaluation of cultural differences.

For most of the novel, Lady Silence has remained onboard Crozier's ship, the one Inuit character the crew come into contact with; she has literally lost her tongue, chewed at the roots; she was at worst seen as a witch, a Jonah, at best as a native who might show them how to hunt. In the final chapters, she saves Crozier and introduces him to the warm 'domesticity of blood and blubber'[30] which Dickens found so repellent. All of a sudden, the great space of the ships, which was home for most of the novel (there is a poignant moment when Crozier abandons ship and simply will not look back on his beloved *Terror*) is stripped of its mask and shown for what it is, an alien, absurd design intruding upon a place for which it is totally unfit, where it brings the corruption of technology. Crozier becomes aware of a different way of negotiating the harsh icy surroundings, of Silence's sensuous body and intelligence, previously screened by racial prejudice, as she communicates with gestures, a cat's cradle of sinews, and most often, simply by mentally sending her thoughts.

Like Lady Silence, the rough Crozier is granted shamanistic qualities, having inherited his grandmother's second sight. When he battles alcohol withdrawal, his first brush with death turns into a trance in which he sees the Thing of the ice as a priest, feeding him the Eucharist – paving the way for the shift from Christian to Inuit myth. Simmons explains away his monster as a creation of Sedna, the goddess of animals, who sought revenge against her enemies but was threatened by her own creation and banished him to the most barren of Arctic regions. Recalling Shelley's *Frankenstein*, Simmons's monster Tuunbaq shifts the stress from scientific hubris to the wish to achieve a balanced relationship with nature. In Inuit mythology, Sedna, whose fingers were cut by her own father and turned into otters, whales and seals, needs to be appeased or she will not give food; the myth represents respect for the animals which are being hunted, and the need for a stable ecosystem through a process of symbolic give and take. Lady Silence teaches Crozier to hunt seals and perform rituals. Simmons replaces traditional Inuit throat singing with a kind of musical intercourse, blurring the boundaries between human and animal, physical and spiritual, as the body becomes an instrument. Taught by Silence to understand *inua*, the all-pervasive soul, Crozier goes native and literally gives up his tongue, offering it to the monster 'in mutual ceremonial silence', while the Northern Lights shimmer in the sky, in a chapter which bears no title, no name and no spatial or temporal indications. The paratext signals the switch from the Franklin expedition to the metamorphosis of Crozier: the final chapter calls Crozier by his Inuk name, Taliriktug, 'strong arm', the name of a survivor.

In a final twist, Crozier meets his own drifting ship. As he climbs the dark phantom hull of the eponymous *Terror*, which has not yet sunk, he finds a corpse in his own cabin, an echo of the Conradian motifs of doubles and ships, metaphors for existential doubts and choices. The skeleton may be one of the sailors who tried to return to the ship, but it also symbolizes Crozier's former self waiting for him; the body reaches out for Crozier, a signal that Crozier needs to resist the vampiric hold of the past, to renounce civilization and the ship of death that embodies the commercial logic of progress. Crozier sets the ship on fire, a sacrificial pyre which recalls the way in which Frankenstein's monster presumably dies, an oxymoronic alliance of ice and flame to exorcize the lie of self-defeating, suicidal and vampiric modern hubris, a reminder (perhaps a rather heavy-handed one) that we all need to sacrifice something in order to preserve whatever may remain of global balance.

Thus the Gothic tale of the ice monster and the lost expedition is made to resonate with the cultural anxieties of our time, no longer Mary Shelley's fear of hubristic science or Hawks's fear of insensitive rulers, be they capitalist or communist, but the apocalyptic fear of ecological blindness. The Franklin expedition becomes the paradigm of colonial misappropriation, trying to cut through the ice for the sake of trade and capitalist consumption rather than paying attention to place itself and its nature or function. In the 1950s, when Hawks made his movie, the Pole and the North were territories disputed by superpowers, Russia, Canada and the United States, much like the 1820s contest between Russia and Britain after the end of the Napoleonic wars, much like today, when countries rush forward to claim territories which may be mined and exploited for the first time thanks to the greenhouse effect. But the threat has now gone global. Atwood, Vollmann and Simmons all draw attention to the soiling of the North, erasing the problem of the apocalyptic time span evoked by Kerridge, because the parable of the past suggests that this is happening now, that the melting ice is a sign of hubris and warped technology, and that the consequences for the Inuit are dire, but are only the prelude to the world's march towards disease and hunger. Towards the end of Simmons's novel, the change brought by technology is glimpsed in a vision of lost birds and dying polar bears, warning that the death of the spirit of the ice, which may be seen as an implacable monster, will only bring global disaster: 'When the *Tuunbaq* dies because of the *kabloona* sickness, the spirit-governors-of-the-sky knew, its cold, white domain will begin to heat and melt and thaw' (710). And the end of the ice will upset the balance of the world.

Notes

1   Richard Kerridge, 'Ecothrillers: Environmental Cliffhangers', in Laurence Coupe (ed.), *The Green Studies Reader: From Romanticism to Ecocriticism* (London: Routledge, 2000), pp. 242–9, at p. 244.
2   Kerridge, 'Ecothrillers', p. 243.
3   Bruno Latour, 'Why Has Critique Run Out of Steam? From Matters of Fact to Matters of Concern', *Critical Inquiry* 30/2 (2004): 225–48. Latour wishes to create a Parliament of Things; his own view of Shelley's story is that it was wrong to abandon the monster rather than create it, that technology is not the problem but rather the refusal to face unforeseen consequences. See Bruno Latour, 'Victor Frankenstein's Real Sin', *Domus* 878 (February 2005), available online at www.domusweb.it/en/magazine/878/.
4   Jen Hill, *White Horizon: The Arctic in Nineteenth-Century British Imagination* (Albany: State University of New York Press, 2008).
5   See Ken McGoogan, *Fatal Passage: The Untold Story of John Rae, the Arctic Adventurer Who Discovered the Fate of Franklin* (Toronto: HarperCollins Canada, 2001).
6   Louis Brannan, *Under the Management of Mr Charles Dickens: His Production of 'The Frozen Deep'* (Ithaca, NY: Cornell University Press, 1966).
7   See Russell A. Potter, *Arctic Spectacles: The Frozen North in Visual Culture, 1818–1875* (Seattle: University of Washington Press, 2007).
8   Margaret Atwood, *Strange Things: The Malevolent North in Canadian Literature* (Oxford: Clarendon Press, 1995), p. 21.
9   Margaret Atwood, 'Introduction', in Owen Beattie and John Geiger, *Frozen in Time* [1987] (Vancouver: Douglas & McIntyre, 2004), pp. 1–8, at p. 6.
10 Guy Debord, *The Society of the Spectacle*, trans. Donald Nicholson-Smith (New York: Zone Books, 1995), p. 15.
11 Debord, *Society of the Spectacle*, p. 22.

12 Margaret Atwood, 'The Age of Lead', in *Wilderness Tips* [1991] (Toronto: McClelland, 1992), pp. 145–62, p. 153. Subsequent references are to this edition and are given in parentheses in the text.

13 Andrew Lambert, *Franklin: Tragic Hero of Polar Navigation* (London: Faber and Faber, 2009).

14 Elizabeth McGregor, *The Ice-Child* (New York: Dutton, 2001).

15 Gwendolen MacEwen's *Terror and Erebus* is a verse drama for radio which was broadcast by the Canadian Broadcasting Corporation in 1965. Gwendolen MacEwen, *Terror and Erebus*, in Meaghan Strimas (ed.), *The Selected Gwendolen MacEwen* (Toronto: Exile Editions, 2008), pp. 38–60.

16 Rudy Wiebe, *A Discovery of Strangers* (Toronto: Vintage Books, 1995).

17 Mordecai Richler, *Solomon Gursky Was Here* (Toronto: Viking Canada, 1989).

18 William Vollmann, *The Rifles* (New York: Penguin, 1995).

19 Dan Simmons, *The Terror* (New York: Little, Brown, 2007). Subsequent references are to this edition and are given in parentheses in the text.

20 Fred Botting, *Gothic* (London: Routledge, 1996).

21 *The Thing From Another World* is a 1951 science fiction film officially directed by Christian Nyby, but Hawks produced it, gave considerable advice and probably directed most of it. The film was released by RKO Pictures.

22 Kendall R. Phillips, *Projected Fears: Horror Films and American Culture* (Westport CT: Praeger, 2005).

23 Jules Verne, *Les Aventures du capitaine Hatteras* (Paris: Pierre-Jules Hetzel, 1866).

24 Edgar Allan Poe, *The Complete Tales and Poems of Edgar Allan Poe* (Harmondsworth: Penguin, 1982), p. 260. Subsequent references are to this edition and are given in parentheses in the text.

25 Mikhail Bakhtin, *Rabelais and His World*, trans. Helene Iswolsky (Bloomington: Indiana University Press, 2008).

26 Edgar Allan Poe, *Arthur Gordon Pym and Related Tales* (Oxford: Oxford University Press, 1994), p. 175.

27 Simmons, *The Terror*, p. 439.

28 Available online at www.trashotron.com/agony/audio/dan_simmons_2007.mp3 (accessed 17 July 2012).

29 Atwood, 'Introduction', p. 2.

30 The expression is taken from Charles Dickens's *Household Words* article, 'The Lost Arctic Voyagers', published on 2 December 1854.

4

David Punter

Algernon Blackwood: nature and spirit

Algernon Blackwood was born in 1869 and died in 1951, and it has been said that he was one of the greatest English writers of ghost stories and supernatural fiction. That is not my comment but one made by H. P. Lovecraft, and it perhaps provides a rare opportunity to agree with something the egregious Lovecraft said.[1] Blackwood was also a writer of children's stories and novels; he was a traveller, particularly in Canada, where some of his best-known stories are set; a sometime newspaper reporter and factory owner; and he had a vast range of spiritual interests, ranging from Buddhism and Hinduism to the Order of the Golden Dawn.

Among his output was a series of psychic detective stories featuring the 'physician extraordinary', Dr John Silence, which were extremely popular at the time they emerged; the last significant publication of his work by a mainstream publisher was, as far as I am aware, the collection of stories called *The Insanity of Jones and Other Tales* by Penguin in 1966, although many of Blackwood's other works, which run to some thirty book-length titles plus a mass of other material, are now available from small presses. His fame in England seemed – wrongly, as it turned out – secured when he embarked on a radio career in 1934, which later took him on to television as a story-teller and led in 1949 to the award of a CBE for services to literature.

Blackwood was interested in science; he was interested in psychology and psychoanalysis, and was an avid reader of Freud; he was interested in various strands of late Victorian and Edwardian mysticism and psychical research. It has been said, no doubt contentiously, that he was the only major writer of supernatural fiction to take the supernatural seriously. And his work is governed by a very particular interpretation of the relations between 'nature' and 'spirit', considered in the widest applications of both terms.

In Blackwood's writings it is possible to find a peculiar, perhaps eccentric, certainly unique form of mysticism which gives rise to a curious kind of textuality. So far I have used words like 'supernatural', but have shied away from the perhaps more obvious notion of the 'Gothic'; this is because Blackwood occupies, in my opinion, a strangely oblique position in relation to the Gothic. In his stories and novels there are certainly ghosts; there are even, occasionally, horrors, and when Blackwood wished to chill the blood he could certainly do so. But we may suspect that that was not his main concern. We might see this particularly clearly if we contrast his work with that of his near contemporary, M. R. James. Where James produces, in stories like 'Count Magnus' or 'The Treasure of Abbot Thomas' (both 1904), a set of supernatural forces which are frequently brutal in their physicality, it is rarely in Blackwood that we as readers can be sure that we are being presented with something physical at all.[2] Whereas the terror in James springs from the thought of what we might be subjected to if we were to see clearly the things which flap and howl at the borders of our vision, in Blackwood we are more likely to run the risk of being, to distort the old critical phrase, 'blinded by insight': there is a kind of euphoria, a kind of rapture in the visions which conclude many of Blackwood's stories, when the curtain inside the mind is torn back and we find ourselves exposed to 'natural' forces vaster than we can comprehend.[3]

The conclusion of many of these events is the opening of the inner eye, but the ascent to the ecstasy of union with nature is fraught with pitfalls and complexities; the main one is death. 'The Dance of Death' (1907), for example, concerns a young man named Browne who has been warned by his doctor that his heart is weak.[4] Oppressed by this discovery, and finding himself invited to a dance despite the fact that he has been warned to undertake no excessive exertion, he goes. He has a poor and uninteresting time of it until he notices across a crowded floor a girl 'dressed in pale green', who always dances with the same man.[5] He asks various people who she is, but not only do they not know, they do not see her at all. The dance goes on: Browne prepares to leave but finds he cannot until he has seen the girl again. As he waits he is assailed by sharp stabs of pain, but then is rewarded when she again appears, now without her previous escort, and they dance. As they dance, the artificial light of the room fades away and is replaced by a more general radiance. It comes, of course, as no surprise at all to discover in the cursory concluding paragraph that he has dropped dead of a heart attack.

Attacks of the heart are all too frequent in Blackwood; perhaps this makes reading his work difficult in the twenty-first century. It is, of course, possible to feel that in stories like this mysticism tips over into the sentimental; or that the sympathy one might feel for the protagonist becomes more like pity, in one of the worst senses of that almost infinitely complex term. What, though, fascinates me about the story is the intensity and smoothness of the transition: the way – unusual, I think, in western literature though more common in, for example, Chinese tales of the supernatural – in which the text seeks, quite overtly, to manage the passage between life and death and to assert a broader view of nature within which these human concerns become petty, trivialized.

There is no fear here: indeed, there is a kind of fulfilment of a hope for escape from what Blake referred to as the 'same dull round'.[6] And that escape is, in fact, into a world of great trees, cool air and open skies, a world of ecological unity writ large. In another Blackwood story, 'The Glamour of the Snow' (1911), the plot is perhaps not dissimilar, though the setting is different: Hibbert, the protagonist, is holidaying high in the Valais Alps, where he is trying to write a book.[7] Torn between the world of the tourists who are his only human companions and the wonders of nature all around him, one night he ventures out skating alone on the hotel ice-rink, and there he meets (as we might have come by now to expect) a girl who skates superbly but whose face is hidden. Over the next few nights, she entices him out of the safety of the hotel and higher and higher up the mountain slopes until at last:

> The girl stood in front of him, very near; he felt her chilly breath upon his cheeks; her hair passed blindingly across his eyes; and that icy wind came with her. He saw her whiteness close; again, it seemed, his sight passed through her into space as though she had no face. Her arms were round his neck. She drew him softly downwards to his knees. He sank; he yielded utterly; he obeyed. Her weight was upon him, smothering, delicious. The snow was to his waist … [8]

Hibbert survives this deathly encounter, leaving behind him, when he leaves the village, an enduring legend of the mad night skier. But it is the blinding, the blindness of these moments of vision which seems to me most emblematic of Blackwood: the series of attempts to convey the sense that, in the end, or perhaps explicitly and particularly *at* the end, nothing can be seen: that the gaze which has been merely impeded by natural objects – again, perhaps the implicit Blake reference is obvious here[9] – comes to be able to pass through them undisturbed so that a different world may be encompassed – through, of course, senses different from the ones which we exercise in daily life, 'expanded' senses which might return us to the occulted animal within us.[10]

I mentioned that at the end of 'The Dance of Death' the protagonist escapes to a world characterized, at least in part, by a sense of oneness with the trees, with forests, and this is another familiar – if for that very reason distinctly uncanny – theme of Blackwood's. We might indeed say that at the heart of Blackwood's discourse of nature there lies something recognizable in contemporary terms as 'ecology', but I should perhaps say now that in my view 'ecology' is not a word with which we should feel particularly comfortable. There is a standing danger (of which some critics are aware) that it can come to signify a static condition, or at least a bounded, non-randomized one, a possibility that while, obviously, all manner of evolution will continue, nonetheless there is the possibility of control over the courses it may take.[11]

To object to such a concept of control is, of course, to land on the side of the demons, from James Lovelock with his wish for the 'accursed species' of humanity to leave the earth forever to her own devices, to those more mild-mannered sceptics who question the constitutive validity of concepts like 'biodiversity' while much of the world's medical effort is devoted to eradicating exactly such maddening proliferations in the world of the bacterium. 'Proliferation', perhaps, is a key word: certainly it would take us from ecology to the stranger and perhaps more apt world, less constrained and less subject to control, of Gilles Deleuze and Félix Guattari, and those notions of theirs which cluster around the 'becoming-animal'.[12]

Or 'becoming-forest'. I want now to move on to two more of Blackwood's stories, 'The Man whom the Trees Loved' (1912) and 'The Willows' (1907).[13] 'The Man whom the Trees Loved' is, put very briefly, the story of one Bittacy, a forester who, having spent all his life caring for trees, is in the end, as it were, 'spirited away' by the forest despite his wife's best efforts to save him. He becomes one with the trees, becomes forest, but in the process necessarily dehumanizes; what is left is, we are told, 'but a shell, half emptied'.[14] Our humanness, as we work with the great forces of nature, becomes revealed, so Blackwood seems to say, as a mere defence: while we are working at the self-appointed human task of control, the natural world is working away against that, undermining boundaries, continually spilling

over and spilling out, proliferating in ways which Deleuze and Guattari
would refer to as 'rhizomatic', overwhelming attempts at order:[15] until,
of course, this endlessly seeping tide makes us so angry that we resort
to slash-and-burn as the only way to exert final control – though let us
not forget that it turns out that, despite what Cormac McCarthy so
devastatingly tells us in *The Road* (2006), scorched forests in fact form
the necessary backdrop to all sorts of vegetative rejuvenation.[16]

In 'The Man whom the Trees Loved', we hear Bittacy's wife speaking:

> She saw that jealousy was not confined to the human and animal world alone,
> but ran through all creation. The Vegetable Kingdom knew it too. So-called
> inanimate nature shared it with the rest. Trees felt it. This Forest just beyond the
> window – standing there in the silence of the autumn evening across the little
> lawn – this Forest understood it equally. The remorseless, branching power that
> sought to keep exclusively for itself the thing it loved and needed, spread like a run-
> ning desire through all its million leaves and stems and roots. In humans, of course,
> it was consciously directed; in animals it acted with frank instinctiveness; but in
> trees this jealousy rose in some kind of blind tide of impersonal and unconscious
> wrath that would sweep opposition from its path as the wind sweeps powdered
> snow from the surface of the ice. Their number was a host with endless reinforce-
> ments, and once it realised its passion was returned the power increased.[17]

'All men kill the thing they love', Oscar Wilde had written fifteen years
previously;[18] but the real question here is about anthropomorphism,
and about what this textual, rhetorical move to spread the emotion of
jealousy across the natural world achieves and what it runs the danger
of destroying.[19] What seems to me most interesting here is the extraordinary complexity of the phrases around the 'remorseless, branching
power', for this is surely, at one level, the encompassing, entangling
power of jealousy; but it translates effortlessly, rhizomatically, into
the power of the forest canopy itself. What would a jealousy be that
is impersonal and unconscious? But perhaps we might reverse this
question: what would be a jealousy be that is *not*, as Iago suggests
to us, impersonal and unconscious, one that continues to see clearly
the object of its wrath? Would this be jealousy at all, or something
more rational, something far more foreign to the regime of the forest,
the 'blind tide' – and here the word 'blind', the notion of blindness,
is crucial – with 'endless reinforcements' which suggests the fear-
some grasp of passion, the utter prevalence of jealousy, in one form or
another, as the very pattern of killing?

'The Willows' is set on the Danube, and a scary region, ecologically
speaking, it is. It is a region which is uncontaminated, pure; it is also,
for that very reason, completely unintelligible; it makes us blind in its

absence of location or bearings. What we have here is a momentary defeat for the forces of ceaseless imperialistic exploration: if the impetus behind such forces is to wipe out the right of nature to hold its own secrets – a situation upon which one of the most astute commentators remains the Roman author Pliny the Elder – then here, for a transfixed and transfiguring moment, invasion is held at bay and challenged for supremacy.[20]

Blackwood uses the interesting phrase 'another evolution not parallel to the human'.[21] It is interesting that in some editions of the story the word 'evolution' is given as 'revolution', and we are all no doubt familiar with the crucial ambiguities borne by the concept of 'revolution' since, at least, Elizabethan times: revolution as the ceaseless turn of the wheel, revolution as the abrupt break with the past. We can probably also sense the critical relation between 'revolution' and 'evolution' – between, on the one hand, the cyclical and the developmental and, on the other, the abrupt break and the slow transmutation. All of these, we may take it, are available models for 'natural' change; but whether Blackwood intended 'evolution' or 'revolution' here, the important thing is that it is 'not parallel' to the human, it bespeaks a 'different' world, a world of *différance*, and it thus suggests to us something of the difficulty, a difficulty which is endemic whenever we speak of matters which we may or may not choose to signify under the word 'ecology', of what it is that we do when we attempt to interpret nature, or indeed even to see it with clarity. We are confronted always and inevitably with a dilemma: either we impose human agendas and strategies on to the world of the other, or we treat that world as its own thing, in which case we may feel that we are awarding it due dignity while in fact our admission that we know nothing of it may rob us of all 'fellow-feeling' in our dealings with it.[22]

There are many directions in which this thought of Blackwood, which I take to be one about the colonialism of the human mind, about the impossibility of interpretation without interference, might take us. One of those many directions would be back to Hegel, whose observations on spirit and nature have never been fully sublated. Here is a brief passage from the *Lectures on the Philosophy of Religion* (1821–31):

> The animal, the stone, the plant is not evil; evil is first present within the sphere of knowledge; it is the consciousness of independent Being, or Being-for-self relatively to an Other, but also relatively to an Object which is inherently universal in the sense that is the Notion, or rational will ... To be evil means in an abstract sense to isolate myself; the isolation which separates me from the Universal

represents the element of rationality, the laws, the essential characteristics of Spirit.[23]

'Aggressive', Blackwood says; 'spiritual agencies' can be 'aggressive'. This, of course, is a question of perception, a question of how we see the potential for breaking down the palisade, for breaking and entering into the island stockade which passes for an image of human invulnerability. We may have now moved beyond Hegel's notion of the universal, but the sense of willed isolation here, while it obviously picks up on conventional Christian notions of exile from the Garden of Eden and the separation from God's mercy represented by the angel with the flaming sword, nevertheless continues to interest, especially, in my view, in the connection Hegel makes here with the realm of law.

The rest of the world, the non-human world is, as it were, beyond the rule of law, despite Doctor Moreau's endless attempts to instil the concept of law into the animal brain,[24] and despite our constant misbelief in the real meaning of so-called 'animal training' – both in the end, as is surely obvious, come down to fear. Fear, despite Tennyson, is nevertheless in one sense inimical to natural development – Hegel again:

> That development which in the sphere of Nature is a peaceful growth, is in that of spirit, a severe, a mighty conflict with itself ... Its expansion, therefore, does not present the harmless tranquillity of mere growth, as does that of organic life, but a stern reluctant working against itself.[25]

The ramifications of this difficult and dangerous line of thinking spread into Darwin, Heidegger and beyond, especially perhaps in that last formulation that the working of spirit is always, in some sense, a 'working against itself'.[26] What would the pleasure or the pain be of sacrificing the rule of law, of renouncing the endless striving against the Blakean selfhood? Well that, as we have seen, is what happens in the case of a number of Blackwood's protagonists; it happens to Bittacy the forester, although whether of his own volition or not becomes a question insusceptible of reply if we accept that he has moved into that realm where, as it were, the 'case is altered' and our preconceptions about natural and physical boundaries dissolve in the bright mist. Here amid the willows, the question is again put as to what would happen if 'our minds would succumb under the weight of the awful spell, and we should be drawn across the frontier into *their* world'.[27] Would we end up writing, as Deleuze and Guattari suggest, like a non-human – like a willow, perhaps (Hardy has more than one good passage about what it is – would be – like to write like a tree)? like a wolf? like a dog?

Like a dog, perhaps: Blackwood's story 'The Camp of the Dog' (1908),[28] which is mainly about the werewolf, the double, is also about trees again, but I will turn instead for a moment to a particular moment in another story, 'The Lost Valley' (1910), where our hero penetrates, not unusually in Edwardian writing, into the heart of a 'lost valley' (as I have said, Blackwood had read a great deal of Freud).[29] What he finds is a curious twist on the Hegelian relation between spirit and isolation:

> he now became distinctly aware that the emptiness of this lonely valley was only apparent. It is impossible to say through what sense, or combination of senses, this singular certainty was brought to him that the valley was not really as forsaken and deserted as it seemed – that, on the contrary, it was the very reverse. … The valley as a matter of fact was – full. Packed, thronged and crowded it was to the very brim of its mighty wooded walls – with life. It was now borne in upon him, with an inner conviction that left no room for doubt, that on all sides living things – persons – were jostling him, rubbing elbows, watching all his movements, and only waiting till the darkness came to reveal themselves.[30]

One thing one might fairly wonder here is exactly what Blackwood means by 'persons'. Plenty of his other work would suggest that a closer approximation to his meaning would be the Buddhist term 'beings', which could, of course, include the multitude of creatures without elbows or, as with dogs, with elbows which we humans perceive to be the wrong way round.

Certainly, to put it in a quite different framework, his perception here could be easily converted into a version of and comment on the notion of the 'empty land' conventional as a founding myth of settler colonies (including, of course, Blackwood's own occasional domicile, Canada); the notion that there is nothing here, that the land is ours to occupy, that the ghosts of previous indigenes, whether they be humans or other animals, are mere intimations we receive because of our fear, that they do not relate to the inevitable return; and so we are reduced again to slash-and-burn or, in V. S. Naipaul's inimitable and more up-to-date term, 'insuranburn'.[31] Can you insure against the exiled dead?

Well, perhaps you can, but only if you know what they are, which would seem difficult under the conditions of a dark, mostly blinded revelation such as the one half-presented to us here. But equally it would only be then that the extreme difficulty, if not the impossibility, of an equal confrontation – or assimilation – between the nocturnal and the diurnal could be achieved. And this, we might say, strikes to the heart of Blackwood's fiction, which takes place in a perennial series of half-lights – and what, after all, could be more ecologically friendly? In the half-light the vast nocturnal advantages of bat, owl and other members of the traditional witches' cauldron can be brought back into line with the poverty of human eyesight; the trickery of red eyes glowing in the dark can be suitably reduced, as it is in another of Blackwood's stories, to mere reflections of the dying embers of a human-built camp fire.

But Blackwood's vision in the 'The Lost Valley' might suggest other directions as well; it might take us forward, for example, to a vision of community where the identity of each individual – human, animal or indeed phantom – need not be a condition of entry. This may sound mystical, and that is probably because in one sense it is, and we should not worry about that: to stay in tune with Blackwood there has to be a certain adoption of mystical values. But in another sense perhaps it is not: because if we are to think about the forces of nature without imposing our imperialist will, delivered for example through the horrifying anthropomorphization meted out to companion animals,[32] then we have to go through a process, at least arguably, of meeting the animal, the 'other world', the world of 'nature', whatever that might mean, on its own terms without imposing what Hegel challengingly and counter-intuitively (as always) refers to as the laws of spirit.[33] I am not sure whether this is something of what Blackwood is trying to intimate in his curious, half-lit, phantomatic stories; but certainly in many of them the narcissistic centralization of the human suffers, if not from displacement, at least from a perceptible set of tremors – tremors of the heart, signs of an angina of the soul – which emanate from a larger, less certain sense of what 'life', in the more general, more proliferative sense of the term, might mean; and from an unavoidable realization of the presence of the almost unheard languages in which something might be replying to, at the same time as undermining, the assertive accents in which humanity tends to deal with those forms of life which it continues to perceive as its inferiors.

We can return from these difficulties to something more recognizably human – if anything by Blackwood is fully recognizable as human – by turning to his story 'The Insanity of Jones' (1907).[34] In one sense, this is a simple tale of madness and paranoia. Jones, a clerk in a fire insurance office, is, we are told, a man who

> had always been tremblingly aware that he stood on the borderland of another region, a region where time and space were merely forms of thought, where ancient memories lay open to the sight, and where the forces behind each human life stood plainly revealed, and he could see the hidden springs at the very heart of the world … So convinced was he that the external world was the result of a

vast deception practised upon him by the gross senses, that when he stared at a great building like St Paul's he felt it would not very much surprise him to see it suddenly quiver like a shape of jelly and then melt utterly away, while in its place stood all at once revealed the mass of colour, or the great intricate vibrations, or the splendid sound – the spiritual idea – which it represented in stone.[35]

Possessed of these convictions, Jones inhabits two contradictory worlds. In one of these worlds, the word of dream, he meets a man – if it is a man; certainly whatever it is, it is dead – who convinces him that, in a previous life some four hundred years ago, he has suffered a terrible wrong and it is his duty to avenge it. He has pointed out to him the perpetrator of this age-old injustice and, utterly persuaded of the justice of his own cause, shoots him several times and then, 'acting impersonally' as he sees it, 'as an instrument in the hands of the Invisibles who dispense justice and balance accounts', places his final shots direct into the man's eyes.

Jones is insane, of course: the title of the story tells us as much. But what is interesting is that his insanity takes, for the larger part of the narrative, a shape almost indistinguishable from the intimations of final, blinding insight with which we have become familiar from others of Blackwood's tales. The belief in the curtain, and in what lies behind the curtain, can, it seems, lead us towards a kind of insight through the blinding of the outer senses; or it can, as in the final paroxysm of this story, lead us into a field where all trace of humanity is buried, emblematized, of course, here in the intolerable blinding of the other. 'The Insanity of Jones' is not a story about the 'natural' world; but it is a story about the delusions of the human, and about the ab-humanity which might be revealed at moments of the most intense stress or pressure.

Perhaps in some ways Blackwood seems old-fashioned, Edwardian to the core: but there can be no doubt that there is a thread which runs through his stories and can connect us to more contemporary thoughts on this notion of the inhuman and on the pathologies through which we might read it. Blackwood's chief characters are, as it were, only temporarily or even parenthetically human: the something else which is going on inside and around them can be thought of as mystical; it can also be thought of as related to Blackwood's readings of Freud, to his conviction that everyday interactions are only a surface layer, a set of egoic fictions, which act as a frail and flimsy cover on a quite different set of aspirations, desires and violences; and it can also be thought of as the pressure of the non-human, the 'animal', on the surfaces of civilization, much as the 'crypt' adumbrated in the psychoanalytic revisionism of Nicolas Abraham and Maria Torok exerts its insistent pressure even though its secret shape can never be known.[36]

My final example from Blackwood is a story called 'The Touch of Pan' (1917) – not to be confused with Arthur Machen's masterpiece *The Great God Pan* (1894), but traversing, in a way, quite similar terrain.[37] But here we have a man faced with a choice: a choice as to whether he will look outward or inward. On the brink of a conventional marriage – and here we are in the familiar Gothic company of *Dracula* (1897) and the eve-of-wedding fantasy – he experiences a series of visions, collected around the figure of a wild girl and of the always hidden form of the god Pan, who cannot be seen and is indistinguishable from the trees whose movements both reveal and conceal his presence. The question is whether he will obey the summons; or, perhaps more accurately, what will be the balance of power and weakness which will lead him into one or the other of the solutions to his impossible dilemma.

The story is virtually postmodern in its hinted indecisiveness; it is not as though Heber, the protagonist, is really even in a position to make a choice. Whatever he may choose has been already laid down for him: the achievements and disappointments which will flow from one or the other decision do not belong to the short-term future alone but are emblematic of a far longer movement of time. And time, as Freud says, does not exist in the unconscious: or if it does, it is looped into baroque patterns, it has lost its beginnings and its ends, its origins and its trajectory into an imagined future.[38] The passing of time, the clear movement from past through present into future, is a mere distraction: rather what one has, what one is destined to live with, is an endless looping of phrase, a process caught in condensation and displacement, a negotiation between spirit and nature.

The most obvious example in 'The Touch of Pan' is the repeated phrase '*In the heart of that wood dwell I.*' What is going on in that phrase, it seems to me, is an attempt to incarnate a world in language: to make a form of words into a magical incantation which is capable of bringing a world into being and which thereby asserts a formative power of language, a primordial power of language, even a metaphorically 'non-human' or 'pre-human' language which will undercut and undermine our attempts to use language for our own anthropocentric ends.

'In the beginning was the word': we might argue that this seems to be true for Blackwood, but then we would come up again against the question of when the 'beginning' might have been. It would seem closer to the truth to suggest that most of Blackwood's stories take the form of recapitulations: they press upon the point at which the everyday shell of the human breaks apart and reveals a different truth, one which exists adrift from the correlates of time and space and yet is at the same time far more deeply embedded in the earth.

In conclusion, let me try to return, as it were, to the heart of the matter. Blackwood's concern is constantly with the heart – the state of the heart, the 'course of the heart'. The involution of the heart places it directly over against the processes of time and history, and furthermore it implies a constant oscillation between life and death, such that one does not simply supervene upon the other and mere human accommodation is superseded by a different order. A quotation from Sartre on Jean Genet is curiously relevant:

> To say 'instant' is to say *fatal instant*. The instant is the reciprocal and contradictory envelopment of the before by the after. One is still what one is going to cease to be and already what one is going to become. One lives one's death, one dies one's life. One feels oneself to be one's own self and another; the eternal is present in an atom of duration. In the midst of the fullest life, one has the sense that one will merely survive.[39]

Some of this is surely recognizable in the context of Blackwood: the condensation and collapse of time, the emphasis on the fatal instant, the attack of the heart, the question of what might be a full life and by what criteria it might be judged. But behind these issues there also seems to be a constant, often partly suppressed questioning of assumptions about human supremacy: the trees, the river, the dog are carriers of a different kind of life, far more long-lived, far more powerful than our own. One of Blackwood's strengths is that he offers no glib answers as to how we might accommodate ourselves to these 'other lives', beyond suggesting that an awareness of them, a temporary lifting of the curtain of denial behind which we mostly pass our time, may mark not only an escape from the confines of that inevitable humanness but also the possibility of rapturous, fully engaged experience which is otherwise not available to us.

Notes

1 H. P. Lovecraft, 'The Supernatural in Literature', *The Recluse* (1927). This chapter in part builds on and develops a previous essay, 'Pity: Reflections on Algernon Blackwood', *ELN* 48/1 (2010): 129–38.

2 See M. R. James, *'Casting the Runes' and Other Ghost Stories*, ed. Michael Cox (Oxford: Oxford University Press 1987), pp. 43–56, 78–96.

3 See Paul de Man, *Blindness and Insight: Essays in the Rhetoric of Contemporary Criticism* (Minneapolis: University of Minnesota Press 1983).

4 In Algernon Blackwood, *The Insanity of Jones and Other Tales* (Harmondsworth: Penguin, 1964), pp. 216–26.

5 Blackwood, *The Insanity of Jones*, p. 219.

6 William Blake, *There is no Natural Religion* (c.1788), in *Complete Writings*, ed. Geoffrey Keynes (London: Oxford University Press 1966), p. 97.

7 In Algernon Blackwood, *Tales of the Uncanny and Supernatural* (London: Spring Books, 1962), pp. 234–55.

8 Blackwood, *Tales of the Uncanny*, p. 252.

9 William Blake, Annotations to Wordsworth's *Poems 1815* (1826), in *Complete Writings*, p. 783.

10 See, for example, Jay D. Glass, *The Animal Within Us: Lessons about Life from our Animal Ancestors* (St Albans: Donington Press, 1998).

11 See Peter Barry, *Beginning Theory: An Introduction to Literary and Cultural Theory* (Manchester: Manchester University Press, 2009), pp. 239–61; Greg Garrard, *Ecocriticism* (New York: Routledge 2004); Hubert Zapf, 'Literary Ecology and the Ethics of Texts', *New Literary History* 39/4 (2008): 847–68.

12 See Gilles Deleuze and Félix Guattari, *A Thousand Plateaus: Capitalism and Schizophrenia*, trans. Brian Massumi (Minneapolis: University of Minnesota Press, 1987).

13 In Blackwood, *Tales of the Uncanny*, pp. 71–143, and *The Insanity of Jones*, pp. 13–64, respectively.

14 Blackwood, *Tales of the Uncanny*, p. 143.

15 See Deleuze and Guattari, *A Thousand Plateaus*.

16 See Roger Underwood, *Australian Bushfire Management: A Case Study in Wisdom versus Folly* (Western Institute for Study of the Environment, 2009). See http://westinstenv.org/ffsci/2009/03/22/australian-bushfire-management-a-case-study-in-wisdom-versus-folly/ (accessed 26 June 2012).

17 Blackwood, *Tales of the Uncanny*, pp. 121–2.

18 In 'The Ballad of Reading Gaol'; see *The Works of Oscar Wilde* (London: Collins, 1963), p. 742.

19 See Sandra D. Mitchell, 'Anthropomorphism and Cross-Species Modelling', in Lorraine Daston and Gregg Mitman (eds), *Thinking with Animals: New Perspectives on Anthropomorphism* (New York: Columbia University Press, 2005), pp. 100–17.

20 See Pliny the Elder, *Natural History*, trans. John F. Healey (Harmondsworth: Penguin, 1991).

21 Blackwood, *The Insanity of Jones*, p. 50.

22 See Lorraine Daston and Gregg Mitman, 'Introduction', in Daston and Mitman (eds), *Thinking with Animals*, pp. 1–14.

23 Georg Wilhelm Hegel, *Lectures on the Philosophy of Religion*, trans. E. B. Speirs and J. Burdon Sanderson (London: Kegan Paul, Trench, Trübner and Co., 1895), Vol. III, pp. 52–3.

24 See H. G. Wells, *The Island of Doctor Moreau*, ed. Brian Aldiss (London: Everyman, 1993).

25 Georg Wilhelm Hegel, *Lectures on the Philosophy of History* (1830–31), trans. John Sibree (New York: Dover, 1956), p. 55.

26 See Margot Norris, *Beasts of the Modern Imagination: Darwin, Nietzsche, Kafka, Ernst and Lawrence* (Baltimore, MD: Johns Hopkins University Press, 1985).

27 Blackwood, *The Insanity of Jones*, p. 50.

28 In Blackwood, *The Insanity of Jones*, pp. 293–365.

29 In Blackwood, *Tales of the Uncanny*, pp. 374–426.

30 Blackwood, *The Insanity of Jones*, pp. 410–11.

31 See, among many other examples, Shula Marks, 'South Africa: "The Myth of the Empty Land"', *History Today* 30/1 (1980): 7–12; and V. S. Naipaul, *A House for Mr Biswas* (London: André Deutsch, 1961).

32 See, for example, James A. Serpell, 'People in Disguise: Anthropomorphism and the Human–Pet Relationship', in Daston and Mitman (eds), *Thinking with Animals*, pp. 121–36; and Anthony L. Podberscek, Elizabeth S. Paul and James A. Serpell, *Companion Animals and Us: Exploring the Relationships between People and Pets* (Cambridge: Cambridge University Press, 2005).

33 See Georg Wilhelm Hegel, for example, *The Phenomenology of Mind* (1807), trans. J. B. Baillie (London: George Allen & Unwin/Humanities Press, 1966).

34 In Blackwood, *The Insanity of Jones*, pp. 189–215.

35 Blackwood, *The Insanity of Jones*, pp. 189–90.

36 See Nicolas Abraham and Maria Torok, *The Wolf Man's Magic Word: A Cryptonymy*, trans. Nicholas Rand (Minneapolis: University of Minnesota Press, 1986), and *The Shell and the Kernel: Renewals of Psychoanalysis*, trans. Nicholas Rand (Chicago: University of Chicago Press, 1994).

37 In Blackwood, *Tales of the Uncanny*, pp. 289–310.

38 See Sigmund Freud, *New Introductory Lectures on Psycho-Analysis* (1933), in *The Standard Edition of the Complete Psychological Works of Sigmund Freud*, ed. James Strachey et al. (London: Hogarth Press, 1953–74), Vol. XXII, p. 74.

39 See J. P. Sartre, *Saint Genet: Actor and Martyr*, trans. Bernard Frechtman (New York: George Braziller, 1963), p. 118.

5

William Hughes

'A strange kind of evil': superficial paganism and false ecology in *The Wicker Man*

At first sight, the British Lion B movie *The Wicker Man* (1973) appears a perfect subject for ecocritical analysis. Summerisle, the fictional Scottish island at the centre of this teleological Gothic drama, would appear to be – if anything – a nearly contemporary experiment in Green living. The film depicts – seemingly with sympathy and, as the opening credits suggest, with a feint of documentary impartiality – a separatist agrarian eco-community which celebrates both pagan folk wisdom and a literal, earthy closeness to both the land and fruitful reproduction more generally.[1] If this in itself were not enough, *The Wicker Man* might also be read as a protracted study into what nature may actually *mean* in the context of a number of alternative, and at times competing, discourses. Nature is a concept which may be defined with equal efficacy through reference to theological, ecological, scientific and pagan perspectives. As a concept under cultural negotiation, it enjoys a fluctuating relationship to a humanity which, via these competing perspectives, may be scripted variously as the privileged and unabashed holder of an enduring Old Testament dominion; the uneasy, guilt-ridden and unworthy steward of a fragile environment; or a co-equal and knowing participant in its mysteries and cycles.[2] All of these conceptions of the human encounter with nature characterize *The Wicker Man* – and, if they are contained within the various perspectives which broker power and knowledge within the film, they are equally germane to how Anthony Shaffer's meticulously constructed and intricate script might be critically approached. It is singularly surprising, therefore, that no ecocritical analysis exists of this frequently cited, and oft-screened, cult classic.

This strange omission might possibly be simply yet another reflex of the apparent reluctance of institutionalized academic ecocriticism to look beyond the evocative but safe fields of Romanticism and wilderness utopia and into the more dangerous wastelands of the Gothic. That said, it may equally be a matter of the perceived emphasis of the film's polemic. The plot of *The Wicker Man* would, at first sight, appear to stress the human interest of the doomed central character, Police Sergeant Howie, over and above the impending ecological disaster that motivates his invitation to Summerisle. Investigating the alleged disappearance of Rowan Morrison, a child whom he comes to suspect has been reserved as a blood sacrifice for the pagan deities worshipped by the islanders, Howie is brought face to face with alternative interpretations of the Christian truths he holds so dear. Some of these encounters are less an act of blasphemy than one of simple defamiliarization: Howie's indignant rejection of Lord Summerisle's doctrine of parthenogenesis, whereby the God of Fire may impregnate a girl jumping through a bale fire, is countered by the Laird's simple observation that the Christian Saviour was 'himself the son of a virgin impregnated, I believe, by a ghost'.[3] Criticism has made much of the evident clash of cultures between the islanders, their leader, Lord Summerisle, and the man the latter mockingly describes as 'a Christian copper'.[4] Indeed, the film almost seems to be an ethical and cultural trap, Howie's repressed sexuality and intolerance of the licence which may exist beyond statute law and Holy Writ contrasting with the islanders' own joyous celebration of the rites of Bacchus and Aphrodite – or their equivalents in Summerisle's Celtic-inflected pantheon. It is these promiscuous primitives who should surely attract the empathy of the metropolitan audiences of 1973, rather than the uniformed representative of dour morality and sexual restraint. It is the final reckoning, where Howie is re-scripted from Fool to martyr, which ethically problematizes all that has been represented before, a point upon which critics of *The Wicker Man* for the most part concur.[5]

There is more to *The Wicker Man* than polemic and polarity, however, and much of the unexplored territory of this provocative film is directly relevant to the preoccupations of twenty-first-century ecocriticism. The encounter between Howie and the paganism of Summerisle is, at its heart, a matter of fundamental cosmology rather than one simply predicated upon inconvenient detail. Overlooked in critical readings of Howie's bewilderment with the islanders' beliefs is the central point that the two religious discourses – Christian and pagan – have distinctively different conceptions of *both* nature *and* the relative place of humanity *in* nature. Nature, throughout *The Wicker Man*, is a contested and contestable concept. It is, for Howie, the top-down creation of a singular Christian deity; for the islanders and their nominal spokesman, Lord Summerisle, it is the pervasive and timeless embodiment of a polytheism that answers to alternative gods. The concept of nature is broad enough, as ecocritics have suggested, to embrace not merely the untouched wilderness but also the domesticated countryside, a terrain modified by the practices, subsistence or commercial, of human agriculture.[6] Indeed, the film's opening credits – which depict, in lingering detail, Howie's flight across Summerisle, taking him from the wild headlands of the coast via the lush, ordered orchards inland, to a landing in a neat, stone harbour – graphically illustrate just how broad both the concept of nature, and the domain of the island's Laird, might be.

In the form of land, and the consequent fruits of that land, nature is the legal property of those who farm and exploit it: Howie, as a rural policeman, is a defender of such things.[7] In Judaeo-Christian theology, the human stands *outside* nature, on top of it even, separated from both God and Eden. Yet, throughout *The Wicker Man*, humanity is insistently imbricated *within* the reproductive cycles of nature, making the conception of ownership perverse, if not inappropriate. The rituals of the Summerisle community anticipate or echo the cycles of the seasons, the two sacrifices at the end of the film recalling the relative place of the human in pagan nature. If not placating hostile deities, modern pagans must at least give something in thanks for, or in anticipation of, the gifts which nature will hopefully bestow.

The problem in *The Wicker Man* is that the literal fruits of nature are not for the children of the island. The dependence of this ideal microcosm of earthy pagan joyousness upon the anonymous corporate world beyond its shores is heavily emphasized. Summerisle fruit is a delicacy distributed profitably in the boldly labelled wooden crates glimpsed on several occasions during the film. Evocative names, of the kind beloved of the marketing industry – 'the renowned Summerisle famous', 'Star of Summerisle', 'Flame of Summerisle' – glamorize and commodify a humble, supposedly natural product, and the two-part structure of these names indicates a sustained and selective strain of development as much as they lay claim to the island's ownership of its fruits.[8] That claim is utterly superficial: on Summerisle, the very earth is the Laird's, and the fruits thereof.[9]

The feudal patronage of Lord Summerisle may not always be exercised in the interests of the islanders themselves. Willow, daughter of the landlord of the significantly named Green Man public house, rebuts Sergeant Howie's request for a dessert apple with the pointed retort that there are 'No apples', because, as she says, 'I expect they have all been exported.'[10] Willow's retort may well be a strategic conceit to stimulate Howie's curiosity, but it still has implications for those involved in the island's alternative form of crop production. To dwell with nature, even on Summerisle, would appear to involve an unavoidable degree of complicity with – and even a dependence upon – the essentially 'unnatural' import/export forces of cash-based commerce. However the islanders choose to venerate the origin of their fruitful bounty, the value of nature must inevitably change as a consequence of commercial interaction. Their goddess is translated into an exchange of coin or a system of credit, a way of buying in the tinned potatoes and artificially coloured broad beans consumed by Howie in the Green Man, or of obtaining wholesale the familiarly labelled bottles of Smirnoff, Haig and Martell that grace the bar of that bucolic establishment. Supposedly, nature and the fruits of nature are valorized differently on this pagan island and beyond its shores, where they pass into the custodianship of nominally Christian distributors, supermarkets and purchasers. Yet because coin changes hands on Summerisle, and the cash registers in the pub and the Post Office ring up identifiable totals in British pounds, shillings and pence, the value of nature will always be compromised there, will always embody something of modernity and the non-pagan.

It is perverse, then, that *The Wicker Man* should have become, as Judith Higginbottom asserts, 'extremely popular with Pagan audiences' – the more so as paganism is, in Higginbottom's words, characteristically attractive to 'people from the Green movement ... eco-warriors and road protestors'.[11] It must be stressed here that the depictions of paganism in *The Wicker Man* do not closely resemble actual British pagan practice in the early 1970s. Well researched though the film is, it advances an approximation or an evocation of contemporary pagan practice, supplemented by historical scholarship. Indeed, the connection between what is depicted in *The Wicker Man* and the contents of Frazer's magisterial *The Golden Bough* (1890–1915) is widely recognized by critics and acknowledged by the film's director, Robin Hardy.[12] Summerisle is regulated, as Hardy suggests, by 'a Pagan faith for our times'.[13] This is the core of the problematic relationship between the island's paganism and its ecology: both are, in essence, timely rather than timeless, and anthropocentric rather than expressing human embodiment within a diffuse and diverse natural continuum. *The Wicker Man* is a work far from congruent with environmentalist aspirations, then or now.

It is a critical commonplace that the central events of *The Wicker Man*, the processional axis, as it were, that elevates Howie's status from secular saviour to sacred victim, are scripted by the Laird and his associates to stimulate the curiosity, and outrage the morality, of the hapless policeman. Lord Summerisle's speech following Howie's rescue of Rowan, his insistence that with Howie now in his ritual position, 'the game is over ... the game of the hunted leading the hunter', merely consolidates the point.[14] The clues scattered gleefully around for Howie's benefit – the obviously missing photograph in the bar of the Green Man, the broken fruit boxes and rotting apples left in the desecrated kirk, the alternating denials and acknowledgements of the missing child's existence received from the idlers at the harbour, from Rowan's mother, sister, schoolfellows and teacher, and the island's doctor and Registrar, all whet his appetite. One wonders, indeed, why there *needs* to be a rather pompous book on pagan ceremonial in the island's tiny Carnegie Library, given that the inhabitants are all seemingly co-religionists and 'a deeply religious people' as Lord Summerisle insists.[15] Of all those present upon Summerisle, Howie alone *needs* that book, which is itself a descendant of the scholarly folklore tradition of Frazer and his associates. Essentially, the scattered elements that have been brought together to make up *this* particular May Day on Summerisle need to be conveniently synthesized so that Howie may project a likely course of events, however unprecedented they may be by mainland standards. That said, Howie is being invited to participate in a popular version of folklore that embraces the whole of the British Isles: the chapter from which he gains knowledge of the composition of the procession he will walk in is teasingly headed 'Britain: Land of Legends'.[16] What Howie absorbs, though, and what are enacted upon him, are scholarly Victorian interpretations rather than indigenous Celtic rites, a folk tradition motivated not by the earth or the seasons but literally provided to give bread, circuses and an opiate for the masses – and a profit for the masters. Howie, perversely, comes to be as much a believer in the sincerity behind the rituals that he has been drawn into as the common people who eventually immolate him.

Due to the substantial editorial cuts imposed upon the film immediately prior to its initial distribution, much of the meticulous chronicling of the island community's collective conversion to a revived paganism was unavailable to the cinema audiences of 1973.[17] Twenty-first-century academics, however, do have access to a restored director's cut of the film and, more importantly, to a crucial portion of Shaffer's script, reproduced as an appendix to Allan Brown's *Inside The Wicker Man* (2000).[18] This extract, which covers the long interview between Howie and Summerisle, is particularly illuminating, and remains an extraordinarily under-used resource in recent criticism of the film. The original dialogue is considerably longer and more detailed than that found in any distributed version of the film, though uncertainty remains as to how much of the script was actually shot.[19] Taken as a context, however, this section of script clarifies 'the true nature of sacrifice' in *The Wicker Man*, and advances a relationship between the human and the natural distinctly different from that associated with the scenes of sexual congress that have historically defined Summerisle paganism in the minds of prurient teenage boys and aesthetically minded film critics alike.[20]

Brown suggests that '*The Wicker Man* takes no sides when Howie and Summerisle describes [*sic*] the benefits of their respective faiths'.[21] The two cosmologies are, in essence, functionally the same in the film – they are mechanisms that underpin repressive social management through superficial (if not misleading) statements about cause and effect, the natural world, and the balances that are enacted between pleasure and guilt, licence and restraint. The paganism of the island is, notably, not indigenous. It is explicitly a Victorian invention, an expedient mechanism put in place as late as 1868 by the first Lord Summerisle, the current Laird's grandfather. In Shaffer's original script, an incredulous Howie is informed:

> In the last century the islanders were starving ... Dutifully, every Sunday, the people – Baptist and Catholic, Presbyterian and Free Kirk bowed as low as their respective religions permitted, to the Christian God and prayed for prosperity. But inevitably none appeared. In due course they came to realize that their reward was to be either in the colonies, or as the various priests indicated in a rare moment of agreement, in the next world. Then in 1868 my grandfather bought this island and set about changing things. He was a distinguished Victorian scientist, agronomist and free thinker – the T. H. Huxley of the Trossachs you might call him. Look at his face. How formidably benevolent he seems, as only a man incredulous of all human good can.[22]

The sergeant is quick to comment 'You are very cynical, my Lord'; Summerisle responds, bluntly, 'I simply know my family, Sergeant.'[23]

The allusion to Huxley, defender of Darwin and wittily truculent opponent to Bishop Samuel Wilberforce at the British Association meeting held in Oxford in 1860, has implications beyond the signification of a crude clash of cultures, secular and spiritual. Huxley, the author of *Evidence as to Man's Place in Nature* (1863), was active in popularizing an intimacy between the animal and plant kingdoms, based upon the ingestion and conversion of protoplasm by both.[24] This is both a scientific hypothesis and an attractive image readily accessible to a pagan community seeking a sympathetic continuity between the animal and the vegetable: witness the names, for example, of the islanders – Oak, Beech, Alder, Rowan, Myrtle – and the trees that eventually grow upon their graves.[25] The first Laird's incredulity regarding the goodness of his fellow man is certainly not in keeping with the resistance to guilt and rejection of original or innate sin associated with modern paganism.[26]

The first Lord Summerisle is thus not a druid, nor even a man having a spiritual connection to the earth. In fact, his attempts to introduce what the current Laird stresses is '*artificial* fertilizer' on to the island having been opposed by 'the fundamentalist priests', he is quick to exploit one vision towards nature against the other. The Laird continues:

> I refer you again, sir, to the spiritual vision of the Celts. These islanders needed little urging. My grandfather simply told them about The Stones – how they in fact formed an ancient temple, and that he, the Lord of the Manor, would make a sacrifice there every day to their old Gods and Goddesses, particularly those of Fertility and Fruitfulness, and that as a result of this worship (Preacher's voice) the barren island would burgeon and bring forth fruit in great abundance. (normal voice) For an atheist, grandfather had a singularly biblical turn of phrase, don't you think?[27]

Needless to say, the improved conditions promoted through artificial fertilizers and the self-interest exhibited by an uneducated population desperate to escape starvation ensured that, allegedly, 'the old Gods defeated the Christian God, and the priests fled the island never to return'.[28] Of course, the current Lord Summerisle is quite aware that this is simply a strategic lie. In the face of Howie's incredulity, he retorts:

> Come, come, Sergeant. As I've already told you, he worshipped science. What he did, of course, was to develop new cultivars of hardy fruits to suit local conditions. Out here we have his original experimental orchard, much developed, of course. Come and have a look.

This seemingly innocuous reassurance to the Christian copper's indignation is, however, more telling than it might first appear. Howie queries whether the second Laird was inclined to 'keep up the Godless charades of your grandfather', only to receive in reply the following statement from Lord Summerisle:

> He became fascinated by the old ways, if that's what you mean. Indeed, he went further. What my grandfather had started out of expediency, he continued because he truly believed that it was infinitely more spiritually nourishing than the life-denying, God-terror of the Kirk. And I might say, Sergeant, he brought me up the same way – to love the music and drama and rituals of the old pantheism, and to love nature, and to fear it and rely on it and appease it where necessary. He brought me up to...
> HOWIE (*shouting*) To be a Pagan.
> *There is a silence between them.*
> LORD SUMMERISLE (*softly*) A heathen, conceivably, but not, I hope, an unenlightened one. [original stage directions][29]

During the interview Lord Summerisle, played by a well-manicured Christopher Lee, is urbane and tolerant, a slight smirk never far from his freshly shaved face. There is a visual hint of irony here, a suggestion that the current Laird holds more to the beliefs of his grandfather than those he has associated with his father.

There is evidence, indeed, that the atheistic grandfather's project continues still, and is realized through a process of cultivation and manipulation that trusts to the alleged certainties of secular science rather than the variable whims of Celtic deities. This much is intimated by the script's specific references to a laboratory, 'equipped as any laboratory would be in a horticultural research station', and by the suggestion that the original orchard of 1868 is 'much developed', its trees 'elaborately tagged and bound', 'small refrigerators' evaluating with what success its fruits may be artificially preserved.[30] Clearly, nature is here restricted by human agency, labelled and contorted, developed and improved by grandfather, father and, implicitly – given the modern equipment involved – son also. Those refrigerators do not appear in any published cinematic print of *The Wicker Man*. The lush, subtropical garden through which Howie accompanies his host, however, is yet another reminder of just how much Summerisle has lost of its native herbage. Palm trees are not native to Scotland.

One must question the sincerity and commitment of a twentieth-century savant who is simultaneously a progressive scientist, a paternalist in the Victorian tradition, a feudal lord, a tribal chieftain, a serving priest – and a conventional Justice of the Peace. Lord Summerisle is an outsider, by education as much as ancestry. His public-school accent betrays an access to the classical and historical texts that would allow the fabrication of a convincing pagan edifice whose deities' bounties were in fact underpinned by calculated scientific practice. On the one hand Caesar's *de Bello Gallico* (the source of the popular pictorial image of the Wicker Man) and Frazer's *The Golden Bough* evoke the atmosphere of Druidry and the past; on the other, the quiet workings of experimental science, which aspire to ensure that the superficially motivated pagan ceremonial appears to bring forth the desired end.[31] *The Golden Bough* is, of course, an anachronism in 1868 – but was widely studied in the twentieth century following the release of a two-volume abridged edition in 1922.[32] This latter is just the sort of book which might repose in dusty splendour on the shelves of a provincial lending library, an uneasy neighbour to more modern and lurid accounts of regional folklore.[33]

Other features of the film's long processional section suggest a hasty *bricolage* of places and periods rather than a well-researched and truly indigenous revival of local custom: the tune 'Oranges and Lemons', played during the swordsmen's game at the Stone Circle, is English in origin, the bagpipes lending it a rather surreal, even playful, air.[34] It is probably the only well-known song about decapitation, and this is presumably the motivation for its inclusion as a ritual element in Summerisle's fabricated mythology.[35] *Sumer is Icumen in*, similarly, appears to have been adopted quite simply because of its antiquity and lyrical relation to Maying – and the 'obby 'oss, Teaser and Punch which feature in the fatal procession all have their acknowledged folk sources that lie far south of Scotland.[36] The whole ritual procession and, indeed, the events which lead up to it are, as Mikel J. Koven rightly asserts, 'an unselfconsciously Victorian perception of Celtic Paganism'.[37]

Taking this into account, it might be concluded that the choreographed events of May Day 1973 are an expedient gesture by the current Lord Summerisle equivalent to those initiated by his grandfather in 1868. After years of fruitfulness, Summerisle's harvest has unexpectedly failed. The present Laird has thereby become a hostage to the explanation proffered by his grandfather – or else, to the myth lovingly perpetuated by his own father. A successor to the now exhausted Victorian cultivar, which one assumes is under development in the laboratory and orchards so recently toured by Howie, will necessarily have to be associated with the divine rather than the scientific for the status quo to be maintained. Howie, no doubt sensing the fragility of the current Laird's position, is explicit on this score, even in the face of a population who believe that his immolation will renew the vitality of their orchards. On the very road to his funeral pyre he breaks free and confronts the collective body of his captors, Lord Summerisle being located physically behind him, the better to show the thoughtfulness and uncertainty of expression that periodically cross his hitherto humorous and confident visage. Howie declaims, at once contemptuous and certain in his demeanour:

> There is – there is no Sun God. There is no Goddess of the Fields. Your crops failed because your strains failed. Fruit is not meant to be grown upon these islands. It's against Nature. Well, don't you see that killing me is not going to bring back your apples?[38]

Howie specifically challenges the tense-faced Laird to confirm the words of his statement. The emphatic firmness of the latter's rebuttal – 'I know it will' – is, however, rapidly undermined by his wavering facial expression as Howie continues his own forecast of the island's immediate ecological future, a forecast which is based as much in the sergeant's appreciation of material science as it is in his reverence for the Christian God displaced by Summerisle's pagan theocracy. The beleaguered policeman continues:

> But don't you understand that if your crops fail this year, next year you are going to have to have another blood sacrifice. And next year, no one less than the king of Summerisle himself will do. If the crops fail, Summerisle, next year your people will kill you on May Day![39]

Summerisle looks undeniably anxious at this pronouncement. The verbal hesitation within his retort, 'They will not – fail', only emphasizes his situation more. The crowd remain implacable throughout, their collective gaze fixed on Howie rather than on Summerisle – though, just as the Laird voices his final, hesitant statement, the harbourmaster, standing to his immediate left, momentarily gazes upon him. If this latter is ambiguous as an index of the test of faith that Lord Summerisle has inadvertently imposed upon his dependents, its vision of a kingly sacrifice is a clear allusion to Frazer. It also proposes the ultimate test of the Laird-Priest's sincerity and devotion.[40]

With its uneasy balance between material science and imaginative spirituality, *The Wicker Man* is without doubt a perplexing work. In essence, Summerisle is a place from which nature – as defined by either of the above standpoints – has been summarily evacuated. On the one hand, a primal though still anthropocentric natural balance based upon indigenous fishing and farming – albeit at subsistence level – has been ousted not merely as inadequate for the basic support of life but also as inimical to the generating of profit. On the other, its replacement is predicated not upon natural selection or an evolution free from manipulation, but through processes which might be regarded as the nineteenth-century equivalent of contemporary genetic modification – albeit with the opposition of priests rather than self-styled eco-warriors.

The utopian vision advanced in *The Wicker Man* is thus far from Green in its implications. If it appears idealistic on the surface, with its lack of shame and imagery of plenitude, it is also deceptive at its very core. It is clearly based upon a lie, constructed and perpetuated to occlude both science and capitalism behind a veil of divinity. Summerisle, as it is depicted in *The Wicker Man*, is as much an experiment in social engineering and social control as it is in modified plant ecology. As such, the island's true correlatives are paternalistic Victorian industrial communities such as Bourneville and Saltaire – the first Lord Summerisle being a thinker cast as much in the mould of John Cadbury or Titus Salt as he is in that of T. H. Huxley. Summerisle is no Brook Farm, no Walden even, for the differences constituted by life offshore, in isolation, in an alternative community are in this fictional case a delusion – as much a delusion, indeed, as the empty rituals which cloak secular science with pagan divinity. *The Wicker Man* indeed anticipates many aspects of current ecocritical and Green concern – but it embodies, equally, a chilling implication that idealistic alternatives may carry, occluded within them, traces of the repressive orthodoxies they claim to resist.

Notes

1 The first frame of the opening credits, which immediately follows the display of the British Lion logo, states 'The Producer would like to thank The Lord Summerisle and the people of his island off the west coast of Scotland for this privileged insight into their religious practices and for their generous co-operation in the making of this film': Robin Hardy et al., *The Wicker Man: The Director's Cut* (Studio Canal, DVD, 2002), Scene 1, 'Mainland'. Allan Brown playfully adapts this conceit as a preface to his *Inside The Wicker Man: The Morbid Ingenuities* (London: Sidgwick and Jackson, 2000), p. vii. The quotation in the title of this chapter is taken from Edward Woodward's Foreword, p. xi.

2 Compare, for example, Genesis 1:28, which is variously anthropocentric and a statement of the Deity's delegation of stewardship (rather than ownership) to humanity; the homepage of the (interfaith) Cornwall Alliance for the Stewardship of Creation at http://www.cornwallalliance.org/about/ (accessed 26 September

2011); and – from a twenty first-century pagan perspective – Rosa Romani, *Green Spirituality: Magic in the Midst of Life* (Sutton Mallet: Green Magic, 2004), p. 5.

3 Hardy et al., *The Wicker Man*, Scene 10, 'Lord Summerisle'. Fire is a prominent element in pagan and Wiccan celebrations at Beltane (from the Celtic *bel-tine*, meaning 'lucky' or 'bright' fire, an allusion which recalls again the solar deity prominent on the flag of Summerisle), a feast and time of sexual licence customarily celebrated annually on 1 May. See Ann-Marie Gallagher, *The Wicca Bible: The Definitive Guide to Magic and the Craft* (London: Godsfield Press, 2005), pp. 66–7.

4 Hardy et al., *The Wicker Man*, scene 10, 'Lord Summerisle'.

5 Brown, *Inside The Wicker Man*, p. 167; A. Catterall and S. Wells, *Your Face Here: British Cult Movies Since the Sixties* (London: Fourth Estate, 2002), p. 141.

6 See, for example, Greg Garrard, *Ecocriticism* (London: Routledge, 2004), pp. 70–1.

7 Indeed, the novelization of the film opens with Howie, an amateur ornithologist, defending a golden eagle's nest as an agent of the state against an acquisitive and destructive collector of rare birds' eggs. The harsh London accent of this latter figure is rendered in marked contrast to the more muted Highland tones voiced by the off-duty policeman and his fiancée. See Robin Hardy and Anthony Shaffer, *The Wicker Man* [1978] (London: Pan, 2000), pp. 6–10.

8 From Lord Summerisle's address to Howie in a scene heavily edited in the final release of the film and effectively part of Hardy et al., *The Wicker Man*, Scene 10, 'Lord Summerisle'; see Brown, *Inside The Wicker Man*, p. 221. Shaffer's original script for this scene is reproduced verbatim as Appendix 7 of Brown's *Inside The Wicker Man*.

9 Cf. 1 Corinthians, 10:26.

10 Hardy et al., *The Wicker Man*, Scene 4, 'The Green Man'. The Green Man, 'consort of the goddess and ancient spirit of the Greenwood', is especially honoured at Beltane – which (though not named as such) is the May Day festival in which the marooned Howie finds himself an involuntary participant: see Gallagher, *The Wicca Bible*, p. 66. Hardy, for one, was well versed in the ritual and folklore of May Day: see Brown, *Inside The Wicker Man*, pp. 25–6.

11 Judith Higginbottom, ' "Do As Thou Wilt": Contemporary Paganism and *The Wicker Man*', in Benjamin Franks, Stephen Harper, Jonathan Murray and Lesley Stevenson (eds), *The Quest for The Wicker Man: History, Folklore and Pagan Perspectives* (Edinburgh: Luath Press, 2006), pp. 126–36, at pp. 128, 127.

12 Higginbottom, ' "Do What Thou Wilt"', pp. 128, 130; Anthony J. Harper, '*The Wicker Man*: Cult Film or Anti-Cult Film? Parallels and Paradoxes in the Representation of Paganism, Christianity and the Law', in Franks et al. (eds), *The Quest for The Wicker Man*, pp. 98–110, at p. 100; Brown, *Inside The Wicker Man*, pp. 24–6

13 Robin Hardy, 'The Genesis of *The Wicker Man*', in Franks et al. (eds), *The Quest for The Wicker Man*, pp. 17–25, at p. 21.

14 Hardy et al., *The Wicker Man*, Scene 18, 'Sacrificial Victim'.

15 Hardy et al., *The Wicker Man*, Scene 10, 'Lord Summerisle'. Much of Howie's reading of the book was cut from the theatrical print; see Brown, *Inside The Wicker Man*, p. 107.

16 Hardy et al., *The Wicker Man*, Scene 14, 'Disturbing Research'.

17 For details of the post-production process, see Brown, *Inside The Wicker Man*, pp. 102–9.

18 Brown, *Inside The Wicker Man*, Appendix 7.

19 Eric Boyd-Perkins, the film's editor, is alleged to have arbitrarily discarded material from the film that he found distasteful, claiming that the footage in question
had never originally been shot on location. Christopher Lee, who played Lord
Summerisle, also suggested in interview that, even in the 102-minute print, 'there's
an awful lot missing. A tremendous amount, not just what I said and did'; see
Brown, *Inside the Wicker Man*, pp. 102–3, 104, 107.

20 The quoted words are spoken by May Morrison, island postmistress and mother
of the missing Rowan, prior to Howie's house-to-house search for the supposedly
abducted girl; Hardy et al., *The Wicker Man*, Scene 15, 'Search Every House'. On
the defining sexual content of *The Wicker Man* see, for example, Patrick Gibbs's
review for *The Daily Telegraph*, 28 December 1973, reprinted in Brown, *Inside
The Wicker Man*, pp. 208–9, or the anonymous review entitled 'They tried to keep
THIS sex film quiet', *Evening News*, 28 February 1974, reprinted in ibid., p. 213.

21 Brown, *Inside the Wicker Man*, p. 183; cf. Brown's Introduction to Hardy and
Shaffer, *The Wicker Man*, pp. xii–xiii.

22 The reference to Huxley and the disparaging remarks regarding the clergy do not
appear in the director's cut of *The Wicker Man*.

23 Lord Summerisle's response does not appear in the director's cut.

24 See, for example, T. H. Huxley, 'On the Physical Basis of Life', *The Fortnightly
Review*, 1 February 1869, pp. 132, 133, 137.

25 The supposed transmogrification of the dead Rowan Morrison into a hare is
another example of this; see Hardy et al., *The Wicker Man*, Scene 11, 'Exhumation'.

26 See Joyce and River Higginbotham, *Paganism: An Introduction to Earth-Centered
Religions* (Woodbury: Llewellyn, 2008), pp. 2–3.

27 The reference to the stone circle and the explicit acknowledgement of the first
Laird's atheism do not appear in the director's cut.

28 Brown, *Inside the Wicker Man*, p. 219.

29 The director's cut renders the central portion of this speech more briefly as 'my
father continued out of love'.

30 Brown, *Inside the Wicker Man*, pp. 218, 220

31 Ibid., frontispiece and p. 73. Caesar's account is discussed in *The Golden Bough*;
see Mikel J. Koven, 'The Folklore Fallacy: A Folkloristic/Filmic Perspective on *The
Wicker Man*', in Franks et al. (eds), *The Quest for The Wicker Man*, pp. 83–97, at pp.
89–90.

32 The alleged Druidic tradition of burning sacrifices in wicker cages is considered in
J. G. Frazer, *The Golden Bough: A Study in Magic and Religion* (London: Macmillan,
1960), Vol. II, pp. 856–9. This is a cheap reprint of the 1922 edition, first published
in 1957.

33 The 1970s was the era in which provincial folklore and regional ghost stories
became exposed to a mass audience through the conjunction of cheap paperback publication and the public library system. Among many such works published at this time, Antony D. Hippisley Coxe's encyclopaedic *Haunted Britain*
(London: Hutchinson, 1973) and the regional volumes such as *Haunted London*
(1973/1975) by Peter Underwood and *Haunted East Anglia* (1974/1976),
reprinted in paperback by Fontana/Collins, are perhaps most representative.

34 Hardy et al., *The Wicker Man*, scene 17, 'Six Swordsmen'.

35 Melvyn J. Willin, 'Music and Paganism with Special Reference to *The Wicker Man*', in Franks et al. (eds), *The Quest for The Wicker Man*, pp. 137–52, at p. 150.
36 See, for example, Higginbottom, '"Do As Thou Wilt"', p. 130.
37 Koven, 'The Folklore Fallacy', p. 83; cf. p. 87.
38 Hardy et al., *The Wicker Man*, scene 19, 'King for a Day'.
39 Ibid., scene 19, 'King for a Day'.
40 See, for example, Frazer, *The Golden Bough*, Vol. I, pp. 349–50, 384–5.

6

Alanna F. Bondar

Bodies on earth: exploring sites of the Canadian ecoGothic

Since the 1960s, Canadian writers have been responding to Northrop Frye's influential musings and consequent stranglehold on defining Canadian cultural identity. As a result, Canadian literature shows consistent patterns of retreat from the 'unnatural' wilderness as non-nurturing mother to seek comfort, instead, in the garrisoned security of a colonial mother-country's psychological and physical fortresses. When asking how Canada might form a cultural identity, based on the evolving nature of early Canadian literature, Frye astutely noted that it is not a question of 'who are we?' but, rather, of inquiring into 'where is here?'[1] For Canadians, 'wilderness is defined as wild uncultivated land, which in Canada includes vast tracts of forest and innumerable lakes and also the Arctic North', but it also has 'multiple functions', not existing exclusively as a thing-in-itself.[2] Critic Gaile McGregor likewise theorizes that wilderness, fundamentally described as alien and 'other', 'is not accessible and no mediation or reconciliation is possible in the Canadian confrontation with nature'.[3] Faced with an unexpected, unexplainable and unimaginable wilderness, Canadians erased pastoral expectations (in contrast to New World American writers) and replaced them, as Margaret Atwood suggests in her thematic summary of the Canadian literary consciousness, with stories of disaster and survival, which fostered (or confirmed) a 'violent duality' within the literary imagination. She adds: 'Canadian writers as a whole do not trust Nature', since Canada is 'the space you inhabit not just with your body but with your head. It's the kind of space in which we find ourselves lost.'[4]

Canadian critic and writer Robert Kroetsch argues that Canada finds 'disunity as unity'; by disrupting metanarratives that define Canada as a strictly a colonial space, readers may begin to understand how outdated ideological constructions trap Canada into fearing 'the other', as it is conceived through multiculturalism.[5] Kroetsch argues that, in Canada, 'the centre does not hold'; consequently, we ought not to fear the postmodern abyss since its decentring of ideological strongholds on subjectivity and cultural identity gives 'new energy to countries like Canada' which have been, in terms of world history, 'invisible'.[6] Echoing Kroetsch's sentiments, Justin D. Edwards asks his readers in *Gothic Canada* (2005) if Canada is an 'uncanny nation' since it is 'an in-between space, caught in-between colonization and post-colonization' where 'intersections cannot but generate paradoxes within Canadian identity and textuality'.[7] Smaro Kamboreli likewise identifies the Canadian writer 'as a diasporic subject, constantly hover[ing] on the edge of an abyss'.[8] In *Unsettled Remains: Canadian Literature and the Postcolonial Gothic* (2009), Cynthia Sugars and Gerry Turcotte explore settler–invader relations that recognize how initial examples of the Gothic mode in Canadian literature reflected, as Frye has argued, 'terror in the face of the unknown wilderness' but show how 'a more recent strain of gothic literature in Canada has been ... more concerned with an interiorized psychological experience of gothic "uncanniness" and illegitimacy'.[9] This development in Canadian literature, which combines Gothic, uncanniness and the postcolonial, according to Sugars and Turcotte 'takes on a variety of possible tacks: fears of territorial illegitimacy, anxiety about forgotten or occluded histories, resentment towards flawed or complicit ancestors, assertions of Aboriginal priority, explorations of hybrid cultural forms, and interrogations of national belonging and citizenship'.[10] Thus, as Edwards contends, Canada 'is strangely familiar and familiarly strange'[11] – and as such, suggests that Gothic representations in Canada are evolving. First, they recognize an early Canadian colonial and masculine-identified Gothic mode in literature that perpetuates false ideological logics associated with binary oppositions (e.g. humanity vs. nature; European vs. indigenous; garrison vs. wilderness); then, they decentre such inherited myths by exposing, mutating and reassigning definitions of monstrosity, mystery and fear associated with 'otherness'.

Canadian texts of an ecoGothic nature, like the Gothic mode itself, make discoveries about cultural fears, anxieties and ancestral/colonial hauntings that expose Canada, and its culturally defined relations with 'wilderness' as a site of Gothic anxiety, as an uncanny space. Canadian authors, liberating themselves from Frye's legacy and Atwood's musings, continue to move beyond compartmentalized thematic interpretations of Canadian literature to more desirable and globally identifiable literatures created by 'skilful shape-changers',[12] consistent with postmodern trends and strategies. Understandably, the 1990s emergence of ecocritical and ecofeminist philosophies within American and British scholarship breathed new life into discussions concerning Canadian cultural identity and its connection to human–nature relations. In this vein, emerging ecocriticism and ecological literatures in Canada have shown ways of decentring colonial hauntings (global, national, personal and regional) that are connected to wilderness fears – regardless of whether their underlying physical threats are present, imagined or irrational. Thus, environmental consciousness, as it is evolving in the Canadian novel, appears ideologically entwined with a Gothic mode imbued with postmodernism, postcolonialism and, frequently, magic realist possibilities. Recent Gothic, ecological and postcolonial texts involve these theoretical perspectives in ways that positively revalue Gothic fears by unearthing previous colonial overtones, biases and/ or cultural erasures. In these cases, fear, particularly of 'the other', is revealed as historical ignorance, perpetuated through a continued desire for control. EcoGothic texts attempt, therefore, to expose how these manifestations of the uncanny have been unfairly propagated within culturally defined labyrinths of racism, sexism, speciesism and fear of the marked and/or sexualized body.

Canadian authors Camilla Gibb (*Sweetness in the Belly*, 2006), Michael Ondaatje (*Anil's Ghost*, 2000), Shanne Mootoo (*Ceres Blooms at Night*, 1996), Eden Robinson (*Monkey Beach*, 2000), Nancy Huston (*Instruments of Darkness*, 1997), Anne-Marie MacDonald (*Fall on Your Knees*, 1996), Robert Kroetsch (*What the Crow Said*, 1978) and Lola Lemire Tostevin (*Frog Moon*, 1994) share recognizable ecological concerns when they strategically explore a culturally encoded body–nature link and revision it from ecocritical perspectives on body image and the denigration of the body. By positioning the human body as the site of Gothic terror (and not exclusively the female body, as is the premise of Camilla Gibb's *Sweetness in the Belly* and Michael Ondaatje's *Anil's Ghost*), these authors make manifest personal hauntings, repulsions, fear and the uncanny – all contained within individuals seeking self-identity and psychological sanctuary. Ultimately, self and other, often contained within the same 'Jekyll and Hyde' person, become recon-

ciled when the body is foregrounded as a recognizable and complex
biotic space which holds membership in a biotic community. With origins in the proto-ecological 'women on spiritual quest' novels that infil-
trated the Canadian literary market in the 1970s and 1980s, Canadian
ecoGothic (or ecofeminist Gothic) novels seek to decentre impulses
(theoretical, literary, cultural or otherwise) of cultural identification
and unity that serve to reinforce social controls and networks largely
based on European, colonial, American and maintained logics of binary
opposition. Moving away from a strictly female-identified Gothic
mode that considers the body as site of Gothic horror, more recent
texts move in a more gender-inclusive direction when they identify the
body (male and female) as the site of mutilation, torture and political
power agendas. *Sweetness in the Belly*, for example, positions the body
as the site of re-membering political power agendas in which bodies
become the landmarks of continued rampages against the earth-body
and bodies-on-earth. Michael Ondaatje's *Anil's Ghost* likewise uses the
Gothic mode to centre/decentre/recentre the survival of the human
body and spirit, particularly those lost in the multifarious labyrinths
of mass graves that mark secret orders for racial (planetary) cleansing.
    These ways of integrating the body in texts are consistent with eco-
logical discussions in which the earth-body (human body) is linked
culturally through metaphor to the body-earth (planet Earth) and
are explored without disrespectful and reductionist arguments that
designate the animal and/or feminine-identified body as disposable,
enslavable and unidentifiable. David Punter challenges this age-old
link between animals and women from a respectful, ecofeminist position which explores how such an association might be transformative
rather than hegemonic and oppressive. In this way, Punter employs
early ecofeminist Ynestra King's concept of 'practical essentialism' and
applies it to postcolonial writing and its Gothic elements.[13] Effectively,
in order to collapse the self–other paradigm within postcolonial and
Gothic literary frameworks, the reader must be or become the monster.
Becoming monster, given how the postmodern reader has come to
read texts and subjectivity as fragmented, unstable and often unidentifiable, may not be as horrifying as it sounds. Referring to an argument
made by Deleuze and Guattari in *A Thousand Plateaus* (1980), Punter
outlines how 'becoming-animal' might

> place a positive value on [prejudices associated with race and animalness] as a
> way of working with the decentring of consciousness, a way of spreading outward

from the merely human and achieving some wider contact with the world beyond
consciousness on which terrain, according to them, things actually happen.[14]

However, according to Punter, this attempt at consciousness-shifting
through literary frameworks is not a question of 'whether it might be
"good" to feel this kind of mystical affinity with plants and animals';
neither is it a question of how 'such an affinity might promote soci-
etal health and serve to dam up violent impulses'.[15] The politics of
the postcolonial complicate ecocritical desires, since the outcome is
wholly determined by the context, the interpreter and the interpretation of 'this reassumption of the attributes of the animal'.[16] Turning
to indigenous knowledges critic Ken Arvidson, Punter adds that his
term 'extreme animism' 'might be seen as a healthy revivification of
the archaic, a remaking of broken connections'; however, it might just
as easily be taken to represent 'a culminative turning of the face away
from power, an abjection into the world of the animal *as it has been
reformulated* by the colonizers'.[17] Ultimately, for this kind of revisionist
strategy to work, Deleuze and Guattari maintain, the emphasis must
remain on 'becoming'. Thus, by destabilizing conventional cultural
ideologies associated with the mutual inclusiveness of body–nature
denigration, ecoGothic texts often choose to explore how the body
is viewed, manipulated and understood as a site of Gothic fear. After
all, it is within the unique cultural and artistic milieu of literature that
emerging cultural fears, anxieties and concerns may be heard, mended
and re-membered so as not to continue to be silenced or garrisoned
unnecessarily against the evolution of a more just and sustainable
biotic community.

The Canadian ecoGothic novel asks to be recognized as transformative in an emerging tradition, since the Canadian postcolonial Gothic
novel is already critically and imaginatively explored as an essential revisionist site for the ways in which we continue to 'settle the
nation, [and] to carve out a sense of homeliness on foreign terrain'.[18]
EcoGothic strategies, thus far, appear to be twofold: traditional Gothic
practices may reflect the origins of an imported and inherited 'garrison
mentality' that may continue to haunt Canadians on an unconscious
level; while postcolonial Gothic writers will employ the Gothic mode
as a way of decentring these fears and unlocking new ways of collapsing
the logic of binaries by recognizing 'otherness' as 'anotherness', as critic
Patrick Murphy advises when exploring otherness within an ecofeminist perspective.[19] The latter approach has the potential to include

inversions of the paradigm that pits Europeans against indigenous peoples. Canada, a vast geographical area, offers a range of bioregional diversity, sociopolitical differences and attempts to celebrate difference, which continue to be marked by its official languages – English, French and Aboriginal. As Arun Mukerjee suggests, being 'different' does not mean being un-Canadian, nor does difference or 'the other' equate with 'monster'.[20] Postcolonial Gothic thus makes promises contained within the frameworks of postmodern, ecocritical and feminist theories to illuminate colonial power structures in which 'colonizer and colonized stand ... as doubles of each other in a relationship that is not so much hierarchical as haunting',[21] and in which 'the monster' (female, mutilated, native, animal, wilderness and so on) is cast in a new light, made possible through revisionist strategies of the postmodern politic. Consequently, the colonizer (male, whole, European, civilized) shadows the subaltern, denigrated and/or oppressed 'other', and becomes the monster himself. In such cases the colonizer is, of course, representational – the mirror reflecting colonial horrors, both past and present.

   Clearly, in Canada, 'here there [still] be monsters', and not simply the 'silent world or fantastical beasts'[22] illustrated by early cartographers exploring the New World – spaces that are vacant, absent and unknown. If we follow Margaret E. Turner, who uses this phrase from early European maps (unfinished, with vast spaces of blank and imagined geography) of a New World Canada, and continue with Frye's musings, we may return to the abandoned question of 'who are we?' and seek its relationship to 'where is here?', in order to unearth mysteries pertaining to monsters. Who are they, really? How were they created? How might they be considered in terms of membership of the biotic community? What might they look like? And who gets to decide? Donna Heiland has observed that the Gothic has provided late twentieth- and early twenty-first-century writers with better ways of decentring values assigned to traditional villains and heroes (and heroines), defined within 'the seemingly rigid divisions that structure the worlds they portray'. Heiland further suggests that 'one is grateful for these moments of confusion – in which villains and victims are no longer so clearly defined' since it is through 'complication, through the embrace of the plural and often fractured visions' that we may find 'lasting solutions to the problems these novels show us'.[23] The fluid nature of Gothic literary frameworks grants agency to such monster-heroes who, as David Punter suggests, are 'genuinely hybrid forms that stand ... at the boundary of what is and what is not acceptable, what is to be allowed to come to the warm hearth of society and what is to be consigned to the outer wilderness'.[24] Ultimately, the postcolonial monster hybrid may frighten readers 'with the prospect of a monstrous hybridity' but it will also implore them to access possibilities 'that might come from those – those divine figures ... who are able to take up the challenge of patrolling the boundaries of what is said to be human'.[25] EcoGothic, held within the theoretical scaffolding of postcolonialism, explores how revisioning a monstrous 'other' that may have once been identified as wilderness, nature and/or the dislocation of the geopsychic self in biotic community, has become as necessary as it is possible.[26]

* * *

In *Femicidal Fears* (2001), Helene Meyers explores the intimate relationship between feminine-identified terrors associated with the Gothic mode and the ways in which, historically, 'the Gothic romance has been preoccupied with women's economic, psychological, and physical vulnerability'.[27] Canadian novelists Nancy Huston (*Instruments of Darkness*) and Lola Lemire Tostevin (*Frog Moon*) recognize how, by perpetuating silence and secrecy around female rites of passage, young girls sabotage sexual identity, self-worth and physical well-being as the result of educational, mythological and cultural encounters with a mysterious and potentially demonic self – as it is associated with the feminine and the female body. Contained within culturally inscribed labyrinths of psychological fear, 'becoming a woman' requires the navigation of treacherous waters whose channels are built and controlled by pedagogies designed to make women doubt their instincts. As Deborah Slicer attests, 'We are encouraged to think of our breasts as enemies. The industry says that ... everything contaminated by the womanly hormone, estrogen, conspire[s] against us. Nature is the mother of a future full of horrors.'[28] As Catharina Halkes suggests, women are up against a complicated past which they must both demolish and salvage from, since women, through their association with 'conquest, possession, domination, "objectification", absence of spirit and passivity, with unpredictability and irrationality' have witnessed how 'the core of both nature and woman have been mutilated'.[29]

In *Frog Moon*, Lola Lemire Tostevin recognizes the body as a place of passion and mystery which ought to be celebrated rather than feared. Tostevin effectively centres Laura's/Kaki's understanding of

her own bodily coming of age within the physical and psychological labyrinths of a Roman Catholic school for girls, only to decentre
it through her character's reactions to visual religious icons. Initially,
Laura (nicknamed Kaki, 'frog', from the Cree word Oma-k-ki, because
she cannot sing, but also symbolic of her ability to adapt) points to
traditional aspects of a Roman Catholic education for girls as barbaric
in the way they associate the body with the profane. Eventually, however, Kaki revisions Roman Catholic protocols that denigrate or disre-
gard the body's sanctity when she incorporates a positive body image
into personalized rituals – rituals that lead her to recognize her own
value and position within a healthy biotic community. In a section that
explores ecofeminist concerns, Tostevin tells how the nuns prepare
their schoolgirls for bedtime, warning each against 'the risk of jeopard-
izing the sanctity of her bodily temple' if she should 'expose any part
of her body to the moonlight at the top of the dorm windows'.[30] These
girls are taught – at all costs – to hide their nakedness from the moon, in
other words, to avoid being seen naked altogether; to do so a girl must
contort her body by becoming as small as possible, effectively erasing
her naked self *every night* by 'crouch[ing] as low as she can under the
make-shift tent' (31). The consequences are horrific, tantamount to
Gothic legend, if a girl does not comply, since girls who are exposed
to the moon will grow long silken hair on their bodies and slanting
eyebrows that meet on the bridge of the nose (32).

Likewise, Kaki's personal experience with the body-sacred is a 'life-
size Sacred Heart at the end of the corridor' (100). This image of
Jesus attempts to 'welcome the new girls with open arms and bleeding
hands', but he has a 'bland expression [that] look[s] sinister' (100).
According to Kaki, 'the statue at the end of the corridor conveyed
only one message. Hope for nothing and there will be nothing to fear'
(100). For this young girl, the Sacred Heart does more than represent
her own silence during her first three months at the convent; it reflects
an internalized space in which her voice would be 'drowned' when she
is spoken to or when someone asks her name. She explains that a kind
of near-death occurs 'in the frantic beating of a heart about to unfold in
her chest, the fluttering of an injured bird. A heart as raw and mangled
as the life-size Sacred Heart at the end of the corridor' (100). Mirrored
to this framed Sacred Heart is a girl caught within a metaphor layered
with social complexity that allies the purity of certain winged biblical
images (such as the dove or the angel) and other 'children of God'
seeking emancipation through abuse, pain and mutilation.

Kaki's description of the Sacred Heart is followed four pages later by her description of a girl's Chimera nightmares. Disassociating herself from the familiarity and comfort of her mother's voice, its 'whoosh like a heart beat. Body talk' (108), Kaki enters the Land of the Chimera where 'young girls are kept in boxes to prevent them from growing; their lips are slit to prevent them from speaking, their skulls compressed to keep them from thinking' (108). Like the framed Sacred Heart – Jesus in a box – Kaki internalizes visual Catholic metaphors that perpetuate grotesque manipulations of the body, which are celebrated while imprisoned within ideological containment. In this way, the body becomes its own Gothic labyrinth of mystery and horror; it is a perpetual burden that offers no options for escape except through heavenly salvation. Ironically, death is therefore not the figure to be feared, but rather the body itself.

Creating familiar Gothic tensions between knowing and not knowing, the body and the psyche, the public and the personal, Huston's young female characters in *Instruments of Darkness* all face ignorance concerning their sexualized bodies. The hostilely agnostic Catholic narrator, Nadia/Nada, a child of a not-so-strict French Canadian upbringing, dismisses Old World superstition but documents, instead, the ways in which feminine psychological fear of the woman's body and delineations between male and female rites of passage may be tracked for centuries; Nadia imaginatively interweaves her own personal story of female sexuality with documented stories of Renaissance-born twins, Barbe and Barnabe. Barbe and her girlfriend, Jeanne, innocently gossip about body-myths in what is for Barbe – a girl without a living mother – a sex-education course born out of rumours, hearsay and barnyard observations. Initially, the girls naively giggle, discovering the potential pleasures of their own bodies, but their delight turns sinister when social strictures concerning the sexualized female body give rise to extreme self-punishment and mutilation. The girls are told how the satanic possession of nuns is connected to the finding of various objects in their vaginas. Included in this particular 'pact with the devil' is 'a piece of a baby's heart that was sacrificed in a witches' sabbath, plus the ashes of a holy wafer, plus some blood, plus a drop of seed from her priest, Father Grandin – because you know, all the sisters at Loudun, said he'd forced them to do it with him'.[31] Another nun, whose story is set as a cautionary tale for Roman Catholic women, finds herself pregnant but rejects herbal abortion remedies since that would mean sending an innocent soul to hell; instead, she chooses to 'cut her own stomach open, take the baby out and baptize it, then smother it – after which she'd die herself' (72). Ultimately, the lesson is clear: this nun chose the 'correct' option since she was rewarded with the knowledge that she was not pregnant, only tested; 'the blood of her moons ... had collected inside her until finally it rose up into her throat' (72). Masked by a fear-inducing religion that privileges the afterlife and denigrates earth-bound existence, the surreptitious stripping of women's personal choices effectively destroys lives – foetal and female. By destabiliz-ing the social construction of these boundaries, Huston un-buries the tombs and unburdens the secrets of the past; in so doing, she revisions the body as a site of Gothic fear, showing how 'the specificity of the female body can easily become a locus for this phobia [the trauma of gender], especially when representations of the female body as a colo-nized, violated space predominate'.[32]

Nadia, in contrast to Barbe, demonstrates how representations of the female body continue to create 'somatophobia, the fear of the body that is projected onto women'.[33] In addition, the human body as a site of colonial trauma (physical and psychological), denigration, sexism and racism likewise presents itself as the 'unsettled' territory in ecoGothic Canadian novels. From an early age, Nadia witnesses the kinds of miscarriages her Roman Catholic mother repeatedly endures because of the Church's outlawing of birth control. Displaced from the ease of knowing, if naively, one's sense of being at home and being at home in one's own skin, the cornerstone of the Canadian Gothic text is that which seeks to 'settle the nation, to carve out a sense of homeli-ness on foreign terrain'.[34] Understandably, this complex relationship within Canadian consciousness necessarily conscripts theories of the uncanny to attempt to explain and/or resolve systems of binaries that construct cultural identities as they are 'tied to the unsettled, the not-yet-colonized, the unsuccessfully colonized or the decolonized'.[35] After all, Nadia's own association is not with a perfect God but with a weaker spiritual entity; she claims that, like that Devil, women are 'double, an oxymoron, a marriage of opposites. *Fourchu et fourbe* ... I thrive on division and derision, I never cease to compare, contrive, seduce, betray, translate' (24).

Nadia's own aborted foetus, which she has named 'Tom Thumb', continues to haunt her by tapping at the window, regardless of her partner's dismissal of abortion as inconsequential since, as he explains, 'God does it all the time! ... What's more, He does it cavalierly, non-chalantly, without batting an eyelash! ... He doesn't give a shit!' (265).

Nadia is not so easily convinced since, ultimately, the abortion took her to the apartments of many molesting would-be rapists who demanded money but did not effectively rid her of the foetus. Furthermore, the successful abortion leaves her body scarred by the psychological conse-quences of sending a part of herself (and not just the foetus) 'tumbling head over heels amidst excrement and dishwater through the pipes of the Chicago sewage system, to be unceremoniously spat a few hours later into Lake Michigan' (263). Despite ongoing and centuries-old depictions of the (female) body as a site of Gothic fear, Huston's text ultimately identifies an ecofeminist agenda when Barbe defies social and historic definitions of her raped, ravished and impregnated body as the site of imposed Gothic terrors. Through a mutual creative pro-cess, both Barbe and Nadia discover liberation in the redefining of the female body as a 'natural' source of pleasure and creative empower-ment when they decentre culturally constructed disconnections of self and body. By identifying how dislocation occurs, unnaturally, these characters move through Gothic paradigms to find ways of forever abandoning imposed devils, fears, ghosts and hauntings.

Just as Huston demonstrates how certain social constructions define the body as unholy and disposable ('God does it all the time'), bodies in *Frog Moon* are unjustly portrayed within Church teachings as tainted and unsacred. Crossing Gothic boundaries between the transcenden-tal spirit and the earth-bound body becomes problematic for Kaki, particularly when Roman Catholic teaching requires its adherents to believe in transubstantiation – that wafers and wine actually turn into the body and blood of Christ in the weekly Mass. In *Frog Moon*, the tradition of Christian martyrs – such as Katrina in Leonard Cohen's *Beautiful Losers* (1966), Wayne Johnston's mother in *The Story of Bobby O'Malley* (1985) and Mrs Dempster in Robertson Davies' *Fifth Business* (1970) – is continued in Laura/Kaki. Kaki starves her-self as a means of gaining control of her own body – a foreign entity to her – and her body's destiny, not unlike Atwood's protagonist in *The Edible Woman* (1969) whose refusal to eat food indicates a much greater psychological unrest. Kaki's more political protest against meat-eating in *Frog Moon* links Roman Catholic fanaticism to everyday reality; her act of starvation, she believes, links her to acts of devotion. Kaki explains: 'If what the priest had said was true, about wine turning into blood and bread into flesh, then nothing good could evolve from this dead meat. She could even turn into a pig' (129). Among mixed personal body images and the practice of eating the saviour's flesh,

Kaki's mind explodes trying to understand the relationships between her body (which she despises), Christ's body (which she eats for spiritual sustenance) and animals' bodies (which she eats to maintain a body she despises). The result is a conscious choice to refrain from the eating/killing of the animals with which she identifies.

Kaki's recognition and development of revisioned spiritual rituals allows the reader access to revised ways of knowing and becoming that avoid perpetuated and prescribed violence against the human body and animals. Kaki's revulsion towards killing masterfully links Jesus' sacrifice to the evening dinner's dead livestock in ways that make her nauseous. The narrator describes the experience as one wherein:

> the thin wafer made flesh, made bloody on her tongue before it dislodges from her palate, scrapes down her throat, along her stomach wall, towards the rot of her bowels. Each morning, as she kneels at the balustrade before crisp linen and lace ... she wonders what morsel of Christ's body she is about to ingest. Which organ, limb, entrails, or wound. Which mucus, marrow, semen. (129)

In a ritual that simultaneously breaks Christian laws, traditions, beliefs and sacred trust, and revisions ritualistic practice, Tostevin carefully blends eroticism and personal spiritual rite, culminating in a fully realized coming of age that incorporates the body with the mind and the spirit. Starving from her refusal to eat food that will sustain her body, Kaki is driven into a blasphemous moment – the novel's climax – that, ironically, simultaneously feeds her spirit and her body. In an act that appears natural, transcendent, God-inspired, Kaki, 'without premeditation', risks expulsion and the consequences of committing a mortal sin when she enters the sacred housing of the chalice to 'retrieve a fistful of consecrated wafers [to] put them into her mouth', repeatedly, as in the ritual of the Catholic Mass, taking fistfuls to represent the ingesting of the 'body of Christ', 'the divine flesh', 'the body of Jesus'. Her aim is for nourishment without oppression and violence, food that 'does away with dependence on food and boiled pigs' (136). In this way, Kaki appears to be seeking a hummingbird's existence by finding a way to live – spiritually and physically – without claiming the lives of others.

* * *

If, as Justin Edwards points out, 'Freud [has no] cure for those who are haunted',[36] then Canadians who cannot, will not or ought not to be settled (which accounts, to some degree, for all Canadian immigrants, generations of immigrants or settlers, and indigenous peoples) are likely to 'internalize ... as part of the geography of the self' an 'externalized *unheimlich* space'[37] – at least insofar as it allows readers and writers to seek answers to questions of cultural, individual or ancestral diasporas. The paradox at the centre of Canadian literature suggests that we are haunted within labyrinths of 'the postcolonial map', where 'histories are mysteriously overlaid' and Canadian authors become 'committed to uprooting or "re-discovering" [their] own ancestors'.[38] Nonetheless, haunting continues to destabilize identity where the ontological status of subjectivity is exposed as 'fluidly transformative'.[39] Within this paradigm, readers of postcolonial and ecological literatures embrace Gothic regeneration as a means of examining certain New World phenomena; Canadian ecoGothic reveals how fears of the other and otherness, self and wilderness, angels and demons may be destabilized within liminal spaces that transgress boundaries and collapse binaries. Here, readers may undertake a different kind of exploration of self and other through a re-charting of Canadian maps of cultural consciousness. It is within this ever-shifting fabric of identity and subjectivity that Canadian literature evolves and takes place, as Edwards summarizes, 'on the ground of indecipherability, a place in which the subject is rarely in control of the boundaries between inside and outside, self and other, which would secure a stable sense of identity'.[40] Unfixing the fixed metanarratives that remain at the core of a nation transfixed by unhealthy and outdated beliefs concerning otherness, multiculturalism and nature is at the heart of Canadian ecoGothic literature.

Notes

1 Northrop Frye, *The Bush Garden: Essays on the Canadian Imagination* (Toronto: Anansi, 1971), p. 220.

2 Coral Ann Howells, *Margaret Atwood* (London: Macmillan, 1996), p. 21.

3 Gaile McGregor, *The Wacousta Syndrome: Explorations in the Canadian Langscape* (Toronto: University of Toronto Press, 1985), p. 27.

4 Margaret Atwood, *Survival* (Toronto: Anansi, 1972), pp. 49, 18.

5 Robert Kroetsch, 'Disunity as Unity: A Canadian Strategy', in *The Lovely Treachery of Words: Essays Selected and New* (Toronto: Oxford University Press, 1989), pp. 21–33, p. 21.

6 Ibid., p. 22.

7 Justin D. Edwards, 'Introduction', in *Gothic Canada: Reading the Spectre of a National Literature* (Edmonton: University of Alberta Press, 2005), p. xiv.

8 Smaro Kamboreli, *Scandalous Bodies: Diasporic Literature in English Canada* (Toronto: Oxford University Press, 2000), p. 22.

9 Cynthia Sugars and Gerry Turcotte, 'Introduction', in *Unsettled Remains: Canadian*

Literature and the Postcolonial Gothic (Waterloo: Wilfred Laurier Press, 2009), p. xi.

10 Ibid.

11 Edwards, 'Introduction', p. xv.

12 Kroetsch, 'Disunity as Unity', p. 28.

13 Ynestra King, 'The Ecology of Feminism and the Feminism of Ecology', in Judith Plant (ed.), *Healing the Wounds: The Promise of Ecofeminism* (Santa Cruz, CA: New Society Publishers, 1989), pp. 18–28.

14 David Punter, *Postcolonial Imaginings: Fictions of a New World Order* (Lanham, MD: Rowman and Littlefield, 2000), p. 145.

15 Ibid.

16 Ibid., p. 148.

17 Ibid., p. 149.

18 Edwards, 'Introduction', p. xx.

19 Patrick D. Murphy, *Literature, Nature and Other: Ecofeminist Critiques* (New York: State University of New York Press, 1995), pp. 4–5.

20 Edwards, 'Introduction', p. xiii.

21 Donna Heiland, *Gothic and Gender: An Introduction* (Malden, MA: Blackwell Publishing, 2004), p. 157.

22 Margaret E. Turner, *Imagining Culture: New World Narrative and the Writing of Canada* (Montreal: McGill-Queens University Press, 1995), pp. 4, 22, quoted in Edwards, 'Introduction', p. xxii.

23 Heiland, *Gothic and Gender*, p. 156.

24 Punter, *Postcolonial Imaginings*, p. 111.

25 Ibid.

26 Borrowing from indigenous knowledges educator Gregory Cajete, ecofeminist critic Patrick Murphy discusses how the *geopsyche* identifies and defines the ways in which the biotic community (flora and fauna, rock formations, climate, weather conditions and so on) has a profound effect on the development of the psyche. Within the individual, there cannot be a divide between 'nature' and 'self' within bioregional understandings of place since it is within the *geopsyche* that 'the soul and intention of the vision are formed' (Murphy, *Literature, Nature and Other*, p. 70). Murphy revisions the *geopsyche* as a theoretical and psycho-spiritual space in which shifts away from cultural perceptions that divide self from other (and thus ghettoize difference as 'strange' and/or 'dangerous') become possible. Through the recognition of one's own *geopsyche*, participants understand how an 'ethics of answerability' can rightfully be grounded in differences 'of perspective or degree[s] of recognition and identification rather than [limited to] a condition of being' (ibid., p. 41). Consequently, the expansion of individual ecological consciousness creates a more holistic and healthy biotic community. If we consider Murphy's contention that 'nothing human is intrinsically "strange", but rather needs to be recognized as "strange-to-me"', then an 'ethics of answerability' can rightfully be grounded in differences 'of perspective or degree[s] of recognition and identification rather than [limited to] a condition of being' (ibid., p. 41).

27 Helene Meyers, *Femicidal Fears: Narratives of the Female Gothic Experience* (Albany: State University of New York Press, 2001), p. 18.

28 Deborah Slicer, 'The Body as Bioregion', in Michael P. Branch et al. (eds), *Reading*

the Earth: New Directions in the Study of Literature and Environment (Moscow, ID: University of Idaho Press, 1998), p. 110.

29 Catharina J. M. Halkes, *New Creation: Christian Feminism and the Renewal of the Earth*, trans. Catherine Romanik (London: SPCK, 1991), p. 151.

30 Lola Lemire Tostevin, *Frog Moon* (Toronto: Cormorant Books, 1993), p. 31. Subsequent references are to this edition and are given in parentheses in the text.

31 Nancy Huston, *Instruments of Darkness* (New York: Little, Brown, 1997), p. 71. Subsequent references are to this edition and are given in parentheses in the text.

32 Meyers, *Femicidal Fears*, p. 34.

33 Ibid., p. 133.

34 Edwards, 'Introduction', p. xx.

35 Ibid.

36 Ibid., p. xxi.

37 Ibid., p. 20.

38 Punter, *Postcolonial Imaginings*, pp. 31, 32.

39 Edwards, 'Introduction', p. xviii.

40 Ibid., p. xx.

7

Shoshannah Ganz

Margaret Atwood's monsters in the Canadian ecoGothic

Margaret Atwood is a name synonymous with Canadian literature and biting social commentary. Atwood has likewise been credited with the creation of a sub-genre of Gothic and Canadian fiction known as Southern Ontario Gothic. The Atwood *oeuvre* of Gothic works includes most famously *The Handmaid's Tale* (1986), *Surfacing* (1972) and *Lady Oracle* (1976). To these I would add two more: *Oryx and Crake* (2003) and *The Year of the Flood* (2009). Ever a timely writer, Atwood's most recent fiction explores what she terms in the final pages of *Oryx and Crake* the 'end game' for the human race.

This chapter explores the possibility of Gothic literature serving as a form to critique environmental destruction and advocate restoration. In fact, I go so far as to suggest that Atwood's *Oryx and Crake* and *The Year of the Flood* are at the inception of a nascent mutation of the Gothic, what I term the Canadian ecoGothic. The chapter explores in particular the monsters in the texts – Jimmy/Snowman, the monstrous human survivor who cares for the Crakers; the humanoid Crakers, manufactured by the real Frankenstein of the text, Crake, who deliberately and sadistically attempts to destroy all human life forms (except one); the various monstrous manufactured and mutated creatures that prey on the surviving humans; and the sexual predators, among others. Atwood plays with all the stock characteristics of the Gothic genre, but with an eye to a world ravaged by climate change – empty warehouses become the decrepit mansions of survivors hiding from manufactured animals and crazed monsters; incestuous love triangles play across and between the two books, and between monsters and humans; there

are various allusions to earlier Gothic works; the hidden room of the
earth's gardeners threatens dark secrets as do the various dark corners
of abandoned infrastructure; barely decipherable messages come too
late; the uncanny familiarity of various scientific and global threats
serves to make the reader uneasy; and an overwhelming sense of foreboding permeates both texts. Atwood is clearly using the markers of the
Gothic to advocate environmental awareness and change before the
crazed monsters at the centre of the text destroy all life forms.

Canadian literature has a long history of writing about nature in
Gothic terms. Historically, nature has been the threat, the ever-present
and fearful monster seeking to swallow human beings whole. Early
Canadian Gothic texts, perhaps most famously John Richardson's
Wacousta (1832), portray human beings as building walls to protect
themselves from threatening nature. This trope of threatening nature
is so prevalent in early Canadian fiction that Northrop Frye describes
early Canada as having a 'garrison mentality', continually engaged in
building walls to protect against the ever-encroaching wilderness.[1]
Atwood, developing on this trope of the Canadian 'garrison mentality',
suggests in *Survival* (1972) that '[t]he central symbol for Canada ...
is undoubtedly Survival'.[2] Accordingly, Atwood writes that for 'early
explorers and settlers, it meant bare survival in the face of "hostile"
elements and/or natives'.[3] Atwood believes that in early fiction the
obstacles were the hostilities of the 'external – the land, the climate' but
that increasingly the fears become internal, 'what we might call spiritual survival, to life as anything more than a minimally human being'.[4]
At the time of *Survival*'s publication in 1972, David Suzuki and other
Greenpeace 'tree huggers' were just beginning the campaign to 'save
the planet' from the threat posed by the monstrous greed of human
beings. It was just around this time that Atwood notes a spiritual 'crisis'
in Canadian fiction. I would argue that it is also around this time in
Canadian literary history that the terms of the equation begin to shift;
no longer is nature the threatening monster but rather increasingly
human beings are seen as monstrous and as a threat to nature, the
natural world and themselves. While Atwood characterizes the shift in
Canadian literature as a relocation of the theme of survival to internal
as opposed to external fears, for many, Atwood included, the internal
fears are focused on the external manifestation of human destruction
of the natural world.

The threat, even the Gothic threat, of human beings to and against
nature began in the 1970s to get public airtime in Canada on the

Canadian Broadcasting Corporation. David Suzuki led the way with books, reports and his TV series *The Nature of Things*. Farley Mowat advanced awareness of the threat of humans against nature with a long list of publications including *A Whale for the Killing* (1972), *Tundra: Selections from the Great Accounts of Arctic Land Voyages* (1973), *Wake of the Great Sealers* (1973), *The Snow Walker* (1975), *Death of a People – The Ihalmiut* (1975), *Canada North Now: The Great Betrayal* (1976) and *No Birds Sang* (1979). In the world of fiction, Wayland Drew's *Wabeno's Feast* (1973) appeared, commenting on the threat human beings pose to the survival of nature in all its forms.

While *Survival* commented on the Canadian motif of the war between humans and the natural world as early as 1972, in the following year George Woodcock said of *Surfacing* that '[t]he environment is the great theme'.[5] However, from the themes of the environment, it took a number of years for Atwood to further develop the connections between nature and the human project to tame nature, resulting in a process of conquest that threatens the very survival of all life. In the interim Atwood wrote extensively in the Gothic mode: *Lady Oracle* makes connections between the Gothic mode and detective fiction; *Alias Grace* (1996) experiments with speculative fiction; and *The Handmaid's Tale* begins to make further forays into the connections between human activity and environmental destruction.

In the early 1990s, a number of these explorations coalesced. Evidence of the growing sense of uncertainty and foreboding posed by human intervention in the natural world began to appear as early as 1991 in Atwood's short-story collection, *Wilderness Tips*. In 'The Age of Lead', a man is dying of an unnamed disease, while a woman is watching a documentary about the reasons for the demise of the Franklin expedition, and in connecting the two stories she gazes around her apartment at the many plastic and manufactured conveniences, wondering which of them will kill her. Writing about Atwood's development from *Surfacing* to *Wilderness Tips*, Coral Ann Howells notes that Atwood

> has moved from representing wilderness to Canadians as their culturally distinctive national space to a much bleaker contemporary revisionary reading, where simple binary nationalist oppositions disappear. In *Wilderness Tips* an identifiably Canadian voice addresses an international audience, arguing for our shared recognition of complicity in her strong warnings against global pollution as wilderness recedes into myth.[6]

During this crucial decade, as the world warmed and campaigns were launched to deny that the effects were human made, three important

journeys influenced Atwood's thinking and writing about the environment. The first was a trip to Australia where Atwood observed, and was
impressed by, the deep connection to nature and dependence on the
environment evidenced by the indigenous peoples. A second journey
to the North laid before her first-hand evidence of the melting of the
polar ice caps (an account of this journey is detailed in 'To Beechy
Island' as part of an essay collection edited by Katherine Govier in 2004
entitled *Solo: Writers on Pilgrimage*). Her third journey brought her to
Toronto airport on the morning of the terrorist attacks of September
11, 2001. Together these journeys, I would argue, fermented into a
growing sense of the imminent threat posed by the increasing loss
of connection between modern human beings and the environment
and each other, and the resulting and clearly accelerating destruction
of the natural world. The connections between human greed, big oil,
environmental destruction and total apocalypse are not that far behind.

Clearly many real landscapes contribute to the future landscapes of
Oryx and Crake and *The Year of the Flood*. The arid deserts of Australia
lend something to the imaginary terrain of these texts. But not surprisingly in the 1990s in terms of the visible results of climate change, the
North still figures most boldly in Atwood's imagination. Certainly the
impact of Atwood's journey into the melting polar region cannot be
emphasized enough. This journey is one that Atwood comes back to
again and again in her discussions of *Oryx and Crake* and *The Year of the
Flood*. But the North is not a new subject to Atwood or a new context
for apocalyptic vision or Gothic horror. The Arctic figures in nearly
all the early environmental exposés as one of the sites for concern
and debate. Not surprisingly, the North has long held a fascination
for Canadian explorers and writers, and its origins as part of a Gothic
landscape lie in Mary Shelley's *Frankenstein* (1818) and the European
imagination of the nineteenth century. While a complete treatment
of the North in Canadian history and fiction and its connection to
the Canadian Gothic imagination is certainly not possible in anything
less than a book-length study, it seems worthwhile to note that it was
during the 1970s that awareness of threats to the North and the fight
for its protection began to enter public debate. Atwood's lecture series
at Oxford University and later book-length study *Strange Things: The
Malevolent North in Canadian Literature* (1995) offers exactly the kind
of treatment of the North in Canadian fiction that I earlier gestured
towards. And the North has been – and is – viewed as a barometer
by which to measure the increasing pace of environmental destruc-

tion and the possible and probable eventual demise of the planet. The North is not the landscape of either *Oryx and Crake* or *The Year of the Flood*, but is undoubtedly part of the real and imaginary landscape out of which the terrifying world of these texts is born.

In the year following the publication of *Oryx and Crake*, Earl G. Ingersoll argued that

> *Oryx and Crake* seems to be set somewhere along the coast of the American South – Where would Atwood find a spot that's warm year-round in Canada? – and the time seems to be later in the 21st century. What has happened takes longer to figure out because this post-apocalyptic world has been some time in the making.[7]

Six years later the progress of global climate change had been so rapid that it seemed likely that the only habitable place on the planet would be somewhere further north, and with the extended vision Atwood offers in *The Year of the Flood* we find that the climate warming refugees have fled the American South. Canadian bestsellers such as Gwynne Dyer's *Climate Wars* (2008) – the data now out of date and with recent studies suggesting more rapid and dramatic changes – suggest scenarios much like the 'imaginary' world of the 'not-too-distant future' of *Oryx and Crake* and *The Year of the Flood*. The 'fiction' of Atwood's world becomes the scenario of contemporary scientific accounts and survival guides. The scholarly articles that repeatedly parrot Atwood's descriptions of her works as 'speculative' seem weak reassurance in the light of her uncanny predictions of market failures in her 2008 *Payback: Debt as Metaphor and the Shadow Side of Wealth*.[8]

In addition, the term Gothic is amorphous at best and has been increasingly applied to a variety of works with a variety of messages. *Oryx and Crake* has historically been referred to as 'speculative fiction', but one of the main problems with this generic marker is that it does not account appropriately for the moral message of the text, nor other aspects that are representative of science fiction.[9] In his 2004 essay, Ingersoll notes that

> *Oryx and Crake* faces the risk inherent in any fiction produced by a writer with a 'message', and readers of SF know how long the genre has had to contend with the criticism that attention paid to a 'message' restricts, for example, the writer's ability to create characters. Furthermore, the setting of the action in a brave new world of perhaps almost a century in the future calls on her to 'do the science' to make that projected world scientifically cohesive and credible. As a number of readers have pointed out, the genres of fantasy and science fiction have traditionally been gendered feminine and masculine, respectively, because until very recently young women have not been encouraged to study the sciences.[10]

Ingersoll states that Atwood must 'do the science to make that projected world scientifically cohesive and credible' for a century in the
future, which Atwood does not do, and it is clear seventeen years later
that the science is already dated. However, part of Atwood's project
is that she does not do the science for the very distant future, but
for today. I would argue that many critics have focused too closely
on this work as 'speculative fiction' and 'science fiction', and by narrowly defining both of these genres have missed much of the amazing
vision and scope of the work. Further, Atwood has readily admitted,
in lectures on *Oryx and Crake*, that she is not a scientist but rather
an author and researcher who has gathered the interpreted data of
scientific research and incorporated only things that have a basis in
reality, or have in fact already taken place, into her works. Expanding
the generic exploration of this work to include the Gothic, in which
Atwood has been a defining author and successful creator for decades,
answers many of the problems posed by the critics. Atwood herself
notes that she is 'interested in the Gothic novel because it's very much a
woman's form'.[11] Further, this manoeuvre from the clearly demarcated
genre of science fiction to the more amorphous Gothic is not without
precedent in Canadian literary criticism. James de Mille's *A Strange
Manuscript Found in a Copper Cylinder* (1888) is considered the first
Canadian work of science fiction. It is also widely discussed as one of
the early works of Gothic literature. The strange yet familiar lands of
A Strange Manuscript and *Oryx and Crake* serve yet a further purpose
in the Gothic genre, becoming a vehicle for the uncanny or, in Freud's
original word, *Unheimlich* – the reminder of home and the unhomeli-
ness of the place contributing to the uncanny qualities of both texts.
Further, the problems raised by Ingersoll with regard to gender are
resolved since women have been writers of the Gothic from its inception. The Gothic has also always been a vehicle for social criticism – the
contention that the moral message of the text undercuts character
development has not to my knowledge ever been a point of criticism
of the Gothic form. Many of the aspects of *Oryx and Crake* that come
under censure from critics when this work is wedged into the genre
of science fiction are cleverly answered and appropriate in a work discussed as Gothic in vision and influence.

   Likewise, while I have often thought of Gothic texts as being focused
on the buried or repressed secrets *of* the past and obsessed *with* the
past, Gerry Turcotte, writing of *Obasan*, notes that '[w]hereas in traditional Gothic, barriers are physical, with locked doors and dungeons

signifying entrapment – here it is memory that imprisons'.[12] Snowman notes of himself in *Oryx and Crake* that '[h]e'd grown up in walled spaces, and then he had become one. He had shut things out.'[13] But in the devastated and present world of *Oryx and Crake* he is no longer able to shut out the memories of the past – in fact his world for the most part revolves around the memories and actions of the past. As the central reporter of the post-apocalyptic world he is both stranded in the future and trapped in the past. Snowman imagines intoning to the Crakers: '*I'm your ancestor, come from the land of the dead. Now I'm lost, I can't get back, I'm stranded here, I'm all alone*' (129). The actions of the past, our own and that of the text, are unburied in the present of the text not only through Snowman's memories, dreams and delusions but also by the Craker children. The Crakers were manufactured to live entirely in the present, but the waste from our past litters the text of their world. The Craker children beachcomb our refuse – broken plastic objects, broken bits of technology, the unburied waste that our culture attempts to bury in landfills. And it seems that while all the great works of art and science have more or less disappeared, the garbage of our culture is still a part of the present. In a typical Jimmy/Crake argument about the value of arts versus science, Jimmy says 'When any civilization is dust and ashes … art is all that's left over. Images, words, music. Imaginative structures. Meaning – human meaning, that is – is defined by them' and Crake responds 'That's not quite all that's left over. … The archeologists are just as interested in gnawed bones and old bricks and ossified shit these days. Sometimes more interested. They think human meaning is defined by those too' (204). The refuse of our age is itself made uncanny when the naive Craker children gather the objects and ask what they are – and Snowman, the receptacle of knowledge of the past, spins stories about the uses of these objects that in the world of the Crakers, where these objects are clearly divested of any usefulness, take on an uncanny quality – familiar, but made unfamiliar.

Language itself takes on an unfamiliar and even uncanny quality that contributes to the Gothic qualities of the story on a purely linguistic level. One of the examples Atwood often offers in her public readings is Snowman's discussion of 'toast'.

> 'What is toast?' says Snowman to himself, once they've run off. *Toast is when you take a piece of bread – What is bread? Bread is when you take some flour – What is flour? We'll skip that part it's too complicated. Bread is something that you can eat, made from ground-up plant and shaped like a stone. You cook it … Please, why do you cook it? Why don't you just eat the plant? Never mind that part – Pay attention.*

You cook it, and then you cut it into slices, and you put a slice into a toaster, which
is a metal box that heats up with electricity – What is electricity? Don't worry about
that. While the slice is in the toaster, you get out the butter – butter is a yellow grease,
made from the mammary glands of – skip the butter. So, the toaster turns the slice of
bread black on both sides with smoke coming out, and then this 'toaster' shoots the
slice up into the air, and it falls on the floor... 'Forget it', says Snowman. 'Let's try
again.' Toast was a pointless invention from the Dark Ages. Toast was an implement
of torture that caused all those subjected to it to regurgitate in verbal form the sins and
crimes of their past lives. Toast was a ritual item devoured by fetishists in the belief
that it would enhance their kinetic and sexual powers. Toast cannot be explained by
any rational means. Toast is me. I am toast. (118–19)

Discussions of a past and familiar object from life, and particularly
home life, unknown and unexplainable to the Crakers and then
explained both to the Crakers and the reader in a way that makes the
word doubly distant and uncanny, highlight another type of refuse
from our culture – language and mythology. These are the conceptual
objects from the past that the Crakers question with regard to meaning
and utility. The uncanny qualities of language likewise contribute to
the major fissures in the text – the unbridgeable divide between arts
and science – and the uncanny persistence of both in the future in the
form of the Crakers and the obsolete words of Snowman. Language
also serves as one of the ghosts of the present, Snowman hearing in his
head and repeating the words of the past from motivational videos and
chirrupy children's videos along with all the words whose meaning is
'toast'.

The other central fissure or danger that Atwood highlights with the
rifts between characters in the text is the role of science in interfering
with or manufacturing life. This is one of the most important Gothic
components of the text, first articulated in a fight between Jimmy's
parents. Jimmy's mother says to his father, 'What you're doing – this
pig brain thing. You're interfering with the building blocks of life. It's
immoral. It's ... sacrilegious', and Jimmy's father responds, 'It's just
proteins, you know that! There's nothing sacred about cells and tissue'
(67). This discussion at the centre of *Oryx and Crake* and contemporary debates about genetic engineering has been part of Gothic literature from its inception. Donna Heiland, discussing *Frankenstein*, notes
that 'the boundaries between culture and nature, human and inhuman,
parent and child, male and female all seem to be threatened'.[14] Fred
Botting shows how 'new methods of reproduction and genetic manipulation ... threaten paternal formations', noting that *Frankenstein* and
Dracula (1897) 'have always been associated with science and tech-

nology'.[15] However, in the case of the Crakers, it is not merely 'monsters' that are created, but rather the potential for replacing all human life with genetically perfect 'models' of human beings. Certainly the Crakers move towards the erasure of all boundaries between human and inhuman and further force questions of who are the monstrous. In physical appearance the Crakers are perfect and Snowman, the supposedly sole human survivor, is an abominable snowman, or an abomination of all that is human.

According to Heiland, 'The novels of Ann Radcliffe state explicitly that we are haunted by ghosts of our own making. In fact, gothic novels have always known this.'[16] This summation of the ghosts of the Gothic or, in wider terms, the monsters of the Gothic was never more true than in the literary forebear of *Oryx and Crake*, Mary Shelley's *Frankenstein*. Gerry Turcott claims that 'monstrous figures stand at the heart of all these gothic tales … haunting, yet also reflecting, a spectral condition. They generally seem, therefore, at once alien and yet strangely familiar.'[17] Sherrill E. Grace notes that 'Canada has plenty of ghosts, and Margaret Atwood knows how to call them up better than most of our writers. Her poems, stories, and novels are often haunted by revenants, ghosts, or gothic presences of one sort or another.'[18] Nothing is more central to *Oryx and Crake* than questions about the cultural production of monstrosity. Punter and Byron note the 'cultural work done by monsters', suggesting that '[t]hrough difference, whether in appearance or behaviour, monsters function to define and construct the politics of "normal"'.[19] But the monsters of *Oryx and Crake*, not unexpectedly for an Atwood text, play games with the reader and the reader is never entirely sure who the 'real' monsters of the text – and the 'real' or fictional world of the text – are, and where they belong, and whether or not they will actually succeed. Atwood leaves the ending open in both *Oryx and Crake* and *The Year of the Flood*, so that the reader is never satisfied as to who the monsters are or whether or not they will survive. In these books, in contrast to most Gothic conventions, the monsters are not conquered and expelled from the world of the text, but rather they are among the planned survivors of global genocide. The message of the Frankenstein of the text is clearly that the 'real' monsters are the humans, and once they have been expelled the new humanoid (monster?) will be able to live in peace and harmony. Seemingly as the text advances the monsters proliferate, and further proliferate from one text to the text that follows. In *Oryx and Crake* the first monsters appear to be the pigoons and other manufactured animals set ablaze to protect humans from real or imagined contamination. But the protagonist as a young boy asks the question that is never really resolved in the text: 'who are the monsters'? Jimmy 'thought of the pigoons as creatures much like himself' (29), and thus the genocidal monsters by extension are the exterminating scientists. This terrifies Jimmy. And as Jimmy grows the question of who the monsters are looms larger. To the establishment as it were, the Corpsecore, Jimmy's rebel mother, who is fighting the monster corporation, is in fact the monster. To Jimmy, in his humorous cafeteria skits, his parents and all adults are monsters, but he himself walks the line by his betrayal of their secrets. Even the computer games the children play demand that they assume the role of monsters and make monstrous and inhuman choices. One such game is *Blood and Roses*, which is described as follows:

> Blood and Roses was a trading game, along the lines of Monopoly. The Blood side played with human atrocities for the counters, atrocities on a large scale: individual rapes and murders didn't count, there had to have been a large number of people wiped out. Massacres, genocides, that sort of thing. The Roses side played with human achievements. Artworks, scientific breakthroughs, stellar works of architecture, helpful inventions. *Monuments to the soul's magnificence,* they were called in the game. There were sidebar buttons, so that if you didn't know what *Crime and Punishment* was, or the Theory of Relativity, or the Trail of Tears, or *Madame Bovary*, or the Hundred Years' War, or *The Flight into Egypt*, you could double-click and get an illustrated rundown[.] (94)

Other internet sites normalize monstrous human behaviours including live suicide and child pornography. Clearly the monsters in these cases are a part of our society and the scathing satire is held up as a mirror. Jimmy and Crake freeze the image of Oryx and the discomfort Jimmy feels as a result of her gaze implicates him for looking. Following a description of her onscreen,

> Oryx paused in her activities. She smiled a hard little smile that made her appear much older, and wiped the whipped cream from her mouth. Then she looked over her shoulder and right into the eyes of the viewer – right into Jimmy's eyes, into the secret person inside of him. *I see you,* that look said. *I see you watching. I know you. I know what you want.* (109)

Later in the text, Oryx ushers in another host of 'real' monsters from her past, beginning with her family selling her to Uncle En, the men who bring her to their hotel rooms, the child pornographers and Jack who teaches Oryx English in exchange for sex. Jimmy rages at these monsters, but Oryx is unwilling to accuse her abusers of being monsters or to view herself as a victim, a familiar stance in Atwood's *oeuvre* of Gothic works. According to Colette Tennant, 'Atwood transforms the genre from one of female victimization to one of empowering awareness'.[20]

Jimmy, even prior to his abominable snowman days, seems monstrous in his manipulation of women with his bottomless need. His rank smell, hairiness and greedy gobbling of Oryx's creatures (the fish) are seen as monstrous through Snowman's eyes in comparison to the citrus-smelling and grass-munching Crakers. Snowman has created a variety of mythologies to explain the world to the Crakers and as such has made himself an indispensable source of lore and information to the new-born humanoid species. The stories he tells explain the pain and suffering of dying humanity that the Crakers witness as they follow Snowman to the seaside, as well as amusing Snowman and parodying Judaeo-Christian stories, while undercutting Craker's plan to create a species without this need to create myth or legend. When Snowman disappears for a few days the Crakers supplant the stories he has told them with their own stories and go so far as to build an effigy of Snowman and chant for his return. This resurgence of the need for religious ritual and ceremony takes on an uncanny quality because of its likeness to our own religious forebears and because of the effigy they create. Snowman says:

> What's the thing – the statue, or scarecrow, or whatever it is? It has a head, and a ragged cloth body. It has a face of sorts – one pebble eye, one black one, a jar lid it looks like. It has an old string mop stuck onto the chin. (429)

And perhaps in this context his monstrous form takes on new dimensions as that of a god of antiquity.

These are only a few of the possible and peripheral monsters of the text. The central moral questions of monstrosity really centre around Crake and the Crakers. Is Crake a *nouveau* Frankenstein, or is he the monster? He manufactures 'better' humans; but he also carefully plots total genocide for the human race. He does this because the human race are destroying themselves and the planet – to save them from themselves, as it were, and to recreate a better-behaved and more environmentally friendly human being. But the Crakers, while looking like perfect humans, also have some bizarrely monstrous markings – when mating they turn blue, and a group of blue-penised men descend on the blue woman. Crakers graze like cattle or rabbits, purr, and have various other manufactured characteristics that are meant to make them suited to the world of the future, but in fact make them rather terrifying, if simple, human-like creatures. Their real monstrosity lies not in their physical proximity to human beings but in the mental vacuity that has replaced the sometimes disturbing but certainly human characteristics – those traits that lead to art and war. The sole human survivor, self-named Snowman after the abominable snowman, is likewise monstrous-looking in a threadbare sheet, with blotchy skin, malnourished, wearing sunglasses with only one lens and manic with loneliness. But perhaps his brokenness, both physical and mental, is where we sense his humanity which we share with Snowman – haunted as we are by our ancestral destruction of the planet and day-by-day destruction of all life to fill our bottomless greed.

In the book that follows, *The Year of the Flood*, there are all the same monsters as in *Oryx and Crake*, but the additional cast includes the God's Gardeners Cult eco-freaks, who, if not intended to be monsters, are at the very least weird; and the pain ball survivor sexual predators, who escape following the apocalypse to continue terrorizing the surviving women. This choir of monsters blurs the lines of what constitutes a monster and ultimately leads all humanity into the role of monster in our participation in destroying life on the planet. At the very least, it forces the reader to question who the monsters are and what constitutes the monstrous.

The Gothic heroine is repeatedly in flight in *The Year of the Flood*, though she does not escape the sexual predation of various monsters. But not only the Gothic heroine, but rather all of the characters are forced into flight by combinations of environmental and human threat. Seemingly none of the characters are immune from the violent threats of crazed and depraved human beings and/or monsters of the texts. While the new Eden on the roof of a city building in the plebes has been transformed into a safe haven for Tobi and others who are fleeing various monsters – sexual predators or Corpsecorp – even the gardener paradise is not immune from the threat of environmental and human-generated violence. Cancer, sickness, betrayal, abandonment and death are all part of the gardener paradise, and before the virtual annihilation of the human species, the Gardener's Eden is destroyed by violent marauders.

In time most of the human race has been destroyed, and as Snowman and other characters venture into the compounds to pilfer what food and supplies they can, the mansions and *faux* antiques become part of an increasingly Gothic landscape. Snowman and others are forced to hide from the wild pigoons in houses with corpses and rotting food, and the compounds emptied of their inhabitants become ghost cities of Gothic proportion. In fact the entire planet becomes one of the trademark graveyards of the Gothic genre – one mass grave and garbage dump that the survivors must navigate. Before the bliss plus annihilation, factories devoid of activity or human occupants loomed like *nouveaux* derelict mansions reclaimed as smelly and recycled squatter units by the God's Gardeners. But even with the cult members inhabiting the vacant rooms, these tomb-like chambers or monuments to the age of industry house secrets far more threatening than the Gardeners' grow opps and mushroom beds – they echo with the ghosts of the past. Pre-Gardener Tobi, for example, is trapped by economics in a small, excessively hot room over a 'real' fur-producing slaughterhouse that smells continually of warm, thick blood. The fancy restaurants boast menus of endangered species, and the secret burger chain is responsible for hiding the evidence of various missing political criminals – only traces of fingernails survive the grinding process to turn up in the burgers and urban legend.

According to Heiland, '[e]vents [in the Gothic] turn on the righting of a wrong that offends the clearly cultural order as well as the seemingly natural one'.[21] And this is perhaps most daringly what Atwood plays at in posing possible solutions to the planetary disaster we are rushing towards. Crake's solution leads to the demise of most of the self-annihilating human race. But the 'fixing' of the world's problems has a ghastly result, and in dying out the melting human zombies, bleeding from their eyeballs, wander the streets and hide in their bathrooms. The various features that contribute to Atwood's work being considered ecoGothic include the setting of our world further ravaged by climate change and made uncanny and terrifying by the devastation wrought by environmental change and global genocide. The feeling of terror generated by the setting is furthered by a cast of characters including monsters of various forms, heroines in flight from these monsters or being tortured and captured by them, various ghosts from the past (including technology and the infrastructure of the world before climate change), and a strange species of humanoid that has seemingly survived.

Ronald Wright's *A Scientific Romance* (1998) similarly features a strange band of humanoids, a survivor from the earlier pre-climate-change world, and a post-climate-change world in which the survivors live in the decaying infrastructure of the previous world and, like the Crakers, cannot read or write but appear to retain the need to create their own strange mythologies with regard to the refuse from the past. Other Canadian ecoGothics are set in the present with ecological signs and wonders that predict and warn about the future demise of the planet. Often, as in *Oryx and Crake* and *The Year of the Flood*, the clear line dividing human and animal or inhuman is blurred, and in texts such as Timothy Findley's *The Butterfly Plague* (1969) the slaughter of animals comes to be seen in terms equivalent to the Holocaust. In Findley's *Headhunter* (1993), the diseases that are infecting the birds threaten the humans with plague, and this is paired with the plague of catatonic and dying children – the result of horrible atrocities committed against all the innocent, animal and human. Wayland Drew's post-apocalyptic world likewise shows the destruction of innocent children – the result of a big company's chemical spill – as one inexcusable event along the path to toxifying the entire planet. Other Canadian ecoGothics, such as Shani Mootoo's *The Cereus Blooms at Night* (1996), pair sexual and colonial oppression with nature and the destruction of nature, but also seem to promise redemption through the tending and replanting of the natural world. Other ecoGothics set in Brazil, such as Andrew Pyper's *The Trade Mission* (2002) and Lesley Krueger's *Drink the Sky* (1999), are less hopeful in their pairing of the human-made destruction of the ecological habitat that indigenous peoples rely on with the overall moral and physical decline of the various power-wielding and abusing characters of the text. And while many of these works feature foreign settings or unnamed places of the future, I suggest that increasingly the threats of ecological destruction presented fictionally in Gothic form will be brought into the present context of Canada, as we become less and less able to look outward for the sources of evil. Certainly we would like to believe that Atwood's ecoGothics are set in the distant future in a place that is not Canada, but the reality seems to be moving towards us as quickly or more quickly than the melting North.

However, while various Canadian ecoGothics share preoccupations with nature and climate change, mental or physical entrapment, worlds over-run by nature or in which the natural world has been devastated, monsters, ghosts and monstrosities, and heroines in flight from sexual predators, Atwood's ecoGothic does not simply leave the reader in this Gothic nightmare world on the verge of violent destruction and the demise of the entire human race. There are some survivors – and most of these are humans who have been trained in survival – and it is at this point that the *The Year of the Flood* takes an interesting shift away from other contemporary Gothics and even ecoGothics. It is not the vanquishing of monsters or the escape of the heroine from sexual predation that in fact resolves the imbalance of these worlds; it is rather the hope offered by the survivors finding each other and together building an ecologically sustainable community for the future. Atwood's *The Year of the Flood* could in fact be read as something of a beginner's guide for the survival of environmental cataclysm. The God's Gardeners instruct their children and by extension the reader in ways to nurture the earth; how to recognize and grow edible and medicinal plants; how to forage and garden; where to find uncontaminated water and how to treat water; how to respect one another and animals and plants; in fact how to prepare to survive ecological disaster and rebuild and re-green the natural world.

Notes

1 Northrop Frye, *The Bush Garden: Essays on the Canadian Imagination* (Toronto: Anansi, 1971), p. 224.
2 Margaret Atwood, *Survival: A Thematic Guide to Canadian Literature* (Toronto: Anansi, 1972), p. 32.
3 Ibid., p. 32.
4 Ibid., p. 33.
5 George Woodcock, *Introducing Margaret Atwood's Surfacing: A Reader's Guide by George Woodcock* (Toronto: ECW Press, 1990), p. 69.
6 Coral Ann Howells, *The Cambridge Companion to Margaret Atwood* (Cambridge: Cambridge University Press, 2006), p. 48.
7 Earl G. Ingersoll, 'Survival in Margaret Atwood's Novel *Oryx and Crake*', *Extrapolation* 45/2 (2004): 162–74. Available online (in an unpaginated but searchable copy) at http://lion.chadwyck.com/display/printView.do?area=abell (accessed 28 June 2012).
8 When I first taught *Oryx and Crake* in 2003, the class discussion was much focused on questions of human-made versus cyclical climate change. Students enjoyed *Oryx and Crake* and discussed aspects of science fiction and fantasy, satire and dystopian vision. The critics echoed much of the same. Recently in teaching *Oryx and Crake* to a first-year class I admitted a fear for the 'not-too-distant future' that I was far from owning when the book first made its way on to the bookshelves. The class discussion focused almost entirely on the reality of climate change, fears and how 'true and factual' the text was proving to be. Students themselves supplied much of the information about climate change and there was only one dissenter who suggested that perhaps climate change was not 'man-made'. The rest of the class did most of the work in railing at his ignorance. This being said – and in an attempt to move beyond the aspect of Atwood's uncanny ability to predict the future – the very real fear generated by this text is not simply produced by the realities of climate change recorded in *Oryx and Crake* and *The Year of the Flood*.
    Days after proposing this paper and the term 'ecoGothic' as a new and nascent

form in Canadian fiction I came across a call for papers for a new book with
Manchester University Press entitled *EcoGothic*. And so while I will blame the
hours of teaching for the resulting slowness and hence loss of claim to the term
'ecoGothic', I would continue to argue that this is a relatively new and emergent
form of the Gothic in Canadian fiction and other world literatures.

9 Gothic science fiction could perhaps be another useful way of discussing *Oryx and
Crake* and *The Year of the Flood*. Critics to date have not discussed these works as
Gothic science fiction, and I am more interested in this chapter in discussing the
Gothic and ecological components of the text than in looking at Atwood's works in
the context of the genre of science fiction.

10 Ingersoll, 'Survival in Margaret Atwood's Novel *Oryx and Crake*', unpaginated.

11 Quoted in Avril Horner and Sue Zlosnik, *Gothic and the Comic Turn* (Toronto:
Palgrave, 2004), p. 129.

12 Cynthia Sugars and Gerry Turcott. *Unsettled Remains: Canadian Literature and the
Postcolonial Gothic* (Waterloo: Wilfrid Laurier University Press, 2009), p. 85.

13 Margaret Atwood, *Oryx and Crake* (Toronto: McClelland and Stewart, 2003),
p. 224. Subsequent references are to this edition and are given in parentheses in the
text.

14 Donna Heiland, *Gothic and Gender* (Oxford: Blackwell, 2004), p. 98.

15 Fred Botting, *Gothic* (London and New York: Routledge, 1996), p. 288.

16 Heiland, *Gothic and Gender*, p. 77.

17 Sugars and Turcott, *Unsettled Remains*, p. 77.

18 Sherrill E. Grace, '"Franklin Lives": Atwood's Northern Ghosts', in Lorraine M.
York (ed.), *Various Atwoods: Essays on the Later Poems, Short Fiction, and Novels*
(Concord, Ontario: Anansi, 1995), pp. 146–66, pp. 146–7.

19 Quoted in David Stevens, *The Gothic Tradition* (Cambridge: Cambridge University
Press, 2000), p. 263.

20 Mary Colette Tennant, *Reading the Gothic in Margaret Atwood's Novels* (Lewiston,
NY: Edwin Mellen Press, 2003), p. 2.

21 Heiland, *Gothic and Gender*, p. 99.

8

Tom J. Hillard

From Salem witch to *Blair Witch*: the Puritan influence on American Gothic nature

In no world but a fallen one could such lands exist.
         (Herman Melville, 'The Encantadas')
But nature is a stranger yet;
The ones that cite her most
Have never passed her haunted house,
Nor simplified her ghost.
       (Emily Dickinson, 'What Mystery Pervades a Well')

When *The Blair Witch Project* hit US movie theatres in October 1999 it became an overnight sensation, creating a media buzz that grew in part because of an extraordinary marketing campaign. An elaborate website, as well as a *faux* television documentary called *The Curse of the Blair Witch* released in advance of the film, led many early viewers to mistake *The Blair Witch Project* for nonfiction, suggesting that its events really happened. We quickly learned that none of it was true – that the events captured in the film were fully staged and acted – but the story (and the film's innovative storytelling method) has remained popular, acquiring almost a cult following. The movie itself tells the story of Heather Donahue, Josh Leonard and Mike Williams, three young film students who set out to shoot a documentary about a legendary witch that supposedly haunts the woods outside Burkittsville, Maryland. All of the film is recorded by the three students themselves, with two cameras, as they wander through the woods over the course of several days looking for clues about the Blair witch. This field research goes awry, however, when they discover themselves lost in those woods, and much worse, they soon realize something is stalking them: a horrifying, unknown terror that is never actually seen on camera. The film ends, as many horror films do, when their lives end. And much to the chagrin of so many moviegoers, we never learn what actually happened or who caused it. All that remains is their film footage, 'discovered' a year later and edited for release as *The Blair Witch Project* (which we are told in an opening title card). At the end, viewers are left speculating.

As much as *The Blair Witch Project* flirts with the possibility of a supernatural force haunting the woods, I am more interested in the story it tells about the failure of twentieth-century convenience and technology to provide survival in the woods. On the fourth day of their ordeal as the trio begins to have trouble finding their way in the forest, Heather optimistically announces, 'It's very hard to get lost in America these days, and it's even harder to stay lost. So, we have that on our side.'[1] One day later, with still no sign of escape, Mike concedes, 'They [the woods] might very well go on forever compared to our footsteps.' But Heather's vehemently optimistic response is telling: 'Not possible,' she says, 'not possible in this country ... Because this is America and it's not possible. We've destroyed most of our natural resources. Let's just keep going.' Taken in context, Heather is not making any explicit comment on environmental devastation. Instead, she is suggesting that given the centuries-old history of deforestation in the United States, it is unlikely that they could remain lost for long in those Maryland woods. At some point, it would seem, they are bound to stumble upon a road, a house or another marker of the modern world. Nevertheless, the film proves otherwise: regardless of the extent of North American deforestation in the late twentieth century, it very much *is* possible to remain lost. Despite their reliance on maps, a compass, backpacking gear and their non-stop filming, they cannot escape; and, ultimately, they are swallowed up by the forest, never to be found again.

Environmental concerns were probably far from the directors' minds when they filmed *The Blair Witch Project*, but nevertheless Heather's statement about the destruction of natural resources provides an implicit environmental subtext that invites us to examine the film through an ecocritical lens, and it opens a space for viewers to consider the fear and horror both aimed at and produced by the natural world in the film. Ecocritics have been slow to address horror films and Gothic literature in general, but in recent years there has been a steady move towards serious and sustained study of cultural representations of anxiety, fear and even hatred directed at 'nature'. Some attention has been drawn to the role and function of ecophobia in both human culture widely considered and in the field of ecocriticism specifically.[2] Such a deep-seated phobia about 'nature' has a long history, and it has been argued that such a sentiment, consciously or not, may lie at the heart of Western culture's long-held desire to alter, change and even destroy those aspects of our environments that (seem to) threaten us. In exploring this history, I find myself following the strand of ecocriticism that builds, as Timothy Clark has described it, a 'broad archive ... tracing different conceptions of nature and their effects throughout the history and cultures of the world'.[3] To this end, particularly compelling is Anthony Lioi's concept of the 'swamp dragon', a figure he posits as 'a model for ecocritical activity that does not shun compromised places and the politics of poison'.[4] 'A swampy, draconian criticism,' he writes, 'will require a new practice of reading, a new attitude toward canon formation, and the consideration of compromised texts as well as compromised environments.'[5] In short, Lioi asks us 'to become the monster under the bed, the thing we dare not touch, the evil bent upon the destruction of civilization'.[6] By not shunning compromised places and by facing the monsters under the bed – or in the woods – we can move closer to understanding our own ambivalent relationships towards the environments in which we live.

Consequently, the key question that drives my investigation here is this: Why did a 1990s film about getting lost and vanishing in the woods touch such a deep cultural nerve? When early advertisements proclaimed that *The Blair Witch Project* 'Does for the woods, what *Jaws* did for the water', what exactly did that *mean*?[7] What does *The Blair Witch Project* tell us about ourselves? Much has been written about the film from a panoply of scholarly approaches, but so far none have sufficiently addressed its ecocritical concerns.[8] If we read the film through a 'green' lens, however, several important storylines come into focus: the inability of three campers to navigate the woods; the failure of modern technology to provide relief or escape; and the deep uncertainty of not knowing what is lurking 'out there', just out of sight. Equally important, Heather's comment about deforestation offers an implicit and unsettling moral: secretly, we may harbour a desire to severely alter, if not outright destroy, some of our natural resources – because to do so is, paradoxically, to survive. These storylines and this 'moral' suggest that the power of *The Blair Witch Project*, as a Gothic text, comes in part from what the film tells us about our own uncertain relationships with the natural world. I agree with Sally Morgan, who has noted that the film plays on 'particular fears and anxieties arising from shared histories, myths, and cultural relationships peculiar to the descendants of the European colonists of North America', and she contends that those fears are related to 'a landscape that remains alien and threatening, irredeemably foreign and hostile even 200 years after its settlement'.[9]

The project of this chapter, then, is to examine some roots of those fears, and to do so I move from the Blair witch of the late twentieth century back in time to the most infamous era of witchcraft in North American history: seventeenth-century Puritan New England. While the 'alien and threatening landscape' that Morgan identifies was part of the European colonial experience regardless of national background, the worldview of the Puritans is particularly interesting in the context of ecocritical studies of fear and nature. When those early settlers came to Massachusetts in the early 1600s, the Calvinist theological framework they brought with them had significant and wide-ranging effects that shaped their interactions with the natural world they encountered. More specifically, as I will demonstrate, the typological understanding of the New World 'wilderness' held by many of these settlers established an important imaginative symbolic structure that allowed them to 'read the world' to interpret signs from God. This symbolic structure, grounded in biblical exegesis and carried out into day-to-day life, not only coloured Puritan textual representations of nature, but also prefigures key characteristics of the literary Gothic mode as it is later developed. As I see it, this pre-Gothic symbolism, while rooted deeply in Puritan theology, has changed and evolved over the centuries, but its basic features can still be located in many (if not most) subsequent Gothicized representations of nature. In short, the Puritans imported to North America a way of reading nature symbolically that both shaped their interactions with landscape and place, and anticipates later metaphoric representations of those landscapes and places in Gothic literature. By looking back in time to identify these characteristics, we can see how *The Blair Witch Project* stands as just one modern manifestation of older, widespread cultural anxieties about the natural world and our relationship to it.

* * *

To get a sense of how the New England Puritans understood their relationship to the natural world, I turn first to Cotton Mather, the Boston minister whose association with the 1692 Salem Witch Trials has made his legacy infamous in early American history. In addition to his renowned status as minister and magistrate, Mather was a prolific author: alongside hundreds of sermons, he published such noteworthy books as *Memorable Providences* (1689), *Wonders of the Invisible World* (1693) and what is usually considered his magnum opus, *Magnalia Christi Americana* (1702). In all of these varied works, one of Mather's primary motives, regardless of audience or genre, is to glorify God and testify to His providential designs. A memorable example of this appears in his 1721 monument of natural history, *The Christian Philosopher*, when Mather makes mention of 'a *Twofold Book* of GOD' which includes 'the Book of the *Creatures*, and the Book of the *Scriptures*'.[10] If we 'read the *Former* of these *Books*,' he contends, "twill help us in reading the *Latter*'.[11] In other words, the natural world – the 'Book of the Creatures' – is a 'book' authored by God, and as a book it can be 'read' and interpreted. Just as important, when read properly this book not only leads to potential religious, spiritual wisdom, but it can also aid reading and interpreting 'the Book of the Scriptures'. For Mather and most of his Puritan brethren, both the earthly world around them and the Bible were divinely created texts – one filled with God's created wonders, and the other with the literal Word of God – available and open to interpretation. Consequently, Mather is able to call the natural world a *'Publick Library'* and offer an invitation: '*Reader*, walk with me into it, and see what we shall find so legible there.'[12]

Mather's use of this public library metaphor is both memorable and significant, for it draws attention to the dual way in which the Puritans perceived the material world around them. On the one hand, they did all they could to eschew earthly, worldly things, understanding that the true prize was the future that awaited in the afterlife – not here and now. But, on the other hand, they also knew that this present world was the product of a divine Creator, and because it was impossible to communicate with God directly, the Puritans believed that '[i]n order to reveal himself, then, it was necessary for God to "veil" his majesty in signs and symbols which man could comprehend'.[13] Thus this world is one in which God regularly intervenes, and all events and phenomena can be interpreted for divine meaning. This focus on '[e]mblem, symbol, allegory', as Susan Manning explains, 'emphasize[s] the doubleness of the puritan vision, the compulsive need to *interpret* the experience in terms of something else, to discover "meaning" in "fact"'.[14]

Such an emblematic understanding of the world can be traced to the ancient biblical exegetical tradition known as typology. In this religious context, typology is a theory used in the Christian tradition to explain the relationship between the Old and New Testaments, wherein events in the Old Testament (the 'types') are seen to prefigure the revelations of Christ in the New Testament (the 'antitypes'). While this tradition is long, complex and difficult for many modern readers to understand, for the New England saints it was an integral part of daily thought. They adhered to the Calvinist 'conviction that Christ is everywhere revealed in the Old Testament, not in his full glory, of course, but in "types and shadows" which are intimations of future fulfillment'.[15] In other words, Puritan typology was not just a way of reading written texts allegorically, of finding connections between Old and New Testaments; the type–antitype structure was understood to describe the historical progression of real-world events. As Thomas Davis reminds us, 'Christian typology … always implies that the two events, promise and fulfillment, have taken place in time as real, historical facts'.[16] Because types were seen as actual prefigurations of future real-world experiences, the New England Puritans read events in their daily lives as the playing-out of God's providential design, and precursors to their experiences could be located in the Scriptures. However the Puritans saw it, 'biblical analogy', John Gatta explains, 'was never far from the imaginative consciousness of literate saints throughout the New England colonies'.[17]

While this typological understanding of the world can be seen at work in nearly any Puritan-authored sermon or history, for an example I turn to one of the most well-known texts from seventeenth-century New England: William Bradford's *Of Plymouth Plantation*.[18] One of the pilgrims aboard the *Mayflower* who established Plymouth Colony in 1620, and an early governor of the fledgling settlement, Bradford penned a history that records those earliest Puritan experiences in North America. In the following passage, Bradford draws on typology to describe his first impressions of the newly encountered land. Writing about his 'poor people's present condition' and describing landfall on the shores of Massachusetts, he laments that:

> Being thus passed the vast ocean, and a sea of troubles before in their preparation … [the pilgrims] had now no friends to welcome them nor inns to entertain or refresh their weatherbeaten bodies; no houses or much less town to repair to, to seek for succour. It is recorded in Scripture as a mercy to the Apostle and his shipwrecked company, that the barbarians showed them no small kindness in refreshing them, but these savage barbarians, when they met with them … were readier to fill their sides full of arrows than otherwise. And for the season it was winter, and they that know the winters of that country know them to be sharp and violent, and subject to cruel and fierce storms, dangerous to travel to known places, much more to search an unknown coast. Besides, what could they see but a hideous and desolate wilderness, full of wild beasts and wild men – and what

multitudes there might be of them they knew not. Neither could they, as it were, go up to the top of Pisgah to view from this wilderness a more goodly country to feed their hopes ... For summer being done, all things stand upon them with a weatherbeaten face, and the whole country, full of woods and thickets, represented a wild and savage hue. ...[19]

The profundity of the isolation that Bradford describes here is difficult for modern readers to fully appreciate. After the arduous passage over the 'vast ocean', these travellers encounter no haven nor solace but rather 'sharp and violent', 'cruel and fierce' winter weather. Instead of the warmth of welcoming inns, they face 'savage barbarians' eager to 'fill their sides full of arrows'. More importantly, Bradford compares the present experiences to those 'recorded in Scripture', drawing a sharp contrast between the past and present at the same time as he reads the one in terms of the other. Similarly, Bradford laments that they could not 'go up to the top of Pisgah to view from this wilderness a more goodly country to feed their hopes'. Whereas Moses before him caught a glimpse of the Promised Land from the summit of Mount Pisgah, here in North America the Puritan settlers do not yet have any such view. Their hope for survival and success rests on faith alone. In this passage, Bradford and company stand poised at the edge of what is imagined as a hostile world fraught with dangers. Instead of a Promised Land, they see only the immensity of an unending 'hideous and desolate wilderness'.

What is apparent in this passage (and elsewhere in Bradford's writing) is the way he explains his experience with the New World 'wilderness' in symbolic terms connected to the biblical past. Rosenmeier explains that 'The Old Testament events and people are [for Bradford] ... more than exemplary, more than static emblems ... for when God's chosen peoples go in search of Canaans, the ancient lives are reenacted. The past lives again in the present.'[20] Put differently,

> the peculiar circumstances of the New England experiment – the New Exodus, the journey through the Wilderness, the establishment of a New Israel, and so on – provided the Puritan with a continuous analogy to the great biblical dramas ... Thus an imagistic consciousness based upon typology pervaded Puritan thought.[21]

For Bradford, then, that first confrontation with the 'hideous and desolate wilderness' was an experience fraught with spiritual significance, and one that resonated with the biblical past. Like the people of Israel before them, the Puritans had crossed a body of water to come to a wilderness, with the purpose of building a new Jerusalem. The Israelites had crossed the Red Sea, the Puritans the Atlantic Ocean, and both groups believed that God was communicating with them.

Amid this symbolic understanding of and engagement with the world – for Bradford, Mather or any Puritan – is the key fact that humankind is divided from 'nature' and only able to approach it as 'a series of inscrutable signs to be "interpreted" for their possible significance', in the words of Susan Manning.[22] Why this division between man and God? The answer is simple. Before all else, the Puritans believed their world to be fallen: although a benevolent God had created the universe, Adam and Eve's transgression in the Garden of Eden had opened the world to suffering and pain. As the Book of Genesis explains,

> to Adam [God] said, Because thou hast obeyed the voice of thy wife, and hast eaten of the tree (whereof I commanded thee, saying, Thou shalt not eat of it) cursed is the earth for thy sake: in sorrow shalt thou eat of it all the days of thy life. (Genesis 3:17)[23]

Moreover, 'Thorns also, and thistles shall it bring forth to thee, and thou shalt eat the herbe of the field' (Genesis 3:18). Because of Adam's transgressions, 'the Lord God sent him forth from the garden of Eden, to till the earth, whence he was taken. Thus he cast out man' (Genesis 3:23–4). As a consequence of his sin Adam and Eve are 'cast out' of Eden and made to live on an 'earth' that is now 'cursed' because of his actions. No longer did humankind live in the Garden, and no longer was humankind free from sin. Consequently, the Puritans (and all humankind, as they believed) collectively bore the burden of guilt for those sins.[24] Indeed, so fundamental was this doctrine of Original Sin that, while learning the alphabet in the *New England Primer,* for the letter *A* every child was taught the refrain: 'In Adam's fall / We sinned all'.

This theological framework of a fallen, cursed world created by original sin was imported to New England, and it shaped the Puritans' experience of the landscape and the natural world they found there. Encountering what seemed to them an unsettled wilderness (despite the inescapable signs of the presence of Native Americans), they read into it – as they did into every aspect of their lives – a religious, biblical symbolism. My argument here is that this symbolic, 'cursed', postlapsarian earth anticipates the settings of the literary Gothic mode a century later, and it possesses interesting implications for ecocriticism.[25]

Scholarship about the literary Gothic has long acknowledged the important function of landscape and nature as settings for Gothic fiction. Ever since Ann Radcliffe's best-selling *The Mysteries of Udolpho* (1794), the sublime landscapes of continental Europe have provided thrilling settings at the same time as they often figure as external markers of characters' interior states. 'The Gothic resides naturally in a landscape of terror,' Christoph Grunenberg writes, 'nurtured by the uncomfortable relationship of the human character and the natural environment.'[26] Allan Lloyd-Smith has described a 'demonic hollowness behind nature' in many nineteenth-century American Gothic texts that may have evolved from Calvinist thinking, and asserts that there is 'a terror of the land itself, its emptiness, its implacability; simply a sense of its vast, lonely, and possibly hostile space that informs the American Gothic and, ultimately, resists any rational explanation'.[27]

Moreover, in articulating a concept of the 'frontier Gothic', David Mogen explains that '[t]he origin of contemporary American versions of the gothic wilderness is the Puritan's initial reaction to the New World', and 'the power of these Satanic associations with the wilderness should not be underestimated'.[28] However, despite such scholarly gestures towards the importance of natural landscapes as Gothic settings, few have explored the ways that these Gothicized settings reveal our (often ambivalent) attitudes towards the natural world.

A quick overview of how the Gothic mode functions is instructive here. Since Horace Walpole published the second edition of *The Castle of Otranto* in 1765 and subtitled it 'A Gothic Story', the literary Gothic mode 'signifies a writing of excess', to quote Fred Botting;[29] and one of its key characteristics is an emphasis on fear.[30] The nature of that fear has shifted depending on the author's specific historical context, but the earliest Gothic fictions typically depict foreign regions centuries in the past, and they simultaneously express desires for and anxieties about the 'excess' of their subject matter. Frequently, the plots involve supernatural activity (or the hint of it), women in danger, ancient castles or monasteries standing over subterranean dungeons or catacombs, the threat of violence and rape, and almost always convoluted family histories, with lost heirs and hidden siblings and parents, in which a secret from the past – usually connected to some scandalous or criminal transgression – comes to light during the tale. As Allan Lloyd-Smith has summarized it, the Gothic 'is about the return of the past, of the repressed and denied, the *buried secret* that subverts and corrodes the present, whatever the culture does not want to know or admit, will not or dare not tell itself'.[31] This notion of a buried secret that eventually comes to light – or memory of a 'primal crime', as it has been called – is central to understanding Gothicized representations of nature.

A typological, symbolic conception of landscape is significant here because of its implications for the Gothic mode. Perhaps more so than most literature, setting is a central convention of the Gothic: the fears the Gothic engages are usually located 'in an antiquated or seemingly antiquated space – be it a castle, a foreign palace, an abbey, a vast prison, a subterranean crypt, a graveyard, a primeval frontier or island', in Jerrold Hogle's words. Moreover, '[w]ithin this space, or a combination of such spaces, are hidden some secrets from the past (sometimes the recent past) that haunt the characters', the same 'buried secret' described by Lloyd-Smith.[32] It might seem strange to read the experiences of the Puritans within such a context because, for them, the natural world of New England was not antiquated but completely new. But at the same time, for the Puritans the New World landscape *does* function as a sort of Gothic castle. It is the wilderness – the fallen, cursed world created when Adam and Eve were expelled from Eden. Like the dungeons, catacombs and castles that later become Gothic set pieces, this fallen landscape is, by virtue of Adam's disobedience described in the Book of Genesis, a locus of that guilty 'secret' of the past: Original Sin. In essence, every encounter with the natural world, every problem and obstacle that it presented, every fear it provoked, served to remind the Puritans of the burden of that inherited sinfulness. Thus the secret, primal crime central to the plots of early Gothic fiction had a predecessor in the Puritan notion of Adam's Original Sin; and one marker of that sin was the fallen natural world – well before the first Gothic novelists transformed it into antiquated castles and monasteries. As the excerpt from Emily Dickinson's poem at the beginning of this chapter suggests, nature *is* a type of Gothic haunted house.

Joel Porte has argued that the terror that marks the Gothic is 'usually at bottom theological', and in his essay 'In the Hands of an Angry God: Religious Terror in Gothic Fiction' he argues for the centrality of religious terror in the early Gothic.[33] Similarly, I would argue that much of the religious fear that appears in seventeenth-century Puritan writing is in many ways itself Gothic (though it precedes the advent of eighteenth-century Gothic fiction), particularly when those fears and anxieties are connected to experiences with the New World landscape.[34] A longer essay than this might explore any number of texts to illustrate such a claim, such as Mary Rowlandson's *The Sovereignty and Goodness of God* (1682), in which she confronts both physical and spiritual trauma when Indian captivity takes her deep into the 'vast and howling *Wilderness*';[35] or Thomas Shepard's 1673 sermon *Eye-Salve*, which addresses the question the Lord asked in Jeremiah 2:31, 'Have I been a wilderness unto Israel?' and explicates 'wilderness' as a place where men 'meet with nothing but wants, and terrour, and woe'.[36] Wherever the Puritans went, it seems, they were never far from a Gothicized landscape reminding them of their own fallen natures.

*   *   *

As the changing, late seventeenth-century world began to fracture and fragment the once-unified Puritan culture, '[t]he normal relationship between cause and effect, sign and significance,' Susan Manning writes, 'was disrupted and the Calvinist set adrift again in a terrifying world of meaningless clues'.[37] Such is always the danger when reading the world typologically: what is at stake when we misinterpret the signs? With such an unstable worldview in mind, I once again skip ahead from the 1690s to the 1990s, from the era of the Salem Witch Trials to *The Blair Witch Project*, and consider the legacy of this *old* idea of a wilderness both real and symbolic. In the woods outside Burkittsville, the three students in the film have their own trouble reading the signs. They never know what it is that tracks them, and neither do we. At various times they posit several possibilities: deer, children, someone playing a prank, backwoods rednecks *à la Deliverance*, or maybe even a witch. One of the few certainties in the film, ironically, is our uncertainty of what is 'out there'. 'Like other liminal monsters occupying the shifting boundary between human, monster, and Other,' Bryan Alexander writes, 'the witch [if it is one] is a creature of blurred and shifting boundaries', which is what makes it that much more frightening.[38]

Because of these shifting boundaries and blurred understandings of what haunts the forest, *The Blair Witch Project* becomes a story about knowing, and *how* we know what we know. More specifically, it is a film about the frailty of knowing with certainty any reliable truth or reality. As Heather, Josh and Mike embark on their quest for knowledge about the history of the Blair witch, the film quickly calls attention to the limitations of the act of knowing. For example, when interviewing townspeople in Burkittsville early in the footage, the filmmakers talk to an older man who explains that '*They say* the woods are haunted up there' (emphasis added). Later, once they've begun exploring the forest, they encounter a fisherman who declares that 'everyone worth their salt around here knows that this area's been haunted by that old woman for years'. Both of these statements, while ostensibly docu-menting folk knowledge about the witch legacy, draw attention to the uncertainty of authoritative knowledge, resting their cases on vague, unnamed sources ('they' and 'everyone worth their salt'). In contrast, early on Heather asserts her knowledge of place. Providing a narrative voiceover while hiking the woods, she describes, 'On our way to coffin rock ... *I know exactly* where we are now' (emphasis added). Similarly, on the way to a nearby old cemetery the next day, Heather uses almost identical words: 'I know exactly where we're going.'

Such assurances quickly fade as their stay in the woods progresses and doubts creep in. The first night camping, when Josh describes hear-ing noises, he asks: 'What's your take on the Blair witch? Do you think she exists?', to which Heather replies, 'I don't know.' On day three, after unsuccessfully trying to find their way out of the woods, Heather says, 'I think it's safe to say at this point that we're lost, and I don't know what to do.' After this admission of *not* knowing, assertions of certainty give way to speculation. By the fifth day all attempts at logical naviga-tion are gone: Mike asks, 'Which is worse, the wicked witch of the east or the wicked witch of the west?' When Heather responds that 'The wicked witch of the west was the bad one', Mike announces 'Then let's go east.' By this point, their misreading of the compass has led them in circles, and Mike has discarded the only map because it was useless to him. Despite what seem to be their best efforts, these three filmmakers cannot successfully 'read' the woods. *The Blair Witch Project* again and again reminds us of their inability to 'read' the signs.

In her discussion of Gothic film, Misha Kavka explains that because '[t]he fearful effect of the Gothic, at least in its literary forms, depends on our ability to cast certain conventionalized images from the text onto the "screen" of our mind's eye', the Gothic is 'particularly suited to the cinema' in its emphasis on 'spectacle'.[39] Thus the Gothic 'tantalizes us with fear' by compelling us to *see*, to *visualize*, the objects of our fear. *The Blair Witch Project*, however, adds an interesting twist to this effect: while the film certainly manipulates the Burkittsville woods as an on- (and off-) screen space, it refuses to present us with any images of whatever it is that follows and torments the three filmmakers. All we see are images of a wooded landscape in the eastern United States. The source of terror remains off-screen and out of sight, so viewers end up casting their own internalized fears on to the 'screen' of their 'mind's eye'. *The Blair Witch Project*, then, is aptly named: Because we do not know who or what haunts them, we 'project' into the forest, on to those off-screen spaces, those things that we most fear.

Such 'projection', of course, is no isolated phenomenon. In many ways, an individual's experience with place or landscape is always coloured by the perceptual framework they bring to it. For instance, describing European 'discovery' and exploration of the Americas, Robert Lawson-Peebles has argued that

> [t]here is ... no such thing as 'the unknown'. Those who are about to enter an undiscovered area project upon it a collection of images drawn from their personal experience, from the culture from which they are a part, from their reasons for travelling, and from their hopes and fears regarding their destination. On occasion these projections are so strong that they shape the terrain they encounter.[40]

Certainly this was case for the New England Calvinists experiencing the landscapes of Massachusetts, who, as Susan Manning points out, tended to 'favour abstraction over actuality and to insist that reality be brought to square with theory'.[41] But this projecting of 'hopes and fears' is also at work in *The Blair Witch Project*. Andrew Schopp contends that 'the film's main point' is that 'the literal woods have been destroyed, but the figurative woods remain. We no longer need the deep, dark, unknown woods encountered by our pioneer ancestors to experience fear and loss.'[42] Instead, it can happen in the relatively finite forests of the rural mid-Atlantic. Almost two centuries ago Cotton Mather invited us to step with him into that '*Publick library*' to read 'the Book of the *Creatures*', but he neglected to tell us that the library may be haunted.

I think about Sally Morgan's claim that, for the Puritans, 'there was an elision of a number of very potent fears, all of which came together in the location of the woods; fear manifested as "Place"',[43] and this does not seem too far from our modern experiences. The 'hideous and desolate wilderness' (so described by Bradford) is just an early version of what becomes the dark dungeon or haunted castle in later Gothic fictions – that fearful space inhabited by threatening characters, creatures or ideas and marked by deep-seated secrets or past transgressions that threaten the status quo. Anthony Lioi asks ecocritics not to shun 'compromised places' and calls for an ecocriticism that focuses 'on the monsters around us' in order to help us 'understand better the dangers we face; it would also admit that we are partially monstrous ourselves ... transforming the guilt of complicity into an appreciation of finitude and impurity'.[44] In a similar vein, Timothy Morton envisions a 'dark ecology' which

> undermines the naturalness of the stories we tell about how we are involved in nature. It preserves the dark, depressive quality of life in the shadow of ecological catastrophe. Instead of whistling in the dark, insisting that we're part of Gaia, why not stay with the darkness?[45]

Examining the shared spaces where ecocriticism and Gothic studies overlap can allow us to begin such work, to consider carefully the terrible comfort that Heather Donahue feels when she states in *The Blair Witch Project* that 'We've destroyed most of our natural resources.'

In *Walden*, Henry David Thoreau admits, 'I believe that men are generally still a little afraid of the dark, though the witches are all hung, and Christianity and candles have been introduced.'[46] Stories like *The Blair Witch Project* remind us that we *are* generally still a little afraid of the woods. And, like the haunted house in any Gothic fiction, the terrors residing in those woods – at least from the seventeenth century onward – are extensions of our own anxieties. Nature may be a haunted house, but its ghosts are our own.

Notes

1 *The Blair Witch Project*, dir. Daniel Myrick and Eduardo Sanchez, Haxan Films, 1999.
2 For further consideration of ecophobia in ecocriticism, see Simon Estok, 'Theorizing in a Space of Ambivalent Openness: Ecocriticism and Ecophobia', *ISLE: Interdisciplinary Studies in Literature and Environment* 16/2 (2009): 203–25, and Estok, *Ecocriticism and Shakespeare: Reading Ecophobia* (New York: Palgrave Macmillan, 2011) as well as my '"Deep Into That Darkness Peering": An Essay on Gothic Nature', *ISLE: Interdisciplinary Studies in Literature and Environment* 16/4 (2009): 685–95.
3 Timothy Clark, *The Cambridge Introduction to Literature and the Environment* (Cambridge: Cambridge University Press, 2011), p. 4.
4 Anthony Lioi, 'Of Swamp Dragons: Mud, Megalopolis, and a Future for Ecocriticism', in Annie Merrill Ingram et al. (eds), *Coming into Contact: Explorations in Ecocritical Theory and Practice* (Athens, GA: University of Georgia Press, 2007), pp. 17–38, p. 23.
5 Ibid., p. 23.
6 Ibid., p. 32.
7 This quotation, included in many early advertisements for the film, is usually attributed to Dave Larsen of the *Dayton Daily News*.
8 A useful starting place for scholarship addressing *The Blair Witch Project* is Sarah L. Higley and Jeffrey Andrew Weinstock (eds), *Nothing That Is: Millennial Cinema and the 'Blair Witch' Controversies* (Detroit: Wayne State University Press, 2004).

9 Sally Morgan, 'Heritage Noire: Truth, History, and Colonial Anxiety in *The Blair Witch Project'*, *International Journal of Heritage Studies* 7/2 (2001): 137–48, at pp. 140, 145.

10 Cotton Mather, *The Christian Philosopher, a Collection of the Best Discoveries in Nature, with Religious Improvements* (London, 1721), p. 8. Available via *Eighteenth Century Collections Online*, http://gale.cengage.co.uk/product-highlights/history/eighteenth-century-collections-online.aspx (accessed 26 June 2012).

11 Ibid.

12 Ibid.

13 Thomas M. Davis, 'The Traditions of Puritan Typology', in Sacvan Bercovitch (ed.), *Typology and Early American Literature* (Amherst: University of Massachusetts Press, 1972), pp. 11–45, at pp. 38–9.

14 Susan Manning, *The Puritan-Provincial Vision: Scottish and American Literature in the Nineteenth Century* (Cambridge: Cambridge University Press, 1990), p. 12, original emphasis.

15 Davis, 'The Traditions of Puritan Typology', p. 39.

16 Ibid., p. 15.

17 John Gatta, *Making Nature Sacred: Literature, Religion, and Environment in America from the Puritans to the Present* (Oxford: Oxford University Press, 2004), p. 20.

18 The first section of Bradford's book, from which I quote here, was written in 1630, although *Of Plymouth Plantation* was not published until 1856. For further details about the book's textual history, see Francis Murphy's 'Introduction' to William Bradford, *Of Plymouth Plantation: 1620–1647* (New York: Modern Library, 1981), pp. vii–xv.

19 Bradford, *Of Plymouth Plantation*, pp. 69–70.

20 Jesper Rosenmeier, '"With My Owne Eyes": William Bradford's *Of Plymouth Plantation'*, in Bercovitch (ed.), *Typology and Early American Literature*, pp. 69–105, at p. 99.

21 Davis, 'The Traditions of Puritan Typology', pp. 44–5.

22 Manning, *The Puritan-Provincial Vision*, p. 7.

23 I use here the text of the 1560 Geneva Bible, which was the authoritative Scripture for the New England Puritans (and the Protestant Reformation in general).

24 As Charles Berryman puts it, the Puritans 'not only accepted the biblical story of the Fall of Man as literal truth, they consequently tormented themselves with the idea of inherited guilt': see *From Wilderness to Wasteland: The Trial of the Puritan God in the American Imagination* (Port Washington, NY: Kennikat Press, 1979), p. 7.

25 Feelings towards the wilderness of the New World were not entirely negative; in fact, they were deeply ambivalent. For the New England Puritans, the wilderness was both a place to be feared and one with sacred, holy possibility. In Daniel G. Payne's words, 'The most prevalent early reactions to the American wilderness revolved around two powerful and often conflicting responses, hope and fear': see *Voices in the Wilderness: American Nature Writing and Environmental Politics* (Hanover, NH: University Press of New England, 1996), p. 9. Because I'm interested in the Gothic implications of Puritan representations of landscape, however, my emphasis here is on its more fearful qualities.

26 Christoph Grunenberg (ed.), *Gothic: Transmutations of Horror in Late Twentieth Century Art* (Boston: Institute of Contemporary Art, 1997), p. 194.

27 Allan Lloyd-Smith, *American Gothic Fiction* (New York: Continuum, 2004), pp. 92, 93.

28 David Mogen, 'Wilderness, Metamorphosis, and Millennium: Gothic Apocalypse From the Puritans to the Cyberpunks', in David Mogen, Scott P. Sanders and Joanne B. Karpinski (eds), *Frontier Gothic: Terror and Wonder at the Frontier in American Literature* (Rutherford, NJ: Fairleigh Dickinson University Press, 1993), pp. 94–108, at pp. 94, 95.

29 Fred Botting, *Gothic* (London: Routledge, 1996), p. 1.

30 David Punter has noted that one of the few things that scholars of the Gothic agree on is that the 'one element which, albeit in a vast variety of forms, crops up in all the relevant fiction ... is fear'; see *The Literature of Terror: A History of Gothic Fictions from 1765 to the Present Day* (Harlow: Longman, 1996), Vol. I, p. 18.

31 Lloyd-Smith, *American Gothic Fiction*, p. 1, emphasis mine.

32 Jerrold E. Hogle, 'Introduction: The Gothic in Western Culture', in Jerrold E. Hogle (ed.), *The Cambridge Companion to Gothic Fiction* (Cambridge: Cambridge University Press, 2002), pp. 1–20, at p. 2.

33 Joel Porte, 'In the Hands of an Angry God: Religious Terror in Gothic Fiction', in G. R. Thompson (ed.), *The Gothic Imagination: Essays in Dark Romanticism* (Pullman: Washington State University Press, 1974), pp. 42–64, at p. 45.

34 Dorothy Z. Baker has written about the influence that Cotton Mather's *Magnalia Christi Americana* had on the production of later Gothic literature in the United States, both in content and narrative form. As she notes, 'the New England gothic is frequently an exposé of Calvinist historical accounts of America and Americans'; *America's Gothic Fiction: The Legacy of 'Magnalia Christi Americana'* (Columbus: Ohio State University Press, 2007), p. 10. Baker doesn't argue for any Gothic qualities in Mather's writing itself, but instead examines the ways in which the 'remarkable providence' narratives within *Magnalia* were later adopted and revised by authors of Gothic literature. She explains, 'in the process of exposing the flawed and unstable narratives that construct an artificial and uncomfortable identity for the nation, nineteenth-century gothic literature frequently proposed alternate versions of America, its history, its citizens, and its historians' (10).

35 Mary Rowlandson, *The Sovereignty and Goodness of God, Together with the Faithfulness of His Promises Displayed, Being a Narrative of the Captivity and Restoration of Mrs Mary Rowlandson*, ed. Neal Salisbury (Boston: Bedford St Martin's, 1997), p. 80.

36 Thomas Shepard, *Eye-Salve, Or a Watchword From our Lord Jesus Christ unto his Churches* (Cambridge, 1673), p. 3.

37 Manning, *The Puritan-Provincial Vision*, p. 22. Manning is discussing specifically the cultural impact of the Salem Witch Trials of 1692, but her assertion rings true for the widespread changes that New England Puritan culture was facing.

38 Bryan Alexander, '*The Blair Witch Project*: Expulsion from Adulthood and Versions of the American Gothic', in Higley and Weinstock (eds), *Nothing That Is*, pp. 145–61, at p. 152.

39 Misha Kavka, 'The Gothic on Screen', in Hogle (ed.), *The Cambridge Companion to Gothic Fiction*, pp. 209–28, at p. 209.

40 Robert Lawson-Peebles, *Landscape and Written Expression in Revolutionary America: The World Turned Upside Down* (Cambridge: Cambridge University Press, 1988), p. 9.
41 Manning, *The Puritan-Provincial Vision*, p. 14.
42 Andrew Schopp, 'Transgressing the Safe Space: Generation X Horror in *The Blair Witch Project* and *Scream*', in Higley and Weinstock (eds), *Nothing That Is*, pp. 125–43, at p. 139.
43 Morgan, 'Heritage Noire', p. 146.
44 Lioi, 'Of Swamp Dragons', p. 33.
45 Timothy Morton, *Ecology without Nature: Rethinking Environmental Aesthetics* (Cambridge, MA: Harvard University Press, 2007), p. 187.
46 Henry David Thoreau, *Walden*, in *The Writings of Henry D. Thoreau*, ed. J. Lyndon Shanley (Princeton, NJ: Princeton University Press, 2004), p. 131.

9

Kevin Corstorphine

'The blank darkness outside': Ambrose Bierce and wilderness Gothic at the end of the frontier

Foundations and frontier

Ralph Waldo Emerson, in *Nature* (1837), writes of the search for a uni-fying theory of nature through science. The problem so far, he suggests, is that no adequate explanation has been put forward to take account of all phenomena: 'many are thought not only unexplained but inexplica-ble; as language, sleep, dreams, beasts, sex'.[1] These terms are extremely evocative for the Gothic scholar, addressing the same concerns as those raised by the Gothic novel of the late eighteenth century and its subse-quent permutations.[2] The literary Gothic was preceded by the use of the term in political debate, where an appeal to pre-Roman 'Gothic' tradi-tions in Britain constituted an appeal to what is 'natural'.[3] This debate is carried over into the New World, where the wilderness found by the settlers becomes the primary source of Gothic terror. In the search for a new Eden, this wilderness becomes a source of both idealism and anxiety. The first part of this chapter will examine the development of wilderness Gothic through the nineteenth century, looking at responses to the environment in the literary and political imagination. The second part will focus on Ambrose Bierce, whose Gothic horror tales offer an insight into the American imagination and the environment. A strand of ecocritical thought runs throughout, with the goal of stimulating a dialogue with the Gothic and situating a nostalgic yet fearful response to the wilderness frontier at the heart of American Gothic.

Wilderness has long been identified as a key component of what constitutes the American Gothic. Allan Lloyd-Smith points out that:

> In the early years of the young United States, the settlers were acutely conscious
> that they lived on the verge of a vast wilderness, a land of threat as much as
> material promise, where many lived in isolation or in small settlements with the
> memories and sometimes justified fears of Indian warfare.[4]

This concept of the wilderness as threatening and Other has been discussed at length by Roderick Frazier Nash in his influential environmental work *Wilderness and the American Mind* (1967). Nash traces the
development of the word through subtle shifts in meaning throughout
the centuries. He identifies 'wild' as being related to 'will' in its earliest
form, so that the term was used 'to denote creatures not under the control of man'.[5] This raises an important distinction from the start, so that
the condition of being wild subverts human reason and logic. Indeed,
the tendency of American Gothic writers has been to move towards an
internalized mode of narrative, allowing Marianne Noble to claim that
'the American gothic is above all a psychological genre'.[6] Gothic as an
exploration of the inner workings of the mind expresses itself perhaps
most fully in Poe, whose notion of perversity implies that among the
creatures not under the control of man might well be man himself.
Lloyd-Smith connects this idea to the wider body politic:

> There is a dark impulse beyond understanding which wreaks havoc, operat-
> ing in complete contradiction to the normative assumption of the early United
> States polity that individuals will always seek to act in their own best interests
> (and therefore might be trusted with democratic self-government and capitalist
> freedom of enterprise).[7]

Emerson's conception of what 'nature' includes covers both the mysteries of the external and internal world, which are not so far apart as
they might at first seem, especially in literature of the fantastic. Maurice
Sendak's celebrated children's book *Where the Wild Things Are* (1963)
makes clear that wilderness is a product of imaginative invention. The
'wild things' of American Gothic have always been found in terms of a
journey that is seemingly outward facing, but ends up in the realm of
the individual psyche.

Nash goes on to trace the evolution of wilderness from meaning
specifically 'the place of wild beasts' (*wild-dēor-ness*) to 'uncultivated
and otherwise undeveloped land ... any place in which a person
feels stripped of guidance, lost, and perplexed may be called a wilderness'.[8] This of course is linked to the word 'bewildered', describing
the very condition that Lloyd-Smith identifies as a founding element
of American Gothic. This can be seen in Charles Brockden Brown's

Edgar Huntly (1799), in which the eponymous protagonist sleepwalks into the wilderness and descends into savagery as he brutally kills several Native Americans he finds there. This is also the central theme of Robert Montgomery Bird's *Nick of the Woods* (1837), whose protagonist Nathan Slaughter lives a double life as both pacifist Quaker and psychotic 'Injun' killer. The figure of the Native American looms large in any discussion of wilderness in early American fiction, being associated consistently with savagery and nature in the Gothic. Nathaniel Hawthorne's 'Young Goodman Brown' (1835), describes Brown's journey into the forest where he fears, 'a devilish Indian behind every tree'.[9] *Nick of the Woods* echoes Bird's own low opinion of Native Americans, made clear in his preface to the 1853 edition, but crucially his indictment is not based on the kind of pseudo-scientific racial categorization that would become fashionable post-Darwin, but on a denial of their culture. In the preface, he criticizes the ideal of the 'noble savage':

> The writer differed from his critical friends, and from many philanthropists, in believing the Indian to be capable – perfectly capable, where restraint assists the work of friendly instruction – of civilisation … but, in his natural barbaric state, he is a barbarian – and it is not possible he could be anything else. The purposes of the author, in his book, confined him to real Indians. He drew them as, in his judgment, they existed – and as, according to all observation, they still exist wherever not softened by cultivation, – ignorant, violent, debased, brutal.[10]

This is an attack on what we would now call cultural relativism. Bird identifies Native Americans with a barbaric state of nature as opposed to 'culture', represented by white civilization. He does not deny their basic humanity, claiming that, 'the Indian is doubtless a gentleman; but he is a gentleman who wears a very dirty shirt'.[11] Rather, he blames circumstance and environment for what he sees as a debased condition. The phrase 'not softened by cultivation' identifies Native Americans squarely with the wilderness, as defined by Nash.

The Eurocentric notion of Native Americans lacking a culture and being identified with nature has been much discussed in postcolonial criticism, but this identification with nature has much to say from an ecocritical perspective, especially given the modern tendency to identify native cultures with responsible stewardship of the land, as opposed to the rapacious and resource-hungry developed world. This sharp dichotomy is an object of some scrutiny for contemporary anthropology, just as ecocriticism seeks to bridge the divide between nature and culture that has developed through the centuries. William Howarth, for example, blames this hierarchy for many of our planet's ills, claiming that 'the dogma that culture will always master nature has long directed Western progress, inspiring the wars, invasions, and other forms of conquest that have crowded the earth and strained its carrying capacity'.[12] This is a Gothic vision of progress, blighted by historical guilt and fear for the future, and one rooted in post-1960s environmental activism. To discover the specific relevance of the nature versus culture debate to American literature we need only go back to 1958 when Norman Foerster proclaimed a view of American history which is now deeply unfashionable in the humanities but extremely pervasive:

> A land of promise, America is virtually without a past. Her children need not look far back to the founders of her civilization, a civilization not yet freed, and doubtless never to be freed, from its European prototype. The story of her culture – of her art, her philosophy, her education – remains to this day an account of the transfer to a new world of the culture of modern Europe, modified, it is true, by the omission of an intimated sense of that August tradition which reaches back to the primitive Northern folks and the ancient Greeks and Hebrews, and by the addition of physical circumstances destined to affect profoundly her mind and heart.[13]

American culture is configured here as simply that of Europe, dislocated from its history and ancestral land. European civilization, in moving to the New World, has lost its status as the pinnacle of the teleological movement of many disparate traditions and has been cast into the wilderness. Teresa A. Goddu blames the currency of such notions as an obstacle to historicizing the American Gothic: 'The Gothic's connection to American history is difficult to identify precisely because of the national and critical myths that America and its literature *have* no history.'[14] In response to this Goddu argues a case for the recognition of such texts as John Neal's *Logan* (1851) and Samuel Young's *Tom Hanson, the Avenger* (1847), claiming that a study of these novels 'fills a gap in the genealogy of American gothicism that begins with Brown and reaches its apogee with Poe, allowing their careers to be read as part of a continuous tradition rather than aberrations'.[15]

Early American literature struggled at first to articulate a distinctive voice; a problem compounded in the Gothic mode by the nation's lack of decaying abbeys and decadent aristocracy. Goddu claims that this problem is solved by the use of native material: 'The Indian, demonized as a devil, and the wilderness, turned into a bloody landscape, not only replace but exceed their British types.'[16] In fact the Native American and the wilderness have a tendency to be conflated in early American

Gothic, and characters have a tendency to be corrupted by contact with either or both, becoming literally 'bewildered'. This is both a matter of historical circumstance and of literary fashion. The Puritan ideology of the early settlers can be detected here, in the profound disengagement from the earthly. America was seen as a potential religious utopia, but at the same time there always existed the danger of contamination from the physical world that shaped their lives. Peter N. Carroll, in his comprehensive study of this period, discusses the importance of their moralistic sermons, or jeremiads, whose prophesied disasters seemed very real during the Indian War of 1675–76, or 'King Philip's War':

> For more than a decade, the Puritan clergy had warned their congregations of the dangers of worldliness and irreligion. But although the ministers forecasted divine chastisements for these sins, the jeremiads remained an abstract rhetorical device ... As the natives swarmed through the wilderness and devastated remote frontier settlements, the colonists became aware of the fragility of their society. The wilderness crisis of 1675 thereby grounded the jeremiads in experience and dramatized the warnings of the Puritan ministry ... Drawn together by the collective terrors of the war, the colonists reexamined the relevance of their social theory and attempted to adjust their ideas to satisfy the needs of a wilderness community.[17]

If the material conditions of existence would form the ideological context of colonialism and mark the Native American as Other, the Native American as bogeyman would later provide convenient material for sensation fiction of the nineteenth century, which often looked back to this earlier period. As Goddu puts it, 'at once a source of the sentimental and the sublime: the nation weeps nostalgically over his disappearance and is excited by the graves that mark his extinction'.[18] Although this can be linked to a sense of literary nationalism, it is worth drawing comparisons with popular writing of the time. Many of these early American novels can be classed in the realm of historical romance, and the great master of the genre, Walter Scott, had experienced success in the early nineteenth century with this same blend of wistful nostalgia and wild adventure, with Scottish Highlanders taking the role of the Native Americans as the last remnants of a vanishing culture, closer to nature and specifically an uncultivated wilderness. Early American writers, then, were very much concerned with nature just as the emergent nation was struggling to subdue its wilder aspects. An important shift in tone to the environment, however, occurs at the moment of Manifest Destiny's seeming victory over this wild land.

Frederick Jackson Turner, in his influential lecture to the American

Historical Association in Chicago in 1893, acknowledged the end of the frontier, citing the 1890 census. He argued that the frontier, in shaping the conditions of the American citizen, also shaped the direction of society. This is summed up in the later published version:

> In short, at the frontier the environment is at first too strong for the man. He must accept the conditions which it furnishes, or perish, and so he fits himself into the Indian clearings and follows the Indian trails. Little by little he transforms the wilderness, but the outcome is not the old Europe ... The fact is, that here is a new product that is American. At first, the frontier was the Atlantic coast. It was the frontier of Europe in a very real sense. Moving westward, the frontier became more and more American. As successive terminal moraines result from successive glaciations, so each frontier leaves its traces behind it, and when it becomes a settled area the region still partakes of the frontier characteristics.[19]

If the story of the expanding frontier articulates a simple dichotomy of civilization against the wilderness, then the end of the frontier marks a more subtle Gothicism, marked by the haunting presence of the past. The 'new product' that is America turns out to bear the traces of previous ownership and stories already inscribed upon it. Turner's thesis suggests that the westward-moving frontier necessitates a continual replaying of the rise of civilization from primitive conditions, a 'perennial rebirth'[20] that shapes a new way of thinking. Tiziano Bonazzi finds religious implications in this:

> By reenacting through frontier experience the 'time of origins', the pioneer reaches back to his archetypal nature and becomes an individual not so much in a utilitarian-psychological or sociological sense as in a religious one. He is the *New Adam*. He has returned to his original true nature. As such he does not need the forest any more ... He is ready to build civilization anew, and the process of social stages can be restored. This is why America reads like a palimpsest of social evolution, and why the whole of America, not the frontier alone makes up the social organism called America.[21]

The palimpsest, as Freud and later Derrida knew, is a haunted scene. The appeal to origins, to a mythical 'nature' with the recreation of Adam, will always be a flawed model, ripe with Gothic possibilities. Indeed, David Mogen, Scott P. Sanders and Joanne B. Kaplinski read Turner's thesis as the 'story of the American Adam, in which Europeans are transformed in the wilderness into a new kind of person, a transformation whose frightening and eerie aspects establish the tradition of frontier gothicism'.[22] Leslie Fiedler writes of the peculiarly American Dream 'of reaching a place of total freedom where one could with impunity deny the Fall, live as if innocence rather than guilt were the

birthright of all men'.[23] If all authors subscribed wholeheartedly to this
view then we would have few examples of post-frontier Gothic to speak
of, yet it has become increasingly difficult to refute Fiedler's assertion
that American literature is, 'bewilderingly and embarrassingly, a gothic
fiction'.[24] The utopian search for origins and truth bears the hallmark of
myth, and often it takes a cynic to puncture myth. Ambrose Bierce was
such a cynic.

Post-frontier Gothic

The end of the frontier saw some remarkable changes to the American
landscape. Most striking from an ecological viewpoint was the near-
extinction of the American buffalo (or properly bison) from the High
Plains, where up to ten million animals were slaughtered between 1871
and 1883.[25] This was in part a deliberate policy intended to weaken the
Native Americans, who had been reliant on the buffalo for food and
clothing for thousands of years. After the slaughter, the buffalo was to
become a symbol of a passing era, as with the increasingly sentimental
portrayal of Native Americans. Rena N. Coen argues this point in a
study of late nineteenth-century artists such as George Caitlin and
Albert Bierstadt:

> We know that there was, in fact, a tendency among painters of the American
> West to view the Indians as 'picturesque' survivors of a dying race and thus
> as pictorial equivalents of Europe's ancient architectural ruins. In this respect,
> the Indian reflected the romantic predilection for the past, the nostalgia for
> that which once was but now was lost or was rapidly vanishing in a suitably
> melancholy decline. More specifically, however, many contemporary literary
> references connect the extermination of the buffalo with the end of Indian life,
> and strengthen a conclusion that such an allegory is intended in visual as well as
> literary representations of the theme.[26]

Coen's argument is ripe with connotations of the Gothic. The aesthetic
appropriation of a bygone era to convey a sense of picturesque doom
accords well with the development of Gothic in the United States.
Wilderness here, as represented in the bodies of the Native American
and the buffalo, takes the place of the ruined castle or abbey, which
in the European mode evoke the idea of power fading into obscurity.
The remnants of the European Gothic can be clearly seen in Poe's
'The Fall of the House of Usher' (1839), where the 'house' takes on
the double meaning of Usher's literal abode and his family lineage as
both are destroyed utterly, unable to adapt to a changing world due to

an inability to, 'put forth … any enduring branch'.[27] At the close of the century, the ending of the frontier and the manifest destruction of an ancient relationship between human and animal as part of a sustainable ecosystem was to establish America's own sense of a lost Eden, sowing the seeds for environmentalist sentiments to come; sentiments that would be powerfully intertwined with a Gothic sensibility.

Ambrose Bierce, who was born in 1842 and disappeared in 1913, lived through the final days of the frontier as well as the event that was to define much of his fiction: the American Civil War. His horror stories are not generally examined through an ecocritical lens, but reading them as such is revealing. 'The Damned Thing' (1893), published the same year as Turner's declaration of the end of the frontier, is particularly intriguing in this respect. The story begins with a coroner's inquest into the death of one Hugh Morgan. This Gothic scene takes place in a candlelit room at night while seven living men, and one corpse, wait to hear the testimony of a young man called William Harker:

> From the blank darkness outside came in, through the aperture that served for a window, all the ever unfamiliar noises of night in the wilderness – the long nameless note of a distant coyote; the stilly pulsing thrill of tireless insects in trees; strange cries of night birds, so different from the birds of day; the drone of great blundering beetles, and all that mysterious chorus of small sounds that seem always to have been but half heard when they have suddenly ceased, as if conscious of an indiscretion.[28]

This description contrasts starkly with the scene in the room, which is one of solemn judiciary process. In fact, while nature goes about its business, of the inhabitants of the room only the coroner seems to share the narrator's awareness of its sensory intrusion. Dead man aside, the party is composed of 'farmers and woodsmen' (98), who do not care to dwell aesthetically on such everyday matters. Nature is reduced to 'environment', or background for human concerns. This is where modern ecological debates come into play. Proponents of deep ecology view environmentalism as inherently flawed in its goal of preserving the natural world as the 'environment' of humanity, necessary yet secondary to our subjectivity. Rather, deep ecology calls for a rejection of anthropocentrism and 'demands recognition of intrinsic value in nature'.[29] Dominic Head argues that 'the Green movement in general is predicated on a typically postmodernist deprivileging of the human subject',[30] yet an attitude not far from this can be detected in Bierce's work as far back as the American *fin de siècle*.

Harker tells his story, which details a hunting trip he took with

Morgan prior to his death. The men see bushes moving but with no animal visible. Morgan is terrified, and it becomes clear that he has previously encountered the creature he refers to as 'that Damned Thing' (100). Suddenly Morgan fires a shot, Harker is knocked off his feet and when he recovers he sees his companion wrestling with a presence, which, though itself invisible, means that he is 'partly blotted out' (101). Morgan's hideously beaten and lacerated body is then revealed in the present by the coroner. In a manner reminiscent of Stevenson's *Strange Case of Dr Jekyll and Mr Hyde* (1886), we are then given an account from Morgan himself, in the form of his diary. The diary consists of philosophical musings on the nature of perception, most relevant among which is the concept that there are sounds inaudible to the human ear. Following this logic, and with recourse to contemporary scientific theory, he claims that the same principle applies to colours: 'I am not mad; there are colors we cannot see. And, God help me! The Damned Thing is of such a color!' (105). Bierce would have been familiar with these ideas through photography, hinted at by his reference to chemistry in the story. The new science of photography was used to document the Civil War, famously by Matthew Brady and Tim O'Sullivan, as well as the Western frontier, where photographers such as William Henry Jackson produced documentary images of natural features and of Native American peoples. John Szarkowski, in an essay on American photography, links it to all the concerns examined here thus far. Noting that its birth coincided with the process of Turner's transformative westward-moving frontier, he claims that:

> As the frontier was an anarchistic force in the development of American civilization, so was photography an anarchistic force in the history of the visual arts ... the ideal pictorial system for a country based upon the principles of individual freedom, political equality, cultural diversity, centrifugal movement, constant experimentation, extemporization, and quick results ... Perhaps more to the point is the fact that North America had no traditional subject matter. It had no ancient history that it knew of, no classical ruins, no romantic medieval monuments, and not even a proper aristocracy.[31]

This takes us back to the question of the Gothic, and what inspiration might be found in this new land. 'The Damned Thing' would suggest that one source might be in emerging technology, what it reveals, and what it has yet to reveal about the world. Perhaps too, the fact that the Civil War was 'the first war to be photographed in such exhaustive detail'[32] and that photographs were commissioned by the federal government of 'vanishing' Native Americans, even as they still endured, suggests that the country was very rapidly imposing a sense of the importance of its own unique history.

On one level the idea of an invisible creature is highly evocative in the context of the near-extinctions of species such as the buffalo in the nineteenth century. The 'damned thing' is a creature that defies human perception, and in positing such a thing the story, like deep ecology, can be said to 'deprivilege' the human subject, here by removing the very possibility of subjectivity. The conception that nature might not be observable by the human subject transforms the relationship radically. In the case of Morgan the roles are reversed and the hunter becomes prey. Bierce's wilderness is a haunted one, seemingly possessed of its own subjecthood. The frontier becomes a space where uncertainty reigns, and even the evidence of the senses can be cast into doubt. Harker fails to persuade the jury, the foreman of which dismisses him by asking, via the coroner, 'from what asylum did you last escape?' (103). In order to preserve a civilized world of legal process and rationality Harker's tale must be excluded from the debate, shut out into the wilderness foreshadowed in the opening paragraphs as a 'blank darkness' of 'unfamiliar noises'.

Bierce's 1891 story 'The Boarded Window' is more explicitly a tale of the frontier, but shares similar concerns. It is set in 1830, on the death of an old man called Murlock, but most of the narrative takes place years earlier, when his wife dies of a fever. This classic use of the Gothic framing narrative, or Chinese-box structure, allows a distance from the facts of the tale, which are ambiguous and strange. It opens with a description of frontier life that shows this distance in its mythologizing of the hardy pioneers:

> In 1830, only a few miles away from what is now the great city of Cincinnati, lay an immense and almost unbroken forest. The whole region was sparsely settled by people of the frontier – restless souls who no sooner had hewn fairly habitable homes out of the wilderness and attained to that degree of prosperity which today we would call indigence than impelled by some mysterious impulse of their nature they abandoned all and pushed farther westward, to encounter new perils and privations in the effort to regain the meagre comforts they had voluntarily renounced.[33]

Bierce's notoriously bitter sense of irony skewers the idealism of the pioneering spirit, portraying the settlers as possessed of a perverse (in Poe's sense of the word) sensibility. They are impelled by their 'nature', which of course is a loaded term in debates surrounding ecology. If humans are indeed part of a symbiotic ecosystem, then the human urge to tame and control the wilderness, which has defined much of our civilization, certainly in the United States, would seem to contradict our assumed place in the natural world. This is perhaps why so much ecological thought, certainly the transcendentalist strand, tends to look back to a pre-agricultural golden age, as represented in romantic notions of the Native American. It is noteworthy that Murlock does not grow crops but hunts for skins in the forest. His previously developed land is slowly being reclaimed by nature, presumably following the death of his wife:

> There were evidences of 'improvement' – a few acres of ground immediately about the house had once been cleared of its trees, the decayed stumps of which were half concealed by the new growth that had been suffered to repair the ravage wrought by the axe. Apparently the man's zeal for agriculture had burned with a failing flame, expiring in penitential ashes. (227–8)

Bierce's use of inverted commas around the word 'improvement' suggests his trademark sarcasm, and his use of the word 'ravage' and the religious tone imply that Murlock's pioneering hubris has been thoroughly humbled by nature. Following his wife's death he prepares the body as best he can and falls into a weary slumber. He is awakened by footsteps, followed by a thump, and reaching out for the table realizes the corpse has gone. Discharging his rifle blindly, the flash illuminates the room to reveal a huge panther dragging his dead wife towards the window it has seemingly used to enter. The final horror is revealed when he examines the body and discovers fresh blood pouring from the throat and a piece of the animal's ear between her teeth, indicating that she had still been alive before the attack.

Bierce's choice of animal is interesting here. 'Panther' is a term that can refer to several species, in the northern United States most commonly the cougar. Historically the term had been used in Europe to refer to a variety of creatures, including mythical ones. It is difficult to think of a more appropriate choice of word to describe a creature from the 'place of wild beasts'. Bierce's choice of place and time are also relevant. Cincinnati, Ohio, sits on the western side of the Appalachian Mountains, where rumours of wild panthers have persisted despite the local extinction of cougars around the turn of the twentieth century. An 1853 book review refers to the feelings of the early Virginia settlers on the eastern side of this great divide:

> In the popular mind of those days, those mountains were regarded as the invincible barrier of the gloomy wilderness beyond, against the advances of civilization.

'Their great height, their prodigious extent, their rugged and horrid appearance, suggested to the imagination undefined images of terror. The wolf, the bear, the panther, and the Indian were the tenants of these forlorn and inaccessible precipices.'[34]

The same review makes an intriguing claim regarding the history of the United States: 'We are fortunate in being a new people; our historians may begin at the beginning, and complete their tale, without being compelled to invoke the aid of superstition or imagination.'[35] Bierce's mode of storytelling, although not claiming historical validity, uses a historical setting to cast doubt on this grand narrative. The creation of national myth involves the casting out of everything that does not fit the model, which is then condemned to return in monstrous form, here through the medium of fiction. Similar examples can be seen consistently in Bierce, including 'The Eyes of the Panther' (1897), where he describes a man in similar circumstances to Murlock:

Charles Marlowe was of the class, now extinct in this country, of woodmen pioneers ... For more than a hundred years these men pushed ever westward, generation after generation, with rifle and ax, reclaiming from Nature and her savage children here and there an isolated acreage for the plow, no sooner reclaimed than surrendered to their less venturesome but more thrifty successors. At last they burst through the edge of the forest into the open country and vanished as if they had fallen over a cliff.[36]

An ecocritical analysis would focus on this opposition of the pioneer and nature as symptomatic of the unhealthy and damaging relationship between humans and the environment more broadly. Yet Bierce, in eulogizing this mythical species, acknowledges its passing. His vision is profoundly Gothic in its assertion that humans, like political orders and indeed conceptions of nature, are transient. Tom J. Hillard has claimed that the Gothic can help steer ecocriticism away from an uncritical idealizing of nature.[37] Bierce's stories do just that, and remind us that nature and wilderness only gain meaning through human interpretation. It is up to us whether we embrace this responsibility, or go on cursing the 'damned thing'.

Notes

1 Ralph Waldo Emerson, *Nature*, in Nina Baym, Robert S. Levine and Arnold Krupat (eds), *The Norton Anthology of American Literature*, 7th edn (New York: W. W. Norton, 2007), pp. 1110–38, at p. 1111.
2 Although it is worth pointing out that the term 'sex' in the nineteenth century referred exclusively to male/female difference rather than sexual intercourse.

3 Fred Botting, *Gothic* (London: Routledge, 1996), p. 28.

4 Allan Lloyd-Smith, *American Gothic Fiction: An Introduction* (New York: Continuum, 2004), p. 37.

5 Roderick Frazier Nash, *Wilderness and the American Mind*, 4th edn (New Haven: Yale Nota Bene, 2001), p. 1.

6 Marianne Noble, 'The American Gothic', in Shirley Samuels (ed.), *A Companion to American Fiction 1780–1865* (Oxford: Blackwell, 2004), pp. 168–78, at p. 170.

7 Lloyd-Smith, *American Gothic Fiction*, p. 48.

8 Nash, *Wilderness and the American Mind*, pp. 2–3.

9 Nathaniel Hawthorne, 'Young Goodman Brown', in *Young Goodman Brown and Other Tales*, ed. Brian Harding (Oxford: Oxford University Press, 1987), pp. 111–24, at p. 112.

10 Robert Montgomery Bird, *Nick of the Woods*, rev. edn (New York: Redfield, 1853), pp. iv–v.

11 Ibid., p. iv.

12 William Howarth, 'Ecocriticism in Context', in Laurence Coupe (ed.), *The Green Studies Reader: From Romanticism to Ecocriticism* (London: Routledge, 2000), pp. 163–66, at p. 164.

13 Norman Foerster, *Nature in American Literature* (New York: Russell and Russell, 1958), p. xi.

14 Theresa A. Goddu, *Gothic America: Narrative, History, and Nation* (New York: Columbia University Press, 1997), p. 9.

15 Ibid., p. 72.

16 Ibid., p. 56.

17 Peter N. Carroll, *Puritanism and the Wilderness: The Intellectual Significance of the New England Frontier, 1629–1700* (New York: Columbia University Press, 1969), pp. 212–13.

18 Goddu, *Gothic America*, p. 57.

19 Frederick Jackson Turner, *The Frontier in American History* (New York: Henry Holt, 1947), p. 4.

20 Ibid., p. 2.

21 Tiziano Bonazzi, 'Frederick Jackson Turner's Frontier Thesis and the Self-Consciousness of America', *Journal of American Studies* 27/2 (August 1993): 149–71, at p. 158.

22 David Mogen, Scott P. Sanders and Joanne B. Kaplinski (eds), *Frontier Gothic: Terror and Wonder at the Frontier in American Literature* (London and Toronto: Associated University Presses, 1993), p. 19.

23 Leslie Fiedler, *Love and Death in the American Novel* (New York: Stein and Day, 1966), p. 143.

24 Ibid., p. 29.

25 John Hanner, 'Government Response to the Buffalo Hide Trade, 1871–1883', *Journal of Law and Economics* 24/2 (October 1981): 239–71, at p. 239.

26 Rena N. Coen, 'The Last of the Buffalo', *American Art Journal* 5/2 (November 1973): 83–94, at p. 84.

27 Edgar Allan Poe, 'The Fall of the House of Usher', in *Tales of Mystery and Imagination* (London: CRW, 2003), pp. 245–69, at p. 247.

28 Ambrose Bierce, 'The Damned Thing', in *The Complete Short Stories of Ambrose*

Bierce, ed. Ernest Jerome Hopkins (Lincoln: University of Nebraska Press, 1984), pp. 97–105, at p. 98. Subsequent references are to this edition and are given in parentheses in the text.

29 Greg Garrard, *Ecocriticism* (London: Routledge, 2004), p. 21.

30 Dominic Head, 'The (Im)possibility of Ecocriticism', in Richard Kerridge and Neil Sammells (eds), *Writing the Environment: Ecocriticism and Literature* (London: Zed Books, 1998), pp. 27–39, at p. 28.

31 John Szarkowski, 'Photography and America', *Art Institute of Chicago Museum Studies* 10 (1983): 236–51, at p. 238.

32 Ibid., p. 241.

33 Bierce, *Complete Short Stories*, pp. 227–31, at p. 227. Subsequent references are to this edition and are given in parentheses in the text.

34 Anonymous review of 'The Institution of the Society of the Cincinnati, formed by the Officers of the American Army of the Revolution, for the Laudable Purposes therein mentioned, at the Cantonment on the Banks of the Hudson River, May, 1783; together with some of the Proceedings of the General Society, and of the New York State Society; also, a List of the Officers and Members of the New York Society, from its Organization to the Year 1851', *North American Review* 77/161 (October 1853): 267–302, at pp. 273–4.

35 Ibid., p. 268.

36 Bierce, *Complete Short Stories*, pp. 38–46, at pp. 39–40.

37 Tom J. Hillard, '"Deep Into That Darkness Peering": An Essay on Gothic Nature', *Interdisciplinary Studies in Literature and Environment* 16/4 (Autumn 2009): 685–95, at p. 694.

10

Andrew Smith

Locating the self in the post-apocalypse: the American Gothic journeys of Jack Kerouac, Cormac McCarthy and Jim Crace

Jack Kerouac's *On the Road* (1957) might seem an unlikely contender as either a Gothic or an ecocritical text. However, it is a book which repeatedly refers to ghosts and in its account of frantic journeys from east to west and back again it captures a sense of the geographical and cultural environment of 1940s and 1950s America in a way which aligns it with ecocritical models of a threatened apocalypse. My argument is that Kerouac's novel provides a version of the 'road' which is echoed in later post-environmental apocalyptic narratives such as Cormac McCarthy's *The Road* (2006) and Jim Crace's *The Pesthouse* (2007). Kerouac also elaborates a version of subjectivity which underpins these later exercises in American Gothic as they all attempt to theorize the relationship between the self and the environment through acts which take place on the frontier. Finally we will see how these texts argue for how the frontier, a type of liminal space like the road, needs to become inhabited by a model of the family which serves as the blueprint for the possibility of social and environmental renewal. It is a move which requires a repudiation of the Gothic as its images of the spectral and the apocalyptic are ultimately challenged by the discovery of what can be affirmed by getting off the road.

At an obvious level, *On the Road* is a quest narrative focalized through the tellingly named Sal Paradise who is in pursuit of a lost Edenic vision that can put back a meaningful spirituality which post-war American social conformity has seemingly stifled. Such a vision is alternative, counter-cultural and represented by the figure of Dean Moriarty – life-affirming, energetic and with a seemingly endless appetite for sex, alcohol and jazz. The journeys across America are also explicitly inner journeys for Sal as he seeks to reawaken an enthusiasm for the kind of vitality that is embodied by Dean. Nevertheless, this potential for an inner revitalization breaks down early in the narrative when Sal recounts waking up in a hotel after having spent the previous day driving with Dean from San Francisco to Des Moines in Iowa:

> I woke up as the sun was reddening; and that was the one distinct time in my life, the strangest moment of all, when I didn't know who I was – I was far away from home, haunted and tired with travel, in a cheap hotel room I'd never seen, hearing the hiss of steam outside, and the creak of the old wood of the hotel, and footsteps upstairs, and all the sad sounds, and I looked at the cracked high ceiling and really didn't know who I was for about fifteen strange seconds. I wasn't scared; I was just somebody else, some stranger, and my whole life was a haunted life, the life of a ghost.[1]

The moment registers not that Sal does not know *where* he is, but rather that does not know *who* he is. The scene is developed to indicate that this sense of loss is related, ironically, to the journey which is undertaken in order to find himself and this is expressed in both temporal and geographical terms, for 'I was half-way across America, at the dividing line between the East of my youth and the West of my future, and maybe that's why it happened right there and then, that strange afternoon' (15–16). The liminality of the ghost thus captures the sense of being in-between places and experiences. However, what the ghost signifies becomes increasingly important to Sal because its putative associations with death and loss suggest a postlapsarian world which cannot accommodate a rediscovered Eden. There is a subsequent encounter with the ghostly which compounds his feelings of loss. This is when he meets an aged indigent traveller who is referred to as 'the Ghost of the Susquehanna', who challenges his preconception that the West is a sustainable metaphor for the frontier, whereas the East (Sal's home) represents a tamed civilization that is associated with a confining domesticity. However, the presence of this 'poor lost sometimeboy, now broken ghost of the penniless wilds' (95) leads Sal to the view that 'there is a wilderness in the East' (95). Sal falls asleep at the local railway station and when he awakens he mulls over the thought that:

> Isn't it true that you start your life a sweet child believing in everything under your father's roof? Then comes the day of the Laodiceans, when you know you are wretched and miserable and poor and blind and naked, and with the visage of a gruesome grieving ghost you go shuddering through nightmare life. I stumbled out of the station; I had no more control. (95)

The tone here is strangely biblical and incorporates a reference to the Laodiceans who were castigated in the Revelation of St John for their lukewarm approach to spiritual matters. The language of the apocalypse and a fallen world inhabited by Sal Paradise indicates that America may well be beyond redemption. Greg Garrard identifies Genesis chapter 3, the account of the Fall, as 'essentially an elegy of lost pastoral bounty and innocence'.[2] Pastoral in an American context has particular associations with a notion of the wilderness and the frontier, associations that are compromised by the image of the territorially mobile Ghost of the Susquehanna. Sal is looking for a spiritual vision which will unite him with place, only to repeatedly find it slips away from him. Dean is linked to this as he is both Beat (defeated) but also 'beatific' (177) and therefore a potential spiritual guide. The text therefore perpetually moves between these corrupted and ecstatic visions in which America is alternately fallen (largely through associations with rural poverty) and endorsed (through temporary urban pleasures). It provides a language of decline and affirmation that is captured in the image of the road as a nowhere place, as being merely a state of transition between places and feelings. As Dean tells Sal 'What's you road, man? – holyroad, madman road, rainbow road, guppy road, any road. It's an anywhere road for anybody anyhow' (229). However, for Sal it is not possible to make a sustainable affirmation because all that exists is 'the raggedy madness and riot of our actual lives, our actual night, the hell of it, the senseless nightmare road' (231). Inner and outer become conflated through a model in which Sal Paradise realizes that Paradise, as a mythic place and as an occulted aspect of himself, cannot be reclaimed.

On the Road should be seen in the context of notions of the frontier. Lynda H. Schneekloth has summarized the position of the male 'frontier hero' as being 'situated between wilderness and civilization' so that he mediates 'the space between the town and the wilds by his knowledge of both worlds. Yet this hero, who negotiates the middle terrain, cannot be a part of either world, cannot settle in the town, cannot make a commitment to other individuals or a community.'[3] While such a view places Kerouac within the context of a post-war reaction to social conformity, it also acknowledges the frontier as a threshold where the inability to belong is conditioned by an idea of the frontier as a space in which the subject is paradoxically both free and lost. The frontier is also at one level a conceptualization of a liminal environmental place in which territory is both mastered and beyond control ('the wilds'). To that degree it takes on the characteristics of what Christopher Hitt has referred to as an 'Ecological Sublime'. Hitt explores Kant's 'Analytic of the Sublime' (1790) and argues that Kant's idea that reason is asserted when challenged by the Sublime represents a moment of self-mastery which informed how writers such as Emerson and Thoreau conceptually mastered an American model of the wilderness. The frontier is thus a mental abstraction but one which is prone to collapsing into Edmund Burke's hypothesis that the Sublime is ghosted by fears of chaos and death – fears which point towards images of ecological disaster in which 'the sublime ... is evoked not by natural objects but by their devastation'.[4] How to inhabit, physically but also ideologically, such a space is the crucial question raised by the road narratives discussed here because, as Schneekloth states, '[a]lthough home and frontier have often been used as oppositions, they are actually dialectically dependent on each other for their meaning'.[5] Ideas about home, belonging and the frontier are also central elements within Cormac McCarthy's model of pastoral.

Megan Riley McGilchrist has noted that McCarthy's *The Border Trilogy*, consisting of *All The Pretty Horses* (1992), *The Crossing* (1994) and *Cities of the Plain* (1998), addresses images of the frontier through an American Gothic idiom which is familiar from Melville, Hawthorne, Twain and Cooper.[6] What is discovered on the frontier is the loss of pastoral (and associated images of freedom) that his characters have been pursuing so that at the end of *The Crossing*, for example, Billy Parham's witnessing of a nuclear test explosion at Los Alamos means that he is confronted by the threatened 'annihilation, not only of landscape, but of an entire way of being human',[7] and in *Cities of the Plain* (set in the early 1950s) only dreamers believe in the American Dream. Robert C. Sickels and Marc Oxoby have claimed that

> The traditional American pastoral vision celebrated at the start of McCarthy's trilogy is forsaken at the end, replaced by what can be called a contemporary American pastoralism, which recognizes that regardless of one's desires a pastoral existence is not merely beyond the frontier, but permanently impossible.[8]

This concern for pastoral has lead McGilchrist to claim that McCarthy's writings 'approach the borders of deep ecology', and so his 'works may be looked at usefully ... through the ecocritical eye'.[9]

The British journalist and political activist George Monbiot has referred to *The Road* as 'the most important environmental book ever written' and the book's cover carries a quotation from Andrew O'Hagan that designates it as 'The first great masterpiece of the globally warmed generation.'[10] The novel focuses on a journey undertaken by a father and son as they head towards the coast. They inhabit a post-apocalyptic world which is in ruins: 'The ashes of the late world carried on the bleak and temporal winds to and fro in the void. Carried forth and scattered and carried forth again. Everything uncoupled from its shoring.'[11] Nothing can grow in this blasted world, so that the unnamed father and son live off old tinned food that they periodically find, while attempting to avoid the organized gangs of cannibals that roam what is left of the countryside looking for others to eat even while within their groups they harvest babies for food. However, although the environment effectively no longer exists it retains a final place within consciousness. The father has a dream, for example, in which he experiences 'the uncanny taste of a peach from some phantom orchard fading in his mouth' (17). The implication is that this prelapsarian world finally disappears when it is no longer recalled. The father feels this strongly when observing:

> The world shrinking down about a raw core of parsible entities. The names of things slowly following them into oblivion. Colors. The names of birds. Things to eat. Finally the names of things one believed to be true. More fragile than he would have thought. How much was gone already? The sacred idiom shorn of its referents and so of its reality. (135)

Language is thus the 'sacred idiom' now hollowed out as its referents disappear, just as the physical world has become 'uncoupled from its shoring'. The novel asks how is it possible to retain some notion of decency in a world which is devoid of any inherent meaning. The father and son repeatedly refer to themselves as 'the good guys' because they fight to maintain moral integrity in a world that is largely defined by hunger and appetite. They, like Sal Paradise, are on a quest which tests their spiritual beliefs, although it is one in which they claim spirituality for themselves.

Sal's encounter with the Ghost of the Susquehanna challenges his notion of an easily divisible East/West America. The father and son also encounter an ageing tramp on the road. In response to the tramp's exclamation that he did not expect to see a child, the father asks 'What if I said that he's a god?' The tramp replies:

> Where men can't live gods fare no better. You'll see. It's better to be alone. So I hope that's not true what you said because to be on the road with the last god would be a terrible thing so I hope it's not true. (183)

For the tramp, the road is dominated by the figure of death who will soon become redundant once everything has died. The tramp's nihilism thus reflects the blasted landscape and implicitly undermines their journey to the ocean, where all they find is 'One vast salt sepulchre' (237). Ultimately for the father there is no spiritual dimension to the world, there is no possible return to a lost Eden which a figure such as Sal Paradise tries to formulate in abstractly spiritual terms. Instead there is merely a possible glimpse of how it was physically constituted. The man notes, 'Perhaps in the world's destruction it would be possible at last to see how it was made. Oceans, mountains. The ponderous counterspectacle of things ceasing to be. The sweeping waste, hydroptic and coldly secular. The silence' (293).

The man dies of a tubercular ailment and the child is taken in by a friendly family who believe in God. However, the boy finds it easier to talk to the memory of his father even if his new surrogate mother suggests that it is because his father had been touched by the divine. The final paragraph laments the end of a world because once gone 'a thing could not be put back. Not be made right again' (307). *The Road* thus echoes *On the Road*'s attempt to discover meaning in a search for some continuing spiritual vision which might hold out the possibility of redemption. Nevertheless, like *On the Road* it ultimately suggests that the world is no longer inhabited by meaning because the world has been destroyed. As Rune Graulund states, 'the nameless man and his boy are constantly on the move, [but] they are in fact not going anywhere. They are always "on the road", but the point of being on the road rapidly dissolves into meaninglessness'.[12] Nevertheless, it is the pursuit of meaning (and the willingness to undertake such a pursuit) which recalls the idea of a frontier life. For McGilchrist, 'the history of American settlement might be said to be about the desire for something, often finally unobtainable, which seems to lie just out of reach, beyond the next mountain range, across the next desert'.[13] In one sense this seems to evoke the sublime in which there is, for Hitt, 'the validation of the individual through an act of transcendence in which the external world is domesticated, conquered, or erased', even if there is the danger that this positive version of the sublime is supplanted by the destructive aspects of technology so that 'ecological catastrophe (as the result of technology) becomes a new source of the sublime'.[14] This blasted landscape thus masters the subject, and this has its roots in Kerouac's spectres even while it entertains a language of the apocalypse that threatens to turn all subjects into spectres. The paradox is that these seemingly bleak frontier visions are not without their optimism. The key to environmental and social renewal is to colonize the frontier

as a place where the home can be re-established and this entails invok-
ing an idea of the home which is implicit to images of the frontier as a
space that needs to be mastered through domestication.

In both Kerouac and McCarthy the road is a place where fragile
identities are tested against the demands of appetite. Sal Paradise's
pursuit of transitory pleasures reworks an aspect of existentialism
that Brian Ireland has claimed as a central element of the road genre,
because '[t]ypically, the characters in existentialist novels are concerned with physical things – the everyday reality of how they feel, how
tired they are, if they are hungry or cold, and so on'.[15] In Kerouac, the
pursuit of bodily pleasures represents a political quest to assert identity outside the models of middle-class, post-war conformity and so it
embraces the life of those on the social fringes such as the tramp, the
hobo and other social and economic drifters; as Victoria A. Elmwood
argues, 'Transients, migratory white laborers, and old-timey drunks
allow Paradise to access an essentialized wilderness associated with
the long gone American frontier and to the mostly extinguished Native
American.'[16] *On the Road*'s use of a Gothic idiom of spectrality captures
this sense of a liminal and restless form of identity in which the pursuit
of self-realization is replaced by an anxiety concerning a loss of self.
As noted, in *The Road* the blasted landscape negates such moments
of temporary transcendence as the focus is on how the alleviation of
hunger marks you out as either one of the 'good guys' or one of the
villains. What it morally means to be a person in this blighted world is a
key theme in the novel as its exploration of the inner life addresses how
an attachment to ethical integrity can be asserted within what appears
to be a Gothic terrain associated with death, hunger and threats of
cannibalism. While Sal Paradise loses a sense of self, the father and
son in *The Road* attempt to retain it by working beyond such Gothic
encounters.

The road and the frontier are both positioned as nowhere places
that nevertheless require some form of habitation. How to inhabit the
uninhabitable is the idea that links images of the frontier, the sublime
and ecological disaster with a notion of the road, and this series of links
is explored by Jim Crace. Crace, a British writer, reworks American
Gothic themes of the road and postlapsarian worlds in his American-
set *The Pesthouse*, which also makes reference to 'the ruined, rusty
way ahead and all the paradise beyond'.[17] This version of America has
also been hit by an ecological disaster which has led to the spread of a
plague-like disease, the flux. The tale centres on Franklin and Margaret,

whom he meets while she is recuperating from an illness in the pest-house (a place of isolation), and a child named Jackie whom they save while on the road – so that they form a surrogate family unit. In the novel communities migrate (here from west to east) because they believe that life will be better beyond certain internal geographical boundaries. It is noted that 'The optimists among them believed that once the river had been crossed, something of the old America would be discovered ... where the encouragements held out to strangers were a good climate, fertile soil, wholesome air and water' (42). Indeed some of a religious inclination regard their ecological catastrophe as a necessary precondition for a return to 'the doors of Paradise' (82) which required the destruction of their fallen world. As in *The Road* it is the journey to the sea which holds this promise. Indeed the sea is sub-ject to the same type of mythologizing suggested by crossing the river; it is noted that 'the ocean' was 'like an old friend' and 'that it roars at you like a cougar, that it smells like blood, that the ocean's got only one bank, that if you drink a cup of it your piss turns blue' (145). In keeping with both *On the Road* and *The Road*, the novel entertains the pos-sibility of a spiritual journey, although one which is formalized by the presence of a religious sect that is opposed to all things made of metal because 'Metal is the Devil's work. Metal is the cause of greed and war' (184). This community of Baptists is presided over by a group of elders whom Margaret sees in physical rather than spiritual terms when she notes of them that 'with so little flesh and so much prominent bone, they seemed huge and corpselike' (196). Their frailty stands in contrast to the giant-like frame of Franklin who seems to embody a physical and moral strength that is a more plausible source of revitalization than that provided by the moribund Baptists, who are murdered by a gang.

As in *The Road*, the journey to the sea is ultimately a disappointment. Franklin notes of the sea that

> It all smelled bad: the weed, the water and the sand, the shells, the battered
> lengths of drift, the pink-gray armored parts of animals that were not spiders
> exactly. He did not like the shore. It seemed ungenerous. Its music was funereal.
> (246)

In *The Pesthouse* the conclusion is that the way forward is the way back. Franklin's dream of escaping America across a dead ocean is replaced when he realizes that 'His dream was not the future but the past. Some land, a cabin and a family. A mother waiting on the stoop' (249). This nostalgia for a rural, conceptually conventional version of the past is key in framing the romance between Franklin and Margaret, in which they, with Jackie, constitute a family unit which indicates that it is possible to begin anew by heading back into the past and back to the west from the east. Franklin had realized this early on during their migration east when he senses that 'he had made a big mistake, that where he truly should be traveling was westward, back to the family hearth, back to mother waiting at the center of abandoned fields' (91). The final lines of the novel emphasize this optimism: 'They could imagine striking out to claim a piece of long-abandoned land and making home in some old place, some territory begging to be used. Going westward, they go free' (309). So, in the end a new form of Eden becomes possible.

However, the notion of the home has a place in both *On the Road* and *The Road*. Kerouac's journeys across America while writing *On the Road* were punctuated by a series of visits to his mother, which also appear in the text as visits to his aunt. Also although his Ghost of the Susquehanna might lead him to question the supposedly overly civilized East of America it does not compromise his vision of the West as a place of potential home. While working on *On the Road* he sent a letter in May 1949 to Hal Chase in which he records that

> Somewhere near Deertrail Colo. the sun was blushing through storm clouds upon a territorial area of brown plains where only one single farmhouse stood … so that the farmhouse, as I conceived of it, was receiving the blush of God himself.[18]

The home represents a point before the apocalypse and it is noteworthy that, in *The Road*, the initial catastrophe recalled by the man is when his wife walks out on them because, as she says, 'We're not survivors. We're the walking dead in a horror film' (57). The break-up of the home or the break-up of the family is what is mourned in these narratives, which suggest that if only families stayed together then all would have been well. Kerouac, for example, in a letter to Allen Ginsberg from June 1949, indicates an ambition to 'wander the wild, wild mountains and wait for Judgment Day', because

> I don't believe at all in this society. It is evil. It will fall … It has all got out of hand – began when fools left the covered wagons in 1848 and rode madly to California for Gold, leaving their families behind.[19]

However, more radically such subtle images of the frontier are not quite so divorced from images of the home as they might initially appear to be. Elmwood, for example, has argued that while Kerouac refutes images of the white, female-controlled, middle-class home, he is nevertheless in pursuit of an alternative image of the home, 'a search in which he turns to non-white subcultures for inspiration and explores a range of occupations trying to find a home that suits him'.[20] As mentioned earlier, Schneekloth sees the idea of the frontier as dependent upon a notion of the home which is being left behind; however, she also acknowledges that the 'the frontier [is] a space to be inhabited, not simply a shifting line between civilization and wilderness'.[21] The seemingly nowhere place of the road is thus the means by which one gets to a potentially inhabitable frontier. McGilchrist claims that McCarthy's *Cities of the Plain* is unusual in affirming the possibility of a return to the type of domesticity that Crace also clearly has in mind at the end of *The Pesthouse*; for McGilchrist the return to the hearth suggests 'that the lone man of the myth of the frontier may have found a home at last'.[22] This raises the question of how the frontier functions as a liminal Gothic space in which identities are lost and recomposed. These movements are also reflected in the view of the landscape which is, as in *The Road*, devastated and functions as an inhospitable but necessarily inhabitable space.[23] The gender implications of these male-authored texts are also clear as they work towards presenting a fairly conventional model of the family as the most appropriate unit through which society can be regenerated. Indeed the images of gender rely on an unexamined assumption that a return to convention provides the only viable way through which to reconstitute the social sphere.

The three road texts discussed here all focus, at different levels of engagement, on the idea of the road and the frontier as a problematic but inhabitable space. The road might seem to represent the journey to the frontier but it is in reality an associated aspect of it. Like the frontier it too is a potentially lawless place in which fragile identities become necessarily renegotiated or reaffirmed. However, such dramas cannot be isolated from the environmental issues that novels such as *The Road* and *The Pesthouse* engage with. The seemingly simple drama about good and bad in *The Road*, for example, indicates either an affirmation of family bonds or their destruction. How to live on the road thus raises issues about social renewal which are linked to a model of the frontier that is associated with environmental factors. McGilchrist, who supports an ecocritically nuanced reading of McCarthy's work, has noted of his Westerns that 'The action ... is continuously mobile: domestic settings are transitory, and are often destroyed or repudiated. Characters seem never to grow, but simply continue in a self-destructive cycle of violence, repetition and loss.'[24] *The Road* is an

extension of this as it is set beyond, if clearly exemplifying, the after-
effects of this 'self-destructive cycle of violence', the antidote to which
is to affirm a sense of place that is established, as it is in *The Pesthouse*,
in a post-apocalyptic environment that promises to provide the space
where one can start again – so that ultimately Sal Paradise's pursuit
of a lost Eden becomes reworked as an attempt to rediscover the possibilities of the prelapsarian. The fact that this is played out in relation
to a blasted environment indicates both the potential for an ecocritical
approach to such narratives as well as how a model of the road shapes
a specifically American mode of representing environmental disaster
and possible social renewal. In this way these texts represents a new
elaboration of a definitively male American Gothic tradition.

The three texts *On the Road*, *The Road* and *The Pesthouse* are structur-
ally very similar as they all involve journeys across blighted landscapes
in search of meaning. There is no sustained explanation for why these
landscapes have been blighted in such ways and as such there is no
demonstrable engagement with a narrative of pending environmental
crisis. While the images of crisis function as a precautionary warning about a possible environmental disaster, they also emphasize the
importance of the family unit, or the home, as the place from which
to start again as the frontier becomes revitalized via a new, non-vio-
lent form of rehabitation. How to construct a view of the world in
post-ecological terms thus rests on a model of family values, which
while politically conservative in its emphasis on the [post-]nuclear
family, also utilizes such imagery as a putatively radical counterpoint
to how the frontier has been conventionally represented (as populated by the potentially self-destructive outcast loner). The ecopolitical
vision of these texts is associated with a language of renewal as in the
end the Gothic is pushed to the margins and its ostensible radicalism contained. This is a view captured in *The Road* when it is noted,
'They were days fording that cauterized terrain. The boy had found
some crayons and painted his facemask with fangs and he trudged on
uncomplaining' (13). Ultimately the Gothic becomes little more than
a child's mask rather than a place for progressing a discussion of the
ecological.

The conjunctions between the Gothic and the ecocritical in these
texts are inevitably conditioned by the fact that *The Road* and *The
Pesthouse* are both post-environmental and, like *On the Road*, are more
interested in what can be reaffirmed than with how an ecological catastrophe can be averted, or indeed explained. Instead the post-apocalypse

seems to provide an opportunity to reassert notions of the family as the smallest social unit that can be salvaged from the Gothic ruins. For this reason the Gothic alignment with an environmental disaster, or with troubled notions of subjectivity which entertains liminal states, is ultimately overcome by getting off the road and finding a new homestead. These texts therefore provide an illuminating example of what happens when writing beyond the environmental apocalypse takes place and a version of a new society is envisioned – one in which the way forward seems, politically speaking, to reformulate the way back.

Notes

1 Jack Kerouac, *On the Road* [1957] (Harmondsworth: Penguin, 1991), p. 15. Subsequent references are to this edition and are given in parentheses in the text.
2 Greg Garrard, *Ecocriticism* (London: Routledge, 2004), p. 37.
3 Lynda H. Schneekloth, 'The Frontier Is Our Home', *Journal of Architectural Education* 49/4 (1996): 210–25, at p. 214.
4 Christopher Hitt, 'Toward an Ecological Sublime', *New Literary History* 30/3 (1999): 603–23, at p. 619.
5 Schneekloth, 'The Frontier Is Our Home', p. 222.
6 Megan Riley McGilchrist, *The Western Landscape in Cormac McCarthy and Wallace Stegner* (London: Routledge, 2010), p. 120. Her argument is that this is the classic American Gothic tradition identified by Leslie Fielder.
7 Ibid., p. 127.
8 Robert C. Sickels and Marc Oxoby, 'In Search of a Further Frontier: Cormac McCarthy's Border Trilogy', *Critique: Studies in Contemporary Fiction* 43/4 (2002): 347–59, at p. 348. See also John M. Grammer, 'A Thing Against Which Time Will Not Prevail: Pastoral and History in Cormac McCarthy's South', in Edwin T. Arnold and Dianne C. Luce (eds), *Perspectives on Cormac McCarthy* (Jackson: University of Mississippi, 1999), pp. 29–45, for a critique of how McCarthy challenges southern pastoral attitudes.
9 McGilchrist, *The Western Landscape*, pp. 46, 18. It should also be noted that McGilchrist includes the work of Wallace Stegner within this discussion.
10 George Monbiot, 'Civilisation Ends With a Shutdown of Human Concern. Are We There Already?', *The Guardian*, 30 October 2007. Quoted by Rune Graulund in 'Fulcrums and Borderlands: A Desert Reading of Cormac McCarthy's *The Road*', *Orbis Litterarum* 65/1 (2010): 57–78, at p. 67.
11 Cormac McCarthy, *The Road* [2006] (London: Picador, 2007), p. 10. Subsequent references are to this edition and are given in parentheses in the text.
12 Graulund, 'Fulcrums and Borderlands', p. 67.
13 McGilchrist, *The Western Landscape*, pp. 145–6.
14 Hitt, 'Toward an Ecological Sublime', pp. 611, 619.
15 Brian Ireland, 'American Highways: Recurring Images and Themes of the Road Genre', *The Journal of American Culture* 26/4 (December 2003): 474–84, at p. 481.
16 Victoria A. Elmwood, 'The White Nomad and the New Masculine Family in Jack

Kerouac's *On The Road*, *Western American Literature* 42/4 (Winter 2008): 335–61, at p. 341.

17 Jim Crace, *The Pesthouse* (London: Picador, 2007), p. 3. Subsequent references are to this edition and are given in parentheses in the text.

18 Jack Kerouac, *Selected Letters, 1940–1956*, ed. Anne Charles (London: Viking, 1995), p. 190.

19 Kerouac, *Selected Letters*, p. 193.

20 Elmwood, 'The White Nomad', p. 340.

21 Schneekloth, 'The Frontier Is Our Home', p. 223.

22 McGilchrist, *The Western Landscape*, p. 214.

23 How to live among such images of death can be linked to ideas of how to dwell within nature itself. In ecocritical thought Heidegger's lecture 'On the Origins of the Work of Art' (1935) has provided a model for how art might in some way dwell within the world by recalling the environmental aspects of particular cultures through seemingly incidental detail (as in Heidegger's analysis of Van Gogh's painting *A Pair of Shoes* [1886] which he relates to the very earthiness of peasant culture). For Heidegger it is poetry which captures a sense of how we can, like a peasant, dwell within the world (by inhabiting the 'word'), and so art can reawaken an attachment to a primal world which enables us to 'be' within it. Nicholas Dungey has explored how Heidegger's notion of dwelling as elaborated in *Being and Time* (1927) constructs a utopian vision in which subjects come to dwell in the world via a shared ethical system in which 'dwelling captures both the objective and subjective conditions of care abiding in each individual and the radius of his or her relationships. These models of care – cherishing, protecting and loving – are ontologically constitutive of who we are' (Nicholas Dungey, 'The Politics and Ethics of Dwelling', *Polity* 39/2 [2007]: 234–58, at p. 241). This image fits with the model of family which the road narratives discussed here either head towards (*The Road*, *The Pesthouse*) or periodically entertain (*On the Road*). Even Kerouac's ostensibly bohemian refutation of the home is replaced by, as Elmwood notes, an alternative pursuit of belonging.

Thomas A. Carlson has attempted a reading of *The Road* via the work of St Augustine and Heidegger, and argues that the novel's images of environmental desolation are counterbalanced by models of possible renewal, in one of which the son is finally admitted into a surrogate family so that '[t]he construction or creation and the loss – both in and of this work – are co-implicated' as the creation of the world is discovered in how it disappears, just as the son retains the ethical vision of his father (Thomas A. Carlson, 'With the World at Heart: Reading Cormac McCarthy's *The Road* with Augustine and Heidegger', *Religion & Literature* 39/3 [2007]: 47–71, at p. 59). Ultimately these narratives affirm the possibility of a renewal of feeling, place and family bonds – the very things which have seemingly been laid to waste. The Gothic world of the apocalypse is in the end obviated by a return to a non-Gothic language of presence which seems to dissipate the pessimistic vision of an end. The Gothic is thus displaced in these narratives as they in non-cynical, if sentimental, moments elaborate a language of transcendence to work through the ecological sublime.

24 McGilchrist, *The Western Landscape*, p. 2.

11

Susan J. Tyburski

A Gothic apocalypse: encountering the monstrous in American cinema

> Wild, dark times are rumbling toward us, and the prophet who wishes to write a new apocalypse will have to invent entirely new beasts, and beasts so terrible that the ancient animal symbols of St John will seem like cooing doves and cupids in comparison. (Heinrich Heine, 'Lutetia; or, Paris', *Augsburg Gazette*, 1842)

A growing number of apocalyptic films from the United States depict humans encountering monstrous versions of nature. In Larry Fessenden's *The Last Winter* (2006),[1] M. Night Shyamalan's *The Happening* (2008),[2] Roland Emmerich's *2012* (2009)[3] and John Hillcoat's *The Road* (2009),[4] nature becomes an avenging force, eliminating troublesome humans from the environment – or, even more monstrous, nature is depicted as an alien entity utterly indifferent to the fate of humanity. Just as humans have, in many ways, appeared to disavow any necessary connection to nature, the natural world in these films seems to reject humanity as expendable. This chapter will explore the following questions: How have traditional Gothic tropes been transformed to explore ecological fears in recent apocalyptic films? And what can we learn about our relationship with the natural world by exploring these modern apocalyptic narratives?

The recent crop of apocalyptic films reflects a growing trend in 'eco-horror' cinema: the transformation of our natural home into a destructive monster. In '"Eco-Horror": Green Panic on the Silver Screen' (2008), Neda Ulaby observes, 'What makes today's eco-horrors different is that the entire *planet* is seen as vengeful and malevolent towards its human inhabitants.'[5] These eco-monsters assume a variety of forms. In *2012*, the earth erupts in a series of earthquakes, tsunamis and volcanic convulsions, causing those of its resident humans who are not immediately consumed to flee in terror. In *The Road*, the planet is ravaged by some unknown force, perhaps a nuclear war or an asteroid, eliminating almost all forms of life. In an especially Gothic twist, a mysterious natural force causes humans to commit suicide in *The Happening*, and in *The Last Winter*, an even more mysterious force causes humans to descend into madness as their environment becomes increasingly more hostile. Despite their individual incarnations, in all of these films the threat to humans is not limited to a single monster but to an all-encompassing monstrous environment.

These monstrous visions of nature are manifestations of eco-anxiety of epic proportions. The term 'eco-anxiety' has surfaced in dozens of news stories, articles and blogs. It has been defined by *Word Spy* as 'worry or agitation caused by concerns about the present and future state of the environment'.[6] In a 2007 story from the *Columbia News Service*, Justin Nobel reports 'a growing number of people have literally worried themselves sick over various environmental doomsday scenarios', and describes a new treatment, 'eco-therapy', to treat the 'eco-anxious'.[7]

A 2009 story by Emily Anthes in *The Boston Globe* chronicles the first known case of 'climate change delusion', in which a 17-year-old youth was admitted to the psychiatric unit of a Melbourne hospital because he refused to drink water.[8] The boy was worried about climate-change-related drought, and believed if he drank water, millions of people would die. The boy's treating psychiatrist has since 'seen several more patients with psychosis or anxiety disorders focused on climate change, as well as children who are having nightmares about global-warming-related natural disasters'. Glenn Albrecht, director of the Institute for Sustainability and Technology Policy at Australia's Murdoch University, has found that changes 'in people's home environment' as the result of climate change are 'sources of chronic stress', which can be measured on 'an Environmental Distress Scale'.[9]

In a recent *New York Times Magazine* piece, 'Is There an Ecological Unconscious' (2010), Daniel B. Smith introduces us to 'solastalgia', a term coined by Glenn Albrecht to describe 'the pain experienced when there is recognition that the place where one resides and that one loves is under immediate assault … a form of homesickness one gets when one is still at home'. Smith goes on to explain that 'ecopsychologists believe that grief, despair and anxiety are the consequences of dismissing deeply-rooted ecological instincts'.

Recent apocalyptic films tap into this eco-anxiety, creating monstrous visions that mirror our fears about the fate of our civilization and the planet we call home. In her 2007 study of millennial horror films in America, *Apocalyptic Dread*, Kirsten Moana Thompson explores 'social anxieties, fears, and ambivalence about global catastrophe' appearing in American films beginning in the 1990s.[10] She explains that the word 'apocalypse' is a transliteration of the Greek word *apokalypsis*, and 'broadly means to "uncover or disclose"'.[11] By creating horrific representations of nature turning on humans, these films uncover our fears and anxieties concerning our relationship with the natural world.

In *The Last Winter*, Larry Fessenden explores the psychological effects of global warming. Like the growing crop of ecopsychologists, he focuses 'on the pathological aspect of the mind–nature relationship: its brokenness'.[12] Fessenden creates an apocalyptic vision of an Arctic icescape which, due to global climate change, is melting and releasing frightening spectres from the depths of the frozen tundra. These apparitions haunt the employees of an American oil company scouting a remote area of the Arctic National Wildlife Refuge, precipitating the descent of the crew into madness and death, and of civilization into chaos.

As the crew confront increasing evidence of the warming landscape, they begin, one by one, to sense a malevolent presence surrounding their vulnerable shelter – a Gothic sensibility that fills the indifferent void of nature with signs and portents. As Joyce Carol Oates explains in her Introduction to the anthology *American Gothic Tales* (1996), the Gothic invests 'all things, even the most seemingly innocuous (weather, insects) with cosmological meaning'.[13] The indifference of the natural world to the crew is emphasized by the stark white background of many of the outdoor scenes – a blank palette upon which the characters project their fears and anxieties.

Gothic portents increase as the film progresses. The young surveyor Maxwell is the first to see ghostly caribou herds running across the tundra at night. He wanders off inexplicably across the icy landscape, spends time staring, mesmerized, at the white box covering an old test well (not unlike the infamous monolith in *2001: A Space Odyssey* [1968]), and returns to the rest of the crew with vague references to something sinister underneath the surface. Maxwell is later discovered out on the tundra, naked, frozen to death in a grisly pose. The company's environmentalist, James Hoffman, is visited by a black crow in his survey hut, and soon after is assaulted by an unusually fierce wind.

When he steps outside to investigate, he sees tracks of a caribou herd in a circle around the hut.

A pivotal moment in the film occurs when a character named Elliott visits Hoffman's hut to retrieve maps and data after Hoffman has been fired from the project for refusing to sign an environmental impact statement prepared by the company. Elliott discovers Hoffman's journal, which records the increasing temperatures around the site, reflects his growing preoccupation with global warming and disintegrates into the apparent ravings of a madman. Elliott is haunted by Hoffman's question: 'What if the very thing we were here to pull out of the ground were to rise willingly and confront us – what would that look like?'

Ultimately, both crew leader Pollack and the environmentalist Hoffman perish as they traverse the tundra seeking help; as they die, they are visited by visions of giant caribou-like monsters resembling the glowing Northern Lights appearing above them in the sky. Hoffman is carried off by one of these ghostly beasts, and as he passively rides through the night sky he relives a childhood memory of running towards the familiar comforts of home after playing in the snow. In contrast, Pollack is violently torn to shreds, battling these visions of nature to the bitter end. Fessenden seems to offer two possible responses to the horrors his characters encounter: we can fight to the end, like Pollack, or, like Hoffman, we can lean back and enjoy the ride to its apocalyptic conclusion.

According to Fessenden, these monster caribou do not really exist in his cinematic world; they are creations of the characters' traumatized psyches.[14] He explains this human need to create monsters, 'Our psychological mechanism to deal with a troubled reality is ... creating monsters and myths and angry gods ... You always look for a scapegoat. It seems so hard to believe that the world could be utterly indifferent.'[15]

In depicting the transformation of our natural environment into something monstrous, we come face to face with our alienation from nature. In *The Last Winter*, Fessenden wanted to graphically expose humans' denial of the reality of global warming.[16] As his characters Pollack and Hoffman debate the significance of rising temperatures, the ice continues to melt and the horrors increase. One by one, the characters in *The Last Winter* become increasingly disoriented and disconnected, and are set adrift in an alien world. Larry Fessenden explains how he explores this concept of alienation in his films, referring to Freud's *The Uncanny*: 'He [Freud] ... talks about not being able to orient yourself back home, which is one of my themes – you can never go home. That's what the uncanny means – that you're basically disoriented from your home and yourself.'[17] This feeling of the uncanny, or disorientation from the familiar, is a traditional element of the Gothic genre.

In *The Last Winter*, Fessenden uncovers and discloses, using brutally graphic images from his characters' psyches, the destructive effects of ignoring our instinctive, essential connection to the natural world. *The Last Winter*'s ghostly monsters are a projection of a communal fear that nature – our original home – is turning against us. As the environmentalist Hoffman writes in his journal, 'Why wouldn't the wilderness fight us? Like any organism would fend off a virus? The world we grew up in is changing forever. There is no way home.'

Fessenden's wild spectres mirror our fears about the fate of our civilization and the planet we call home. Unlike the majority of apocalyptic films, however, Fessenden does not end on a hopeful note of surviving humans rebuilding civilization from the ashes.[18] At the end of the movie, Abby, the sole survivor of the crew's ordeal, wakes up in an empty hospital and, as a newscaster cheerfully details the growing weather disasters assaulting the planet, discovers the corpse of a suicidal doctor hanging from a rope in an office. She wanders out into what appears to be a chaotic, watery landscape – and the screen fades to black. We are left to imagine the horrific consequences of global climate change.

The monsters of *The Last Winter* are a chilling metaphor for the destructive natural forces our consumerist society has unleashed, and a fascinating transformation of traditional Gothic tropes to explore modern crises and fears. In *The Gothic* (2004), David Punter and Glennis Byron identify the Latin roots of 'monster' as 'monstrare: to demonstrate' and 'monere: to warn'. They explain: 'From classical times through to the Renaissance, monsters were interpreted either as signs of divine anger or as portents of impending disasters.'[19] The spectral monsters released in *The Last Winter* serve both of these purposes: they herald the coming of an irrevocable apocalypse and manifest the horrors of this apocalypse in gruesome detail.

The troubled characters in *The Last Winter* are haunted by a common nightmare – the destructive monsters unleashed by global warming. In addition to addressing our fears about climate change, recent American apocalyptic films also tap into the national memory of the terrorist attacks of September 11, 2001. Fessenden began writing *The Last*

Winter in November 2001, shortly after the attacks on New York City and Washington DC, which he describes as 'a very oppressive, anxious time'. According to his 'Director's Notes', he worried whether this paranoia will be 'the ironic end to man in the twenty first century? That the rational still loses out to fear and delusion.' Fessenden translated his experience of post-9/11 national paranoia into *The Last Winter*'s wild spectres – delusions of a traumatized community.

Watching two planes fly into the World Trade Center and the ensuing horrific events unfold in graphic detail on national television destroyed Americans' illusions of personal or national invulnerability. Psychologists Tom Pyszczynski, Sheldon Solomon and Jeff Greenberg dissect this experience in *In the Wake of 9/11: The Psychology of Terror* (2002). They define 'terror' as 'a uniquely human response to the threat of annihilation'.[20] Humans are uniquely self-conscious, which includes an awareness of our mortality. Our vision of life is, therefore, a source of both 'awe and dread'.[21] Most of the time, according to Pyszczynski, Solomon and Greenberg, we keep 'the ever-present potential terror of death' at bay through cultural constructs which convince us that we 'are beings of enduring significance living in a meaningful reality'.[22] According to this theory of 'terror management', we create this sense of significance through '1. faith in a culturally derived worldview that imbues reality with order, stability, meaning, and permanence; and 2. belief that one is a significant contributor to this meaningful reality'.[23] Thus, belief in human agency is an essential element of terror management.

Terror management theory provides helpful insights into the way apocalyptic narratives tap into our deepest fears by stripping away this sense of 'order, stability, meaning and permanence', and replacing it with a vision of destructive chaos. We see this technique used in *The Last Winter*, as the crew gradually descend into madness and despair; the film ends with a scene suggesting the complete breakdown of society. Of the four films discussed in this chapter, however, *The Road* presents the bleakest picture of a post-apocalyptic world.

The Road, adapted from the Pulitzer prize-winning novel by Cormac McCarthy, is a meditation on survival in a post-apocalyptic, ash-grey landscape, stripped not only of most forms of life but also of all semblance of civilization. The roads along which our heroes – a father and a son – travel contain mere shadows of their former society, lifeless except for other roving, desperate humans. An oppressive sense of vulnerability permeates the film, exacerbated by the father's desperate attempts to feed his son and keep him safe from bands of roving cannibals, who feed on the only live food source which remains – humans. Not only does *The Road* depict a hellish post-apocalyptic nightmarescape, but it turns out that the monsters, in the form of cannibals, are us.

Former artefacts of our consumer culture become prize objects crucial to the survival of the father and son. They use a shopping cart to carry their scavenged possessions. They 'shop' the aisles of burned-out grocery stores and abandoned homes for provisions. We learn that the boy's mother committed suicide to avoid a potential rape and gruesome death at the hands of cannibals and, in doing so, destroyed their nuclear family unit. The father carries a gun with two bullets and shows his son how to use it to kill himself, if that horrible option becomes necessary.

The father and son are travelling towards the southern coast, in the hope that it offers a better environment. Along the way, they narrowly escape falling prey to various groups of cannibals. They encounter a strange old man with whom the boy urges his father to share their limited provisions. They are robbed and then encounter the thief on the road with their possessions. Instead of killing him, the father strips him bare and leaves him, devoid of shelter, clothing or sustenance, to his inevitable fate – an image that serves as a metaphor for the ultimate vulnerability of the entire human race. The boy challenges his father, arguing that the punishment – leaving the thief completely vulnerable to certain death – is too cruel for his crime. The father ultimately repents, and attempts to relocate the thief, but is unsuccessful.

The Road's central concept of life-affirming agency is found in the boy; his moral sensibility is an inspiring example to his father, as well as to the film's audience. Near the end of the film, after the pair reach the coast, the father, suffering from injury and illness, lies dying. The boy tells his father that he wants to die with him; the father instructs the boy that he needs to continue to 'carry the fire'. After his father dies, the boy meets a man, a woman, two children and a dog travelling along the coast. He decides to join them; the movie ends with the woman embracing him, leaving the audience with a vision of a reunited nuclear family unit, and perhaps a chance to re-animate the devastated planet.

The Road explores the role of humans in a devastated, postapocalyptic world. What can one do in the midst of a universally hopeless situation? The answer seems to be to endure, preserving as much as we can of our human spark, or impulse towards agency, for as long as we are able – and when we can no longer do so, to leave this world with dignity and honour. Living in line with honourable principles – 'carrying the fire' – allows us a kind of graceful, noble end, as the father achieves, with his son's help, near the end of this film. These honourable principles are crucial cultural constructs allowing us to keep darkness and chaos at bay.

Because of its heroes' stubborn insistence on survival, *The Road* is strangely life-affirming. Ecocritical scholar Greg Garrard, who traces the development of 'apocalypse' as an ecocritical trope from Zoroaster in 1200 BCE through modern environmental writers, cites rhetorician Stephen O'Leary in distinguishing between 'comic', or life-affirming, and a 'tragic', or destructive, 'frames' for apocalyptic narratives.[24] One distinguishing feature between these two 'frames' is the existence of human agency. In tragedy, the hero (or anti-hero) is powerless to alter his ultimate fate.[25] In comedy, the hero is able to craft his own fate and shape his own destiny in a way that affirms the continuation of human life.

Jack Morgan, however, suggests that horror, not tragedy, is actually the dark side of life-affirming comedy. Gothic monsters are antithetical to organic unity. Morgan describes this concept of Gothic monstrosity:

> As opposed to the comic sense of life or tragedy's dignified sense of death, horror embodies a sense of anti-life or unlife; it takes note of the demarcation between the wholesome and the unwholesome, the healthy and the monstrous – a clarity essential to organic life.[26]

The Gothic apocalyptic narrative employs monsters to generate a feeling of horror and revulsion, and may be the ultimate Gothic tale, as it portrays the disintegration not just of a specific individual or a specific place, but of life itself.

The contrast of comic versus horrific approaches to apocalyptic narratives is especially apparent in a comparison of *2012* and *The Happening*. *2012* offers a decidedly anti-Gothic perspective on the apocalypse. It takes a tongue-in-cheek approach to the imminent destruction of the world, turning the catastrophe into a special-effects-fuelled amusement park ride. It depicts the breakdown of our natural world first as an entertaining spectacle, and then as a problem to be overcome by human ingenuity. The spunky determination displayed by *2012*'s hero, Jackson Curtis (engagingly played by traditional romantic comedy lead John Cusack), in the face of global disaster serves as an excellent illustration of the 'brainy opportunism' demonstrated in 'an essentially dreadful universe' that is the essence of comedy.[27]

While a series of earthquakes and tsunamis devastate the planet, our hero rescues his ex-wife Kate, his children Noah and Lilly, and his wife's new partner, Gordon Silberman, from a series of disasters, taking us along for the thrilling ride. Despite a continuous stream of apparently hopeless scenarios, Curtis overcomes all obstacles and not only survives the catastrophic destruction that surrounds him, but manages to reunite with his nuclear family, thanks to the convenient demise of Silberman during the course of their adventures. *2012* portrays this family unit as the life-preserving nucleus of American society, which presumably will go on to repopulate our devastated planet. The entire film affirms the patriotic cultural constructs – love of family and country – especially prevalent in American society since 9/11. Like the 'fire' carried by the boy in *The Road*, adherence to these essential values serves to keep the chaos of an unruly planet at bay.

In portraying rebellious nature as a problem to be solved, or a challenge to be met, Emmerich's *2012* is the most obviously comic – and therefore essentially anti-Gothic – American apocalyptic film to emerge in recent years. In contrast, M. Night Shyamalan's *The Happening* employs Gothic apocalyptic tropes to convey a slowly evolving sense of horror. *The Happening* begins with the sound of the wind behind an eerie melody accompanying the opening credits. This melody gradually becomes more menacing, and we notice that the clouds are moving past in an unusually swift, abnormal manner. The presence of wind permeates Shyamalan's film as an increasing menace that surrounds the human inhabitants of our planet. Like the white Arctic canvas against which the characters project their anxieties and fears in *The Last Winter*, the wind, as well as the rustling greenery, become the raw materials from which the characters in *The Happening* – as well as the audience – create eco-conspiracy theories.

The film opens in New York City's Central Park, where we see individuals sitting on park benches or strolling along, enjoying the day. The breeze picks up; some people become disoriented, begin repeating themselves and start slowly walking backwards. A woman on a park bench removes a hair pin and stabs herself in the neck. The scene moves to a construction site a few blocks away, where workers are gathered in a small group, telling stories and laughing. They are suddenly interrupted by a person falling off a skyscraper; rather than being an isolated incident, this person is soon joined by numerous others leaping to their deaths. We are soon shown other scenes of humans engaging in spontaneous, gruesome acts of self-destruction around New York City.

We then meet our hero, Elliot Moore, a high-school science teacher who is lecturing on the mysterious disappearance of honey bees and what implications such a disappearance could have for our planet. One of his students suggests that it is simply 'an act of nature and we'll never fully understand it'. This class is interrupted by the principal, who arrives to announce that there 'appears to be an event happening', and sends the students home. Terrorists are suspected of leaking some kind of airborne toxin in New York City, which somehow blocks humans' 'self-preservation mechanism'. Elliot and his wife Alma quickly join Elliot's friend Julian and his daughter Jess on a train leaving for Philadelphia.

Before the train arrives in Philadelphia, however, it stops in a small town in Pennsylvania because its crew lose contact with 'everyone'. Julian is anxious to find his wife, who is headed for Princeton, and leaves his daughter Jess with Elliot and Alma so that he can catch a ride in that direction. Along with his fellow travellers, Julian ultimately succumbs to the strange affliction rapidly spreading across the east coast, slitting his wrists after a gruesome car wreck.

Elliot, Alma and Jess get a lift out of town with a horticulturalist and his wife. The horticulturalist, an engagingly odd character with wide, strange eyes, believes that the 'event' is caused by plants. He explains that plants can release chemicals, communicate with each other and 'target specific threats', and have been known to react to human stimuli. As this group encounters others on their journey, they conclude that plants along the east coast are targeting large populations of humans, and decide to split up to avoid triggering a toxic reaction from the local fauna.

Elliot, Alma and Jess find themselves travelling the open country-side of rural Pennsylvania with smaller and smaller groups. The three of them end up in a dilapidated farmhouse with a very strange older woman, who eventually succumbs to the neurotoxin. Before the neurotoxin reaches Elliot, Alma and Jess, who embrace in the middle of the yard expecting the worst, the 'event' apparently reaches its 'peak', and the world suddenly returns to 'normal'.

Originally titled *The Green Effect*, the film's title was changed to *The Happening* in order to keep the reason for the apparent attacks against humans a mystery. As Shyamalan explains in a special features interview found on the DVD, '[f]ear is based on the unknown' and is exacerbated in situations where 'you've lost your bearings'. In *The Happening*, he creates a gradual unmooring from our complacent reality, as the characters slowly realize that every green thing that surrounds them could be emitting a dangerous neurotoxin, so that the very air needed for life becomes an instrument of death.

While *The Happening* seems to end with yet another affirmation of the nuclear family, Shyamalan does not let us off the hook so easily, and plants the seeds of a future apocalypse before the final credits roll. Three months after 'the event', Elliot, Alma and Jess are living together happily in New York City; Alma is pregnant. In the background of this scene of domestic bliss, a TV talk show host interviews a scientist about the 'event'. Echoing the comments of Elliot's student at the beginning of the movie, the scientist states, 'This was an act of nature and we'll never fully understand it.' He then suggests that this 'event' may have been 'a prelude' or 'a warning, like the first spot of a rash'. The scientist explains that 'we have been a threat to this planet', and if the event 'had happened in one other place …' Neither Elliot or Alma pay any attention to the scientist on television.

The film ends with a scene in a park in Paris, similar to the opening scene in Central Park. We see a couple of young men walking along, enjoying the day. Someone screams. One of the men begins repeating himself; the people in the park stop and stand still. The other man looks behind him, and says 'My God.' The screen goes black. The final credits roll against a background of boiling storm clouds, and more creepy music mixed with the sound of the wind. Ultimately, *The Happening* offers only the illusion of agency, and suggests that we are headed for an even larger and more pervasive deadly 'event' – perhaps eliminating humans entirely from the face of the earth.

In reviewing these four recent American films, we are presented with various choices in dealing with the 'entirely new beasts' of a potential apocalypse. We can adopt the can-do attitude of *2012*, relying on faith in human ingenuity to adapt to any calamity that may arise. We can place our faith in a more mystical vision, determined to stubbornly endure and 'carry the light' of humanity as long as possible, like the heroes in *The Road*. We can graciously accept our fate and succumb to the inevitable, superior power of nature, as Hoffman does, or fight to the death, as Pollack does, in *The Last Winter*. Or we can simply continue our normal, multi-tasking routines, oblivious to the hints of potential horror that lie at the periphery of our daily lives until it is too late, as M. Night Shyamalan suggests at the end of *The Happening*.

Whatever our response, nature will be waiting – and perhaps watching. As Larry Fessenden reminds us, 'horror is not a genre. It's a reality.'[28]

Notes

1 *The Last Winter*, dir. Larry Fessenden, IFC Films, 2006.
2 *The Happening*, dir. M. Night Shyamalan, Twentieth Century Fox, 2008.
3 *2012*, dir. Roland Emmerich, Centropolis Entertainment, 2009.
4 *The Road*, dir. John Hillcoat, Dimension Films, 2009.
5 Neda Ulaby, '"Eco-Horror:" Green Panic on the Silver Screen', *All Things Considered*, NPR, 14 June 2008, http://www.npr.org/templates/story/story.php?storyId=91485965 (accessed 3 July 2009).
6 'Eco-anxiety', *Word Spy*, http://www.wordspy.com/words/eco-anxiety.asp (accessed 3 July 2009).
7 Justin Nobel, 'Worried about Environmental Doom? Go See an Eco-therapist', *Columbia News Service*, 13 March, 2007, http://jscms.jrn.columbia.edu/cns/2007-03-13/nobel-ecoanxiety (accessed 2 July 2009).
8 Emily Anthes, 'Climate Change Takes a Mental Toll', *The Boston Globe*, 9 February 2009, http://www.boston.com/lifestyle/green/articles/2009/02/09/climate_change_takes_a_mental_toll (accessed 13 February 2009).
9 Quoted in Daniel B. Smith, 'Is There an Ecological Unconscious?', *New York Times Magazine*, 27 January 2010, http://www.nytimes.com/2010/01/31/magazine/31ecopsych-t.html (accessed 2 June 2010).
10 Kirsten Moana Thompson, *Apocalyptic Dread: American Film at the Turn of the Millennium* (Albany: State University of New York Press, 2007), pp. 1–2.
11 Ibid., p. 3.
12 Smith, 'Is There an Ecological Unconscious?'
13 Joyce Carol Oates, 'Introduction', in *American Gothic Tales* (New York: Plume Penguin Books, 1996), p. 2.
14 Dr Nathan, 'Dreaming Alone: The Larry Fessenden Interview', *Quiet Earth*, 28 October 2008, http://www.quietearth.us/articles/2008/10/28/Dreaming-Alone-The-Larry-Fessenden-Interview (accessed 2 February 2009).
15 Sam Adams, 'Phantom Menace: *The Last Winter*'s Larry Fessenden Envisions the End – with Monsters', *Philadelphia City Paper*, 3 October 2007, http://www.city-paper.net/articles/2007/10/04/phantom-menace (accessed 3 July 2009).
16 Larry Fessenden, 'From the Director', Notes (August 2006), http://www.glas-seyepix.com/html/notlw.html (accessed 7 May 2009).
17 Dr Nathan, 'Dreaming Alone'.
18 Wheeler Winston Dixon, *Visions of the Apocalypse: Spectacles of Destruction in American Cinema* (London: Wallflower Press, 2003), pp. 2–3.
19 David Punter and Glennis Byron, *The Gothic* (Oxford: Blackwell, 2004), p. 263.
20 Tom Pyszczynski, Sheldon Solomon and Jeff Greenberg, *In the Wake of 9/11: The Psychology of Terror* (Washington, DC: American Psychological Association, 2002), p. 8.
21 Ibid., p. 15.
22 Ibid., p. 16.
23 Ibid.
24 Greg Garrard, *Ecocriticism* (London: Routledge, 2004), pp. 85–107.
25 Stephen D. O'Leary, *Arguing the Apocalypse: A Theory of Millennial Rhetoric* (Oxford: Oxford University Press, 1994), p. 68, citing Kenneth Burke, *Attitudes*

toward History (Berkeley: University of California Press, 1984), p. 3, and Susanne K. Langer, *Feeling and Form* (New York: Charles Scribner's Sons, 1953), p. 326.

26 Jack Morgan, 'Toward an Organic Theory of the Gothic: Conceptualizing Horror', *Journal of Popular Culture* 32/3 (Winter 1998): 59–80, at p. 65.

27 Langer, *Feeling and Form*, p. 331, quoted in Morgan, 'Toward an Organic Theory of the Gothic', p. 63.

28 Adams, 'Phantom Menace'.

12

Emily Carr

The riddle was the angel in the house: towards an American ecofeminist Gothic

Ecofeminist literacy: three propositions

One: feminism involves the social analysis of structures of domination.
Two: ecocriticism explores the theoretical principles of life's interdependence.
Three: there is no three to what I know.

Three: ecofeminism, as I define it, occurs at the intersection of gender justice, animal rights and environmental conservation. It goes beyond active intervention in the specific historical conditions of production and reproduction of coherent categories of men and women, wilderness preservation, reservoir management, recycling programmes or alternative energy experiments, bicycles, health food stores, PETA, cruelty-free shampoo and engendered or endangered species to remake our (human) attitude towards our (natural) world at the cellular level: the level of language. It is coyote from the start and this is one of the reasons we need it. Donna Haraway argues that '[p]erhaps our hopes for accountability, for politics, for ecofeminism, turn on revisioning the world as coding trickster with whom we must learn to converse'.[1] I want to add 'word' to 'world': first and foremost, we must change our writing practices if we want to rearticulate social subjectivity as 'a shape changer, who might trouble our notions – all of them: classical, biblical, scientific, modernist, postmodernist, and feminist – of "the human"'.[2] Any hope for an ecofeminist conscience hinges on our ability to imagine outside the bounds of the 'common' language.

Being literary, as Anne Carson puts it, 'desensorializes the words and reader'.[3] A reader must disconnect herself from her other sensory impressions to concentrate on sight. Language, as we know it, 'separates words from one another, separates words from the environment, separates words from the reader (or writer) and separates the reader (or writer) from [her] environment'.[4] Our literacy, in other words, has significant psychological impact on our daily experience of the world; it creates, on the one hand, the illusion that there is a world and there are selves to be conveyed in language and, on the other, that there is a language that can create a world or a self. Either way, language is something inserted between consciousness and things and works to propagate the illusion that we inhabit a dialectical world of subject and object.

Ecofeminist literacy, as I understand and practise it, intervenes in the rhetorical construction of the politics, history and memory that is commonly known as humanity. It teaches us strategies for dislocating our anthropocentric assumptions about, for example, who speaks and for whom;[5] what it means to suffer; the logical fallacies and cultural blind spots that lead to the supremacy of the 'sentient'; the linguistic sleight of hand that turns bodies into commodities; and the deep-rooted (however we might try to deny it) assumption that our obligations to our home, the Earth, and the creatures that inhabit it are economic rather than ecological. Ecofeminist literacy is not so much a theory as an invitation: to debunk the singular survival and ethical centrality of the human self. What's specifically ecofeminist in this invitation is the need to:

1. Continue the transmogrification of the 'sane', the 'responsible', the 'whole', the 'reliable', the 'useful' and the 'necessary' that began with the inclusion of women and men and women of all races into the category of humans with rights – to own and inherit property, to guardianship of children, to be paid for services rendered, to vote, to birth control, to the pursuit of happiness…

2. Articulate the real costs of the continued linkages between woman (whoever she might be) and any body (a chicken or a cyborg or Eden, our Earth) that resists its economic currency.[6]

3. Restore consciousness, inventiveness, intention and cultural context to 'other' animals (and this includes women and children).

4. Investigate what happens when the object of alterity of which one presumes to speak begins 'to lose its status as an object, a given, already set thing' to which one can refer as if one 'were not involved in its construction'.[7]

5. Model, as an alternative to anthropocentrism, biodegradable thought: 'a thought for composing beings, for being decomposed and recomposed, for being compost'.[8]

6. Revisualize the human intelligence that is language so that intuition, instinct and emotion are valued as valid ways of knowing and important sources of morality.

7. Reconnect language with sensory experience – no, more than that, with *carnal participation in the world.*

The moral of ecofeminism is quite simply this: the world quite literally suffers from a lack of imagination.

Second novels! Such accursed children!

I mean it: *the world quite literally suffers from a lack of imagination.* So I will start with a characteristically Gothic move: the transgression of a boundary. Reading beyond the canon is one lesson we should learn both from ecofeminism and from the Gothic. We *know* canons are essentially literary institutions or social contracts that create specific publics for particular texts. And yet we continue to produce our scholarship according to the dictates of the popular and the long-lived. We might, for example, expand the scope of our conversations about the female Gothic to include contemporary women writers but we're all still talking about the same writers: in America, for example, Margaret Atwood, Alice Munro, Shirley Jackson, Angela Carter, Toni Morrison and so on. What we need – in any genre and using any critical apparatus – is to talk about *more* women writers and more diversity of women writers. In the Western world, white male writers continue to occupy an overwhelming majority of the space of literary production.[9]

In winter 2011, the Canadian poet and feminist activist Sina Queyras offered the following advice for challenging this trend on her *Lemonhound* blog:

1. An all women's issue is not the answer.
2. Demand a more vigorous and diverse literary weave.
3. Make a path for female intellectuals.
4. Don't let the bastards make you bitter.
5. The art of pitching isn't hard to master.
6. Biggen your ideas and aim straight at the canon.[10]

Through my case study of Joy Williams's strangely beautiful, marvellously disobedient and very Gothic second novel *The Changeling* (1978), I intend to do just that: aim straight at the canon and demand a more vigorous and diverse literary weave. In the early days of imagining this essay, I thought I would chart an American ecofeminist Gothic lineage from Shirley Jackson (whose international canonical status, I think we all can agree, scholarship has already secured) and Joy Williams (who is widely taught in creative writing workshops in

American MFA programmes but who is not treated by academics as an object of either scholarship or pedagogy and whose reputation remains a distinctly American phenomenon). I felt that it was essential that I *locate* my approach to ecofeminism in the twenty-first century in America because that is the world I have inhabited for most of my life. I still believe that. However, nearly a year later, in the now of writing, I have quite intentionally decided to locate my ecofeminism *outside* the canon and *without* lineage.

What I want – no, more than that, *need* – to do in this essay is carve out a uniquely American ecofeminist Gothic space for Williams. Williams embodies a darkly rebellious strain of what Gertrude Stein has called our 'wholehog American optimism'. By which I mean both maverick and caring. Williams believes very much in the now and the self. However, she also understands our American penchant for reinventing ourselves through radical individualism and turning the future into a cold commodity through the feeding frenzy of the now as utterly preposterous. As a writer and an activist, Williams wants more than what she calls the false sentiment of 'lyrical recall'.[11] She wants to *be*.

In *Ill Nature* (2001), her essay collection, Williams writes – not surprisingly – in an 'unelusive and strident and brashly one-sided' style (175) about commercial shrimping, safaris, Cabbage Patch Dolls, the Unabomber, John Audubon, the sunny eccentric packaged playground that is Florida, *in vitro* fertilization and the 'indulgent American women … clamouring for babies, babies, BABIES to complete their status' (79); about the extinction of wildebeests who, with their 'big, cubistic heads and mismatched features' are 'dying over and over again against the indifferent fence with the water just beyond it' (39–40); in praise of the shark and former punk-metal headliner Wendy Williams, who in middle age moves 'from the right to be smutty to the right to die violently by her own hand' (100); and about her own decision to preserve one acre in the Florida Keys because she 'did not feel that the land was mine at all but rather belonged to something larger that was being threatened by something absurdly small, the ill works and delusions of – as William Burroughs liked to say – *homo sap*' (113).[12]

Williams's politics are definitively non-, anti- and counter-conventional and, like the Gothic, celebrate the often terrifying consequences of articulating what should have gone unsaid, the mysterious and sometimes sinister underbelly behind the clean white porch of normal American life. Williams does not write to reassure: not herself and certainly not us. She writes out of an ethical imperative to reorganize the moral and ontological ground with which intentional human beings interact meaningfully not only with each other but also with the ecologies they have chosen (not perhaps willingly but merely by virtue of their belonging to them) to take responsibility for.

And I want to be very careful here: ethical is not the same as sane, responsible or normal. Ethical, as Williams imagines it, means changing the mind that conceives, and accedes to, that composition of the real we acknowledge as world.[13] In his introduction to Fairy Tale Review Press's thirtieth anniversary edition of *The Changeling*, Rick Moody sums the story up as:

> chiefly concerned with the lucky and unlucky fortunes of a drink-afflicted young woman called Pearl (and the resonances with the identically named urchin of Hawthorne's *Scarlet Letter* don't seem out of place, summoning up as they do the Gothic scaffolding of that romance). Pearl, who works hard to escape the clutches of a sinister extended family on an island enclave of the Northeast, nonetheless, after surviving a plane crash, finds herself back in the domestic fold, desperately looking for another method of egress, while the feral children of the island gather around her. Among them is her own estranged son, Sam, who may or may not have been swapped with an even more wild child in the disorderly aftermath of her aeronautical accident.[14]

That is it, more or less. The plot, however, also includes – in no particular order – shoplifting, abduction, marriage, seduction, masturbation, menstruation, an electrical storm, a scene in which Pearl mistakes her son Sam for a deer, a scene in which Pearl refuses to eat birthday waffles, a shopping expedition to a gay and civilized resort town, a life-sized puppet show in an abandoned church metamorphosed into a community centre, fish soup and a conversation about Faust to piccolo music at The Silent Woman, a madwoman in the attic, family conflict with supernatural histories, a retelling of *Scheherazade*, divine punishment, outlandish personifications, mixed metaphors, surreal imagery and death.[15] Death by accident, death by kitchen knife, death by shotgun, death by fable, death by education, death by suggestion, death for no reason at all, death at the hand of God, death for the love of a young interning priest and death by intoxication.

Readers who want to know *what the moral is* or perhaps, merely, *what really happened*, will find themselves forced to sit back and relax. True to the Gothic genre the real and the unreal, the domestic and the grotesque, the alluring and the terrible coexist. The everyday is collapsed with the nightmarish; distortion, dislocation and disruption become the norm. Williams's ecofeminist Gothic romance literally enchants 'while it explodes in the reader's face'.[16] The story Williams tells is so unreal, so alarming, so precise really. Some strands of its Gothic imagination and some strands of the contemporary ecofeminist Gothic thus forage into issues of beauty (as agency) versus the beautiful (as thing), desire (how it looks) versus love (what it means), the problem of becoming a person you did not intend to become, the myth of marriage, who has the 'social sanction to define the larger reality into which everyone's everyday experiences must fit in order that one can be reckoned sane and responsible', and the links between questions of autonomy and that of living well:[17] not limiting autonomy to a frame of mind or a social condition but drawing attention to 'voice (and silencing), power (appropriation and transcendence), nature (as opposed to formation and culture), [and] gaze (framing, specularity, fragmentation)'.[18]

It is thus important to mention, before I embark on my reading of it, that when *The Changeling* was first published in 1978, it was burned and buried alive in a review by Anatole Broyard in the *New York Times*. Williams's first book had been nominated for the National Book Award and there was an eager and not insubstantial audience awaiting the publication of her second. At the time, Broyard was, nonetheless, ruthless in his reading of the very kinds of linguistic innovation that I now praise for their ecofeminist resonances. In the final paragraphs of the review, Broyard writes:

> I believe it would be a salutary exercise for both reader and writer if we begin to take the rhetoric of the avant-garde literally, to assume that the words on the page mean what the dictionary says they do. When Miss Williams writes, 'Oh to bring back the days when stars spoke at the mouths of caves', I feel entitled, perhaps even obliged, to ask, 'Which days were those?' When she writes, speaking of Pearl, that 'she was young but some day she would be covered with ants', I want to know how the author can tell that she will be covered with ants and how I am expected to employ this information.
>
>   When Miss Williams writes that 'Pearl dropped the brush and gripped her breasts and her eyes and her head in one complex and despairing gesture', I propose to object to that image on the grounds that I can't visualize it. When I read of the children's 'condor eyes' or of 'the tremendous human darkness', I am not going to give the author the benefit of the doubt. There have been too many doubts and too many benefits, and perhaps Miss Williams has fallen victim to them.[19]

Phrases like 'when stars spoke at the mouths of caves', 'some day she would be covered with ants' and the children's 'condor eyes' are precisely the sort of linguistic relocations that remind us of all we miss out on when we blindly accept whatever is currently being assumed to be True. There is a pre-cultural, pre-discursive approach to 'reality' that does not rely on the autonomous human intellect but rather accepts that our perceptual and conceptual relationship with the world is fraught with ambiguity. This kind of organizing intellect is not avant-garde but *necessary*:[20] if, that is, we are to overcome our collective illusions and conservative categorical identifications with 'human' nature, 'human' creation, 'human' activity, 'human' intelligibility and 'human' rights.

What is human nature changes – it can, and must. Likewise people.

Fortunately, history has decided to give 'Miss Williams' the benefit of the doubt; the University of Arkansas reissued the novel in 2008. And just what, one must ask, has changed? Moody hypothesizes that 'the late seventies, with their punk rock nihilism and their Studio 54 fatuousness, were perhaps not properly situated to understand' the challenges of Williams's 'arresting improbabilities of magic realism', surrealistic folklore and 'modernist foreboding'.[21] In an interview with Tao Lin, Williams herself speculates:

> [t]he late 70s were a tough time for women novelists. We were supposed to be feminist, engaged, angry. It was really, weirdly, a very conformist time ... *The Changeling* is about a guilty young drunk named Pearl on an island with feral children. The prose is lushly stark and imaginative, the method magical, even demented. Feminism did not need a guilty drunk![22]

I am more inclined to agree with Williams. At a time when women are actively asserting the significance of *women's* literature and *women's* rights, Pearl is not a good role model.[23] She lacks free will, hope or optimism; she is woman at her most polluted:[24] all 'bodily urges and meanings'.[25] She avoids significance 'as the bird does the snare ... Each moment that occurred lay mute within her, a buried stone, contained from and irrelevant to herself, an event with neither premonition nor consequence' (39). She feels that, if she could find 'a way of knowing who one was', she would 'not just be fucking all the time', which she does because she is not a contented person who has possessions or a child or is interested in and knowledgeable about 'a kinky subject, for example hockey or sharks' (39). Newlywed, she shoplifts in a foolish and very clumsy attempt to 'do something she had never done before and in that way discover something about herself' (40).

Not only does Pearl break the law stupidly and without any sense of purpose, she also does not seem to experience the right kind of

emotions when others die; she has neither ambition nor occupa-
tion; her agenda never quite seems to include anyone – including the
reader – besides herself; she lacks parental instincts and lives 'by sensation rather than intention' (72). Pearl, for example, leaves her all-
American, level-headed young husband for an enigmatic, handsome
and very rich Byronesque stranger named Walker who abducts her
to the 'family' island in 'the North', where she bears his bastard son,
whom she later claims is not her own but instead a changeling, 'something she had witnessed' (229). When Walker dies in a tragic plane
crash after finding her drunk in a cheap motel near Miami airport, she
eschews organized and comprehensive grown-up society for the incoherent, immoral, bewildering world of children and drink. She does not
want marriage; she does not want motherhood; she is, simply put, the
Adulteress and a bad mother.

The Adulteress. Animal, sexualized and without rights.[26]

A difficult heroine for any second-wave feminist to swallow.

What's at stake in the initial 'failure' and later 'success' of Williams's
novel is, indeed, not a question of its literary or artistic merit but rather
one of timeliness. As Anne Williams writes,

> [t]he advent of feminist criticism in the early 1970s coincided with a decline of
> the 60s mass market Gothic – a genre rigidly conventional in its female centered
> narrative and on its insistence that the author of the formula be a 'woman speak-
> ing to women' ... This convention and the popularity of the mode for the female
> audience could only distress a reader newly conscious of women in literature.
> For these stories seemed to confirm – both explicitly and covertly – the patri-
> archal view that what women want is a good (wealthy) husband, that getting
> married is the story of a woman's life, and that women (like Gothic heroines) are
> essentially passive and prone to hysteria.[27]

The women who star as Gothic heroines in the mass culture phenomenon epitomize everything that is wrong with conventional assumptions about the category of the feminine: its moral ambiguousness,
continual threat of self-dissolution, willingness to substitute recognition or love for independence and agency, and capacity – like animals
or the earth – for unnecessary suffering and seemingly endless giving
of, as Michelle A. Massé writes, 'person, property, attention, deference,
devotion, and identity'.[28]

Pearl, however, despite how she might characterize herself, exceeds
the prototypical 'good girl' of the 1960s Gothic; she is never only
or simply a victim. In fact, her decision to exclude herself from
'culture' – defined as 'the circulation of signs through the system of

marriage'[29] – can be read as a strategy for 'authoring' her own fate. Pearl is, for example, alienable but not property. Her body is the object of another's desire but is never made 'real'. Outside the system of marriage exchange, she is literally unlocatable. And this – at least in the twenty-first century in America – gives her agency.

The sexual politics of meat

It is worth, therefore, making a brief digression into the sexual politics of meat. The first sentences of *The Changeling* are these: 'There was a young woman sitting in the bar. Her name was Pearl' (23). Pearl was raised by God-fearing and kind-hearted parents, and her once-upon-a-time *seems* normal enough:

> people sat around her eating pretzel logs. The management advertised it as being cool and it was. There was a polar bear of leaded glass hanging in the center of the window. Outside it was Florida. Across the street was a big white shopping center full of white sedans. (25)

Pearl was holding her baby in the crook of her right arm; his name was Sam and he was, 'in fact, a very nice baby' (26). Tomorrow Pearl would cut her hair, put on a dress the right weight for the weather; she would forget the past; she would 'make every effort to relegate the gigantic physical world to its proper position' (27).

Through a series of flashbacks and flash-forwards, we quickly learn, however, that Pearl's problem is not just the drink; or at least it was not originally the drink. It is pure Gothic: Pearl is, like Daphne du Maurier's Rebecca and before her Charlotte Brontë's Jane Eyre, secluded on a lonely island populated by a dozen over-stimulated prepubescent orphans, more or less, who worry about 'nuclear power and volcanoes and Beethoven's deafness', and four or five adults, more or less related to Walker, the secretive, alluring and slightly threatening master figure who has kidnapped her, more or less (30). Thomas, Walker, Miriam and Shelly are family. Lincoln is Shelly's husband. Pearl suspects the old woman is Walker's mother and, thus, Sam's grandmother but also knows that she might in fact be nothing more than a phantom, some aspect of Pearl's 'fatuous, remorseful, and destructive self' (102).[30]

Pearl is no one – or, at best, the father of Walker's son, Sam. She briefly escapes to Miami but Walker tracks her down and, after striking her, says in a pleasant voice:

You should get out a little more, Pearl. You've become too self-obsessed. Get off
the island a bit. Don't go far. Go to Morgansport and have your hair done. Go to
a movie. Go to the fairgrounds and ride the wooden horses. (74)

Like the unnamed narrator of Charlotte Perkins Gilman's 'The Yellow
Wallpaper' (1892), Pearl is from the very beginning of the story made
to believe that the reason for her unhappiness – and, as a consequence,
failure to properly perform 'wife' and 'mother' – is the failure of her
own imagination.

Pearl's fears, however, are not those of an over- or under-active
imagination but rather arise from the nature of reality itself. It is the
'meaningless hazards' of life that haunt her gin-fuelled nightmares. The
world that slumbers beneath the world of appearances is, for Pearl, 'the
same world, both painful and boring at once, savage and playful, radi-
ant and hideous, benignant and inspired' (152). It is a world in which
a pilot flies 'serenely into the aurora of grasses that was the Everglades'
and flesh and metal fuse; 'damaged and distorted' objects give 'no clue
as to what they once had been' but seem 'cruelly, senselessly alive'; 'a
fishing feeding creature whose destiny had crossed a more powerful
and inept one' dies by the impact of a plane crash; owls feed on 'the
abundant meat of despair'; a baby covered with ointment and lying
on greased paper looks 'much like fish *en papillote*'; the bones of fishes
bang 'in their sockets like guns going off'; in a stinking swamp people
are 'metamorphosing into so much meat and probate' (81–6).

This fantastic cocktail of the monstrous, the seared and the intoxicated is a particularly powerful articulation of Carol J. Adams's ecofeminist theory of the sexual politics of meat. With her triple exploration
of sex, politics and meat, Adams encourages an attentiveness to the
political and ethical dimensions of the discourses that turn bodies (of
women, of animals, of the Earth) into absent referents: artefacts of
language that are to be confronted, avoided and/or redefined. Absent
referents (like water, meat or woman) refer to 'something or someone
that has a very particular, situation life, a unique being' that 'is converted into something with no individuality, no uniqueness, no specificity, no particularity'.[31] Absent referents offer origin, replenishment,
service; they refer not to actors but to mobile, man-made commodity-
concepts we cannot do without. Adams's theory motivates us, thus, to
consider how terms like 'chick', 'hamburger', 'bitch', 'veal' and even
'environment' are in fact dissociative manoeuvres that relegate the
actual woman, animal or ecology to some periphery or backdrop role.
What are our *real* wants and needs when it comes to the consumption

of animal flesh and which language uses are we willing to accept when talking about feminine and non-human creatures?

I mean it. What *are* our real wants and needs? Under what kinds of discursive constraints is self-constitution or reconstitution as a personal and historical subject possible? Whether or not we eat meat, what is the real damage we do when we go along with the language practices dictated by Culture-At-Large? Consider, for example, the self-deceptions that are regularly practised not only when we ordinary, moral, conscientious people eat meat but also and more importantly when we consent to labelling women with terms that 'derive from domesticated female animals: cow, pig, sow, chick, hen, old biddy'.[32] We need new ways of speaking that do *not* precede and pre-empt political responses to our Others or action on behalf of those Others.

Let us review: Pearl (yes indeed, so aptly named!) starts the day with half a gallon of cold white wine and transitions to gin and tonics at dusk. She is 'removed from everything, floating through space, exorcising longing' while she listens to the children's garbled theories about sex, love, birth, whales, dreams and the Bible (131–2). Once Pearl 'thought that she was crazy and that she might get well. She thought that she had to be herself. But there was no self. There were just the dreams she dreamed, the dreams that prepared her for her waking life' (240). Now, having become a wife and a mother, she is tired of the adult's life of decorum (witnessing and responding) and she wants to expose the skeleton inside, to 'make manifest the death within' (225). That or she wants to become 'the animal inside her', 'the little animal curled around her heart, the beast of faith that knew God' (225). Or maybe she wants to live, as a child or an animal, 'without mediation or exception', her mind 'smooth and sunny' (210, 216).

Pearl has many theories for her addiction. She drinks, for example, to get beyond the understanding reflected in the oval irises of her son's eyes. She drinks 'in the hope that her drunkenness would produce a clarity that would usher her into effective love' (133). She drinks to feel 'her whole body gleaming with it' (133). She drinks so she will not become confused about the passage of time. She drinks out of a 'simple desire for communion with the essential ultimate' (168). She drinks because she is 'mad and homeless … furthest removed from the blessing of God' (172). She drinks because '[t]o become a woman was to become a question when as a child one was all swift and shining answer' (173). She drinks because she feels she is 'renting space here in this life' (200). She drinks because she is Pearl, the Adulteress: the quintessential American absent referent.

She tells herself these things, at any rate. What she tells the children when they ask is that she drinks because it makes her bones blossom:

> The children love the image of it and could see the truth. They could see a fragrant branching tree of bones transformed into flowers. But when they kissed her they could taste only the unhappiness in which she dwelled. They could taste no sweet blossoms at all. (110)

Addiction, after all, is not a strategy and no one knows when it is finished.

Rerum concordia discors[33]

The Changeling's apocalyptic penultimate scene is starkly Gothic: Shelly is drowning in the children's pool, Miriam is unconscious on the kitchen floor, Lincoln lies with blood on his mouth in the sauna, Thomas is beating Pearl and calling her a bitch, Pearl and Thomas have fucked or Thomas has raped Pearl, Pearl has had a baby a few days before and still hurts from it, the children are tearing Thomas apart and it is their birthday, the old woman has forgiven Pearl, she is not angry with her any more, she will leave now. And Pearl herself? She is 'the drunken vision scarcely outlined in the darkness, the inchoate body of the dream at last perfectly recalled' (244). She crouches on the wet ground and listens to the sound of the animals breathing in the summer night:

> Puuuuurl Puuuuurl it's my turn let me let me! He's like a cyborg maybe don't cry Trip read about them a long time ago he says they'll use a brain to fly the brain of an unborn child is the perfect thing to use on an otherwise unmanned flying ship it can go everywhere it can know everything when he smiles it stops raining all over the world it's just a mirror there all greasy so greasy you could write on it the world is happening everywhere at once isn't it nice not there here it's gloomy there Pearl it's empty too the harm's been done they're not here not truly you're the only person here and you're with us the others live in a mad world in the midst of strangers you remember that the struggle to love to eat to beware. (244–5)[34]

What 'moral' there is to *The Changeling* is about narrative rupture, linguistic dissolution and violent, carnal death. Pearl's exhausted imagination, finally, is no match for the struggle between time and herselves, between a survivor's guilt and a mother's need to provide a future for her child. *The Changeling*'s final chapter is to all intents and purposes an inarticulate, intoxicated, unpunctuated six-page run-on sentence that quite literally ends with 'no words': 'we are with you there that's it quiet now there are no words for what you think Pearl there are no words for us words turn back Puuuuurl' (250).

Rather than ending in any way we understand a narrative to, Williams's novel works backwards along the evolutionary spiral to return the written word to its pre-literate, more sensible roots.[35] Punctuation, as American poet Brenda Hillman argues,

> was developed to bring out meaning in the oral delivery of [written] words. When the idea of punctuation began, marks were inserted by readers or scribes, not, for the most part, by writers ... so silent reading and the art of punctuation arrive in the same few centuries, bringing a different relation between interpretation and experience itself.[36]

I agree: punctuation creates hierarchies within sentences, privileges some clauses while subordinating others, closes some words and opens others, makes syntax happen, creates rhythm and emphasis, regulates silence and forms 'pre-meaning events'.[37] Punctuation ostensibly 'guides' readers through what would otherwise be a labyrinth of words. Punctuation, however, also limits words' possibilities, signalling one meaning over another and, in effect, turning words themselves into absent referents: 'bloodless', 'flat-footed', 'lost', 'cold' and 'mechanistic' artefacts 'increasingly disengaged from [their] association with the natural world'.[38]

There are, indeed, real costs to conforming to standard grammatical practices. When, for example, we hold to our anthropocentric standards of communication we forget that 'the most eloquent signs of pain, human or animal, are non-linguistic'.[39] The reality is that it would behoove us – as responsible citizens – to relearn how to listen to, for example, the feminine, the frightening and the irresistible. The reality is that life is confusing and words, with their propensity for exaggeration, for the fabulous, for the colloquial, for the melancholy, the obscene, the forbidden and the unspeakable, are such a bad witness. The reality is that entropy, collision and chaos are in fact useful strategies for refusing to become 'irretrievably part of a collectivity with only mass communications to shape its hopes, formulate its values and arrange its thinking'.[40]

And just what is the alternative? A kind of intelligence that emerges at the interstice between identity and non-identity: intelligible and unintelligible, rational and irrational, sensible and senseless. I said it before and I will say it again: don't expect answers. The reality is that, at its best, ecofeminism encourages us to ask the necessary questions.[41]

Has Pearl, for example, 'brought this disaster down upon them with her foolishness, her selfishness' (82)? Has the 'little sober person inside her risen up' and, as Pearl feared, strangled her, the 'little person being no friend' (208)? Like the prototypical Gothic heroine, are all her wounds in fact self-inflicted? Is the novel's final incoherent act in fact suicide?

And just what, in these postmodern days, are we making of suicide? Is Pearl's suicide a response to the hopelessness of excavating a free or original humanity beneath the layers of anthropocentric and patriarchal oppressions? Or can Pearl's suicide be, as Cesar Pavese writes, an 'act of ambition'?[42] If it cannot be redemption, can it be deliverance: the *right* to die tragically, and at a time of one's own choosing? Can we read suicide as enacting the poststructuralist idea of decentring the 'sane' or 'normal' human subject? Or is the moral this: that death (like nature or the human) exists as 'a collective illusion'?[43] Death is not death? Is there in fact no death at all but, as Blaise Pascal writes, merely 'the thought of death without dying', a double life past reinvention?[44] Could Pearl's suicide be a way of addressing un(re)solved feminist questions: does, for example, the female subject continue to (as in the early days of feminism) be symbolically fraught? And did feminism cause this and then fail to provide the answer?

Three: there is no three to what I know.

Three: the reality is that we are latecomers to the conversation that is life on this planet, Earth.

Three: the ecofeminist writes to serve not herself and not others but rather the realm of 'what lies beyond or behind the precarious web of semiotic constructions'.[45] She uses language in ways that challenge anthropocentrism, that dangerous frame of mind that turns the status of animals into a 'peripheral, even unworthy, concern'; children into 'those heirs, those hopes, those products of our species' selfishness, sentimentality, and global death wish'; and the word *environment* into – among other things – a 'marketable concept' with 'economic currency'.[46] The ecofeminist adapts, adjusts and improvises. She goes coyote: developing wiles for surviving, thriving and transcending the selves that are given us.

It will not be easy. There are few models available. Expanding the human consciousness while at the same time articulating that transformation in human terms so the rest of the species can – at least to some degree – understand it is a difficult task. And yet, now more than ever, when we are finally beginning to recognize and understand our role in destroying the ecologies of which we are only one small part, it is a *necessary* task.

Notes

1 Donna Haraway, *Cyborgs, Simians, and Women: The Reinvention of Nature* (New York: Routledge, 1990), p. 201.

2 Donna Haraway, 'Ecce Homo, Ain't (Ar'n't) I a Woman, and Inappropriate/d Others: The Human in a Post-Humanist Landscape', in J. Butler and Joan W. Scott (eds), *Feminists Theorize the Political* (New York: Routledge, 1992), pp. 86–100, at p. 98.

3 Anne Carson, *Eros the Bittersweet* (London: Dalkey Archive Press, 1986), p. 49.

4 Ibid., p. 50.

5 When I say anthropocentrism I am referring, following Haraway, to that strand of Western humanism that privileges 'the Enlightenment figures of coherent and masterful subjectivity, the bearers of rights, holders of property in the self, legitimate sons with access to language and the power to represent, subjects endowed with inner coherence and rational clarity, the masters of theory, founders of states, and fathers of families, bombs, and scientific theories – in short, Man as we have come to know and love him in the death-of-the-subject critiques' ('Ecce Homo', p. 87).

6 The body is, as Haraway writes in *Simians, Cyborgs, and Women*, a fungible concept that includes 'the human, the natural, and the artifactual' (187).

7 J. Bennett and W. Chaloupka (eds), *In the Nature of Things* (Minneapolis: University of Minnesota Press), p. xvi.

8 Jed Rasula, *This Compost: Ecological Imperatives in American Poetry* (Athens, GA: University of Georgia Press, 2002), p. 27.

9 See, for example, poet, critic and activist Amy King's 'The Count' on the website *Vida: Women in the Literary Arts*. The Count is an easy to read pie chart that details the percentage of male and female writers reviewed in major American publications like *The New York Times*. See http://www.vidaweb.org/the-count (accessed 17 July 2012).

10 Sina Queyras, 'The Gatekeepers and the Glass Ceiling, Notes Toward an Essay on The Count', *Lemonhound*, 24 February 2011, http://lemonhound.blogspot.com/2011/02/gatekeepers-and-glass-ceiling-notes.html, n.pag. (accessed 17 July 2012).

11 Joy Williams, *Ill Nature* (New York: Vintage, 2002), pp. 117. Subsequent references are to this edition and are given in parentheses in the text.

12 When Williams sold this acre, she protected its ecologies by including these deed restrictions: 1) The land could never be subdivided. 2) Buildings were restricted to one house and cottage taking up no more land than the originals. 3) The southern half of the property had to be left in its natural state as wildlife habitat (*Ill Nature*, p. 116). As a result, many realtors refused to even attempt to sell the property and Williams spent almost a year finding the right buyer.

13 Williams, *Ill Nature*, p. 62.

14 Rick Moody, 'Foreword', in Joy Williams, *The Changeling* (Tuscaloosa, AL: Fairy Tale Review Press, 2008), p. 14.

15 I mean this quite literally; the narrative scaffolding is sinuous and slinking, like a game of cat-and-mouse.

16 Williams, *Ill Nature*, p. 176.

17 R. Hubbard, 'Introduction', in R. Hubbard, M. S. Henifin and B. Fried (eds), *Women Look at Biology Looking at Women: A Collection of Feminist Critiques* (Boston: Hall, 1979), pp. i–xii, at pp. viii–ix.

18 Rachel Blau DuPlessis, 'Corpses of Poesy: Some Modern Poets and Some Gender Ideologies of Lyric', in L. Keller and C. Miller (eds), *Feminist Measures: Soundings in Poetry and Theory* (Ann Arbor: University of Michigan Press, 1994), pp. 69–95, at p. 71.

19 Quoted in Dwight Garner, 'Joy Williams's 30-Year-Old-Comeback Novel', *The New York Times*, 21 April 2008, http://artsbeat.blogs.nytimes.com/2008/04/21/joy-williamss-30-year-old-comeback-novel/, n.pag. (accessed 3 June 2011).

20 In fact, creative writers and literature scholars in the United States would (and do) consider Williams's *oeuvre* to be 'mainstream' rather than avant-garde.

21 Moody, 'Foreword', p. 13.

22 Tao Lin, 'An Interview with Joy Williams', *Bookslut* (November 2008), www.bookslut.com/features/2008_11_013681.php, n.pag. (accessed 3 June 2011).

23 In the United States in the 1970s and 1980s, women were fighting for the right to contraceptives, to divorce by mutual consent, to the equal division of common property, to equal pay, to federal financial assistance and to abortion.

24 In her essay 'Dirt and Desire: Essay on the Phenomenology of Female Pollution in Antiquity', Anne Carson argues that, since Aristotle and Hippocrates, the female identity has been characterized as pliant, porous, mutable, lacking both the power to control her boundaries and any sort of reliable concern for them: 'Women, then, are pollutable, polluted and polluting in several ways at once. They are anomalous members of the human class, being, as Aristotle puts it, imperfect men … They are, as social entities units of danger, moving across boundaries of family and house, in marriage, prostitution, or adultery. They are, as psychological entities, unstable compounds of deceit and desire, prone to leakage.' Anne Carson, *Men In the Off Hours* (Toronto: Knopf, 2000), pp. 130–152, p. 143.

25 Joy Williams, *The Changeling* (Tuscaloosa, AL: Fairy Tale Review Press, 2008), p. 72. Subsequent references are to this edition and given in parentheses in the text.

26 I am referring to rights of all kinds: inheritance rights, parental rights, land rights, human rights even.

27 Anne Williams, *Art of Darkness: A Poetics of the Gothic* (Chicago: University of Chicago Press, 1995), p. 7.

28 Michelle Massé, *In the Name of Love: Women, Masochism, and the Gothic* (Ithaca, NY: Cornell University Press, 1992), p. 22.

29 Haraway, 'Ecce Homo', p. 94.

30 It is difficult to determine exactly what role the old woman, who might or might nor be Sam's grandmother, plays in Williams's story. According to Pearl, the old woman is raising Sam and giving him the hope that Pearl cannot. Pearl believes that Sam loves the old woman but to Pearl, she is a figure of the monstrous feminine,

a terrible and primal being: 'belonging to a world so little realized, that it seemed preferable to ignore her. The others did. They had, as far as she could tell, forgotten she existed ... She lived half like an animal in her room, but then again, half not, rather a dignified and rapacious matriarch with a face shaped by age and conviction into the edge of an opposing weapon' (150). Pearl is convinced that her son converses with the old woman (who might, very well, be nothing more than a figment of Pearl's own monstrous imagination) as 'it is said animals converse with death' (154).

31 Carol J. Adams and Marjorie Procter-Smith, 'Taking Life or "Taking Life?"', in Carol J. Adams and Marjorie Procter-Smith (eds), *Ecofeminism and the Sacred* (New York: Continuum, 1993), pp. 295–310, at p. 298.

32 Emily Carr, 'Interview with Carol J. Adams', *dandelion* 35/2 (2010): 29–38, at p. 35.

33 According to Friedrich Nietzsche, the 'discordant concord of things': *The Gay Science*, ed. Walter Kaufman (New York: Vintage, 1974), p. 56.

34 According to Pearl, animals are children, or like flowers or stars – 'part of one large animal of God, the heart pounding and never breaking' (244).

35 I mean 'sensible' in the double sense here, both as a sane and realistic approach to a problem or a situation and as those faculties by which the body perceives physical stimuli.

36 Brenda Hillman, 'A Cadenced Privacy', in M. McQuade (ed.), *By Herself: Women Reclaim Poetry* (Saint Paul: Graywolf, 2000), pp. 172–86, at p. 174.

37 Ibid., p. 175.

38 Williams, *Ill Nature*, p. 5.

39 B. Rollin, *Animals Rights* (Amherst, MA: Prometheus Books, 2006), p. 32.

40 Malcom Muggeridge, *A Third Testament* (New York: Ballantine Books, 2004), p. 81.

41 The taboos against speaking out against the culture of meat eating, for example, are subtle, strong and complex. Often, being nice – even being intelligent – means going along with the communal deception. Part of vegetarians' reluctance to speak out in certain public situations is, of course, respect. But we do ourselves and the larger world real damage when we go along with the taboo of silence.

42 Williams, *Ill Nature*, p. 102.

43 Ibid., p. 67.

44 Ibid., p. 4.

45 Bennett and Chaloupka (eds), *In the Nature of Things*, p. xi.

46 Williams, *Ill Nature*, pp. 133, 89, 107.

13

Sharae Deckard

'Uncanny states': global ecoGothic and the world-ecology in Rana Dasgupta's *Tokyo Cancelled*

> Nature takes its revenge for the debasement of the human being to an object of
> power, to raw material. (Adorno and Horkheimer, *Dialectic of Enlightenment*)[1]

Given that the world-system is a thoroughly differentiated physical
environment divided between zones of production in which peripheral
environments suffer heightened resource extraction and environmental
degradation in an age of accelerating climate crisis, developing a methodology attentive to the systemic nature of combined and uneven development across the world-ecology is an urgent task for environmental
literary studies. Adorno and Horkheimer argue that the Enlightenment's
production of a duality between externalized nature and internal human
nature serves to rationalize human domination of the material world,
but also threatens an eventual revolt of nature.[2] Adapting Fredric
Jameson's theory of the political unconscious, Adrian Ivakhiv has called
for a 'global-meteorological reading practice' of the 'geopolitical unconscious' in order to reverse 'ecological unconscionization', the ideological mystification of ecological destruction.[3] Ivakhiv argues that the
Cartesian project has 'repressed the entire network of biological interdependencies and corporeal confraternities that shape and structure
our material existence'.[4] Thus, he proposes 'a geopoliticized ecocriticism' to excavate ecopolitics in their 'latent and indirect manifestations'.[5] Ivakhiv's analysis of how such phenomena as military-industrial
nuclearization, petro-dependency and neo-imperialist devastation of
Mesopotamian environments are manifested as uncanny returns of the
repressed, storms of 'monstrous excrescences, gothic or sublime', is con-

fined to contemporary films such as *Magnolia* (1999) and *The Ice Storm* (1997).[6] However, in this chapter, I will attempt to elaborate a praxis for reading the capitalist world-ecology in Gothic literature, exploring how literary form can embed the social-ecological contradictions of capitalism. I offer here a case study of 'global ecoGothic', reading the viral excrescences and monstrous transformations of human bodies into vegetable matter in Rana Dasgupta's *Tokyo Cancelled* (2005) as Gothic apparitions that register the world-ecology, particularly the ecological regimes corresponding to neoliberalism and financialization.

Before turning to the novel, I wish to outline the elements of my literary methodology, which employs a geographical-materialist approach to texts informed by a world-systems-inflected environmental history of the ecological phases of capitalism. Ivakhiv's reformulation of world-systems theory opens up the possibility of a reading practice attentive to how texts register the uneven space–time sensorium of capitalist modernity, interpreting how unequal divisions of labour are inextricably linked to different phases of ecological extraction:

> The world-system [is] not only a political-economic one, in which social relations and psychic realities are predominantly shaped by the uneven economics of global capitalism, but also a political-*ecological* one, in which the warp and woof of uneven development and global inequality are directly related to the ways in which advanced industrial capitalism both commodifies and thoroughly transforms the natural world and our relationship with it.[7]

However, the environmental historian Jason W. Moore goes beyond Ivakhiv, arguing that the capitalist world-system is *itself* a 'world-ecology', a 'dialectic of plunder and productivity – appropriating nature's "free" gifts outside the commodity system to maximize labour productivity'.[8] He proposes that the history of capitalism can be understood not merely as having 'ecological dimensions' but as being constituted by a series of *ecological regimes* and *ecological revolutions*. Ecological regimes are the 'relatively durable patterns of class structure, technological innovation and the development of productive forces ... that have sustained and propelled successive phases of world accumulation'.[9] Because plunder exhausts the non-commodified relationships that allow capital accumulation to proceed, capitalism is always in search of new commodity frontiers for extraction and appropriation. According to Moore's studies of plantation monocultures and mining regimes in the Caribbean, the rapid appropriation of commodity frontiers undermines the socio-ecological conditions of profitability typically within 50–75 years in any given region, encountering not only biophysical limits to extraction but also the scarcities which 'emerge through the intertwining of resistances from labouring classes, landscape changes, and market flux – all specific bundles of relations between humans and the rest of nature, specific forms of *oikeios*'.[10] When ecological regimes are exhausted and no longer able to produce ever-greater ecological surpluses, thus failing to maintain the conditions of accumulation, then ecological revolutions occur, characterized by the extension of exploitation to new geographies, the extraction of new commodities, intensification of existing forms of extraction and the production of new technologies and social–nature relations.

Moore identifies three key phases among the ecological regimes of the *longue durée* of capitalism: colonization and plantation in the early modern period, the partition of Africa and the integration of Indian and Chinese peasantries into the world economy under high imperialism, and the neoliberal regime of accumulation via dispossession emerging from the 1970s. He argues that finance capital is itself an ecological regime:

> Financialization now seems to be actively driving the end of cheap food, resources, water and pretty much everything else. The large-scale penetration of finance capital into the global reproduction of human and extra-human nature represents a new era of nature–society relations in capitalism. From the agrofood sector to working-class households that depend on credit cards to pay groceries and medical bills, global nature has become dependent on a circuit of capital premised on accumulation by financial means rather than industrial and agricultural production. Finance capital in the neoliberal era has penetrated everyday life as never before, and in do so doing, has sought to remake human and extra-human nature in its own image.[11]

As David Harvey argues, capitalism perpetually displaces its contradictions through sectoral relocation, so that 'the geographical landscape of capital accumulating is perpetually evolving, largely under the impulsion of the speculative needs of further accumulation'.[12] Each ecological revolution only resolves the contradictions of the previous ecological regime by displacing and reconfiguring them on an expanded scale, producing cyclical crises and progressively deepening what Moore and John Bellamy Foster call the 'ecological rift', elaborating Marx's argument that the international extension of the town–country division of labour produces a 'metabolic rift' that enervates workers and drains the soil of nutrients:

> [Large] landed property reduces the agricultural population to an ever decreasing minimum and confronts it with an ever growing industrial population crammed

together in large towns; this produces conditions that provoke an irreparable rift in the interdependent process of social metabolism, a metabolism prescribed by the natural laws of life itself. The result of this is a squandering of the vitality of the soil, which is carried by trade far beyond the bounds of a single country.[13]

Bellamy Foster extends this trope beyond the exhaustion of soil nitrates to argue that capitalism's inexorable logic of accumulation creates a metabolic rift between society and nature, severing basic processes of natural reproduction and forcing periodic reorganizations of nature–social relations, which never heal the rift, but merely intensify it.[14] In the world-ecology, peripheries are drained of raw materials, minerals and nutrients, while cores are in excess, unable to process the waste, forced to relocate not only industrial production but also waste to peripheries. As anthropogenic climate crisis accelerates, the finite limits to resource extraction will intensify the social–ecological contradictions within capital. The totality of the world-ecology seems to pose an impossible challenge to representation. Yet it is precisely because the social and environmental transformations produced within the peripheries by the international division of labour are starker that the socio-ecological contradictions of the world-ecology are more visible in peripheral cultural forms, thus providing an interpretative horizon. As Elizabeth DeLoughrey and George Handley observe,

> Virtually every model of global climate change indicates that the global south is particularly vulnerable to the predicted increases in weather extremes, such as more prolonged droughts, more intensified but less frequent rainfall and flooding, rising sea levels, shifting migrations of flora and fauna due to temperature increases and even earthquakes.[15]

Stephen Shapiro has proposed that catachrestic narrative devices and genres such as the Gothic recur in literary history at similar moments in the recurring cycles of long-wave capitalist accumulation.[16] The Gothic originated in the transition from feudal economies based on land ownership and patrilineal property rights to bourgeois capitalism, registering in its phantasmagoria the medieval affects and remnants not wholly incorporated into the 'modern' regime of commodity relations. For Shapiro, world-systems theory

> relates political geography to economic history by mapping long waves of economic expansion and contraction caused by the intrinsic falling rate of profit generated by capitalist regimes of accumulation against the spatial reorganization of commodity chains.[17]

He thus proposes that structural homologies can be drawn between the aesthetics of subunits located at the same point within the recurring rhythmic cycles of commodity regimes – not necessarily the same point in chronological time – of the Kondratieff waves marking the boom-and-bust cycles of capital under its various reconfigurations. If ecology is added to this formulation, then ecoGothic can be understood as not only figuring the social deformations relating to the economic reorganization of societies, but also the reorganization of social–nature relations around different commodity regimes and the periodic exhaustion of ecologies. The cyclical, periodic emergence of catachrestic literary devices would register the conjuncture of fading and emergent ecological regimes, prognosticating ecological revolutions in nature–society relations, each more pervasive than the last. As Michael Niblett argues, 'World literature will necessarily register, at some level, ecological regimes and revolutions ... since these organize in fundamental ways the material conditions, social modalities, and areas of experience upon which literary form works.'[18] The violence attendant on ecological revolutions that radically reorganize forms of labour, everyday practices, subjectivities and bodily dispositions cannot help but permeate literary representations of social experience.

However, I will contend that the ecoGothic can be read not merely in the implicit manifestations of a geopolitical unconscious. Rana Dasgupta is representative of a generation of writers from the (semi-) peripheries of the world-system who consciously reactivate the potential of literary and oral forms developed in earlier regimes in order to critique the ecological regimes associated with the present phase of neoliberal, post-Fordist accumulation. Dasgupta is British-Indian, Canterbury-born, but resident in New Delhi, where he moved after giving up his job as a marketing consultant to become a writer. In an essay on the future of Indian fiction, Dasgupta contends that contemporary Indian novelists 'are not particularly concerned anymore by their country's colonised past [but rather] by its expanding, imperial future'. They imagine the novel form in Lukácsian terms as capable of representing the totality of social relations and figuring the metabolic rift, thus 'closing gaps in social perception' between classes blind to the pillaging of peripheral environments, peasants and tribals 'so remote for them as to be entirely unsubstantial' by using novels as 'effective laboratories ... that help to generate the full and coherent reality whose absence is currently so sapping to this society's life and spirit'.[19] The form and aesthetics of Dasgupta's own *Tokyo Cancelled* are constructed to correlate social–nature relations across multiple cores and peripheries in the world-system.

Modifying the narrative apparatuses of the Arabian Nights and Chaucer's *Canterbury Tales*, the book comprises a cycle of thirteen stories told by travellers stranded in a Tokyo airport shut down by a blizzard on the eve of a G20 summit and anti-globalization protest. The travellers' tales are set in the present, describing seemingly irreal events in urban cores and semi-peripheries around the world, and are linked by a frame narrative describing the travellers' interactions in the airport terminal. In *Tokyo Cancelled*, cities are uncanny spaces where the juxtaposition of the archaic and modern temporalities of combined and uneven development is registered most visibly. Their urban ecologies are characterized by what Mike Davis calls 'magical urbanism', the national temporalities, settlement forms, ecologies and levels of development, modes of wild capitalism and criminal economies which link cores and semi-peripheries, as when Asian pirate economies and black-market organ trades interpenetrate the metropolises of Europe.[20] The thirteen-story cycle dramatizes the traumatic impact of ecological revolutions on local ecologies and subjects in multiple world cities from Delhi, Istanbul, Lagos and Beijing to Paris, London and Tokyo. Recognition of complicity with global capitalism – its exploitation of peripheral ecologies through biopiracy and exhaustion of commodity frontiers; its reification of the human and of the nonhuman – is figured as returns of the repressed: outbreaks of magical plagues, hyperfecundity, sublime metamorphoses, the physical transmutation of humans into trees, birds, stone or other natural elements. The spectacles of financialization, post-Fordist consumption and outsourcing in the post-industrial societies of the cores are figured as uncanny states of the body: a plague of mass amnesia instigated by futures-trading in the City of London, a Goldman Sachs banker in Paris who is secretly a changeling, a woman's corporeal transformation into a department store in New York.

Fredric Jameson has famously called for the invention of new aesthetic forms to project 'a global cognitive mapping' of 'the world space of multinational capital'.[21] For Dasgupta, the paradox of narrating the totality of the world-ecology is that 'the more the world becomes interwoven the less it seems possible to tell a single, representative story of it – yet the connections are real and lived'.[22] In an interview he explains that the narrative structure of *Tokyo Cancelled* is intended to capture 'the idea of a unity that is architectural and dispersed' and to encapsulate 'the form of a map, a network'.[23] The narrative's time is deliberately compressed into one night even as the space of the stories rhizomatically traverses global geographies, freezing the motion of the traveller-storytellers in order to map the circulation of capital, labour and commodities across the world-system. The book generates a structure of linked tales that can 'admit the distances between places' but also reveal 'metaphors and analogies that connect them', what he calls a 'story-cycle' or a 'novel-in-fragments'.[24]

Dasgupta's designation of this structure as simultaneously 'more archaic' and 'more contemporary than either "novel" or "short stories"' is significant, suggesting its potential to embody incongruous mixtures of residual and modern formations and to transfigure the peripheral experience of ecological revolution in uncanny, irrational or magical terms.[25] Anthropologist Michael Taussig has observed that cultural formations consisting of fantastic reactions to 'nonfantastic' reality arise in peripheral societies as critiques of their violent integration into capitalist modes of production, citing examples of how the imposition of plantation and mining regimes produced popular tales of the devil.[26] In Dasgupta's contemporary tales, the Gothic registers the phantasmagoric transition to neoliberal ecological regimes, characterized by financialization, heightened privatization, intensified asset-stripping of peripheries, new forms of exploitation of biocapital, off-sourcing and the move from production to consumption in post-industrial cores. The tales self-consciously reactivate 'archaic' literary devices that had encoded earlier transitions (such as feudalism to bourgeois capitalism) in order to represent intensified subordination to the logic of the commodity form and to express the sensation of 'patent unreality' in the era of millennial capitalism.

The stories are preoccupied with the new forms of representational and mechanical technologies associated with neoliberal capitalism, particularly finance capital, speculation and biotechnology. Neoliberalism has been marked by a proliferation of biochemical, genetic, nanotechnological, robotic, computer and IT technologies, marking new commodity frontiers in capitalism's commodification of human and extra-human nature. In *Biocapital*, Kaushik Sunder Rajan critiques what he calls 'technoscientific capitalism', the marriage of biotechnology and market forces that has led to the corporatization of life sciences.[27] He argues that life sciences have become significant producers of both economic and epistemic value in the late twentieth and early twenty-first centuries, and that political-economic regimes are co-produced with the biological sciences. Just as the dot.com bubble was driven by information technologies, this phase of neoliberalism is dependent on biotechnology and the extraction of surpluses from new sources of biocapital, both human and non-human, whether through what Vandana Shiva has called 'biopiracy' of indigenous knowledge and peripheral environments or through genetic, pharmaceutical and surgical alterations of the human body.[28] The corporatization of science challenges its methodologies, epistemic assumptions and teleology. For Rajan, the rush to invest, patent and market biocapital is not primarily motivated by a positivist aim to progressively improve human life, communities or ecologies, but rather by inhumane economic imperatives. Biocapital generates new forms of abstraction of commodities, alienating not merely labour, but biological processes. As Jason Moore argues, since the 1970s' neoliberal turn, finance capital has 'decisively reshaped the rules of reproduction for the totality of nature–society relations – extending, horrifically, to the molecular relations of life itself'.[29]

For the remainder of this chapter, I will focus on four exemplary stories, two set in post-industrial European cores, and the other two in centres of development in the global South. In *Tokyo Cancelled*, the tales set in urban cores of the First World register the post-industrial shift from production to consumption and the spectacle of financialization, as well as the deepening exhaustion of the frontiers of appropriation which signals a crisis within neoliberalism. Anxieties about the patriarchal, heteronormative order of social relations that is allied to capital and yet seems threatened by new technologies that undermine the social and symbolic function of the family as a site of social and biological reproduction are expressed by a host of conflicts between fathers and sons throughout the stories. Paternal characters are guilty of acts of great violence, and are allied with the patriarchal order of capital, as corporate executives, investors, innovators and bankers. Children are dispossessed of their inheritances, deprived of access to resources or the prospect of a future. Families are haunted by simulacra, doppelgängers, twins, clones and automata, including a sex doll which comes to life in a masochistic reimagining of Hoffmann and stalks her Japanese owner (whose company is engaged in the biopiracy of South American plants), all figuring cultural anxieties about the 'monstrous' products of neoliberal technoscience. These doubles register the increasing fragmentation of autonomous human subjectivity and embody what Paul Virilio calls the 'industrial production of a personality split, an instantaneous cloning of living man, the technological recreation of one of our most ancient myths, the myth of the *double*'.[30] Furthermore, the proliferation of simulacra encodes a new level of commodity relations in which the image has become the final form of commodity reification.

In 'The Memory Editor', the consumer's appetite for a world transformed into sheer images of itself, for spectacles manufactured by industries which generate illusions of authentic experience, is encapsulated in a plague of amnesia that originates in the City of London and spreads through the world. Seeking to capitalize on the crisis, a multinational corporation creates a new product, 'Memory-mine', which bundles an individual's personal memory on to CDs, carefully excising any painful memories of social violence or inequality. Their extraction technology represents the apotheosis of the commodification of the human and the fragmentation of the body into alienable products, enabling the very stuff of human psyches to be sold. However, the corporation soon disintegrates when the plague of individual memory loss is superseded by the collective cultural amnesia generated by the company's products. The total fragmentation of social relations triggered by the corporation suggests the social and biophysical limits posed to the extraction of biocapital. The memory-mine is an image of commodity logic in which exchange value has been generalized to the extent that the very memory of use value is effaced, erasing the remaining traces of the division of labour and the sphere of production, and replacing the human subject with the corporate 'person'. The millennial form of neoliberal capitalism reconstitutes the human psyche, hollowing out modern subjectivity so that it is no longer defined by individual, familial or national identity, or in the previous capitalist *ethos* of economic productivity and rationality, but rather as 'an effect of images, consumer objects and the lifestyles they conjure up'.[31]

The plague of memory-loss, like other bodily disorders and transformations throughout the stories, is an uncanny realization of the ascendancy of speculative finance and its reorganization of social–nature relations. Capitalism's treatment of humans and extra-nature as resources to be exploited interchangeably results in a final erasure of the most basic component of human consciousness, memory, without which humans can be nothing but zombified consumers, driven to functionless, irrational consumption. In this story, the focus is on First World alienation, rather than on workers in the peripheries whose lives are transformed into dead labour to feed capitalist production. The ecoGothic transformation foregrounded is not the vampiric extraction of surpluses that drains wage-slaves of their labour vitality, but rather of identity itself. The only character to preserve his memory, Thomas, the estranged son of an arrogant stockbroker, is portrayed as obsessed with an irrecoverable past, photographing the city in an attempt to capture the spectre of the residual whose absence haunts him. In the story's fairy-tale ending, he becomes the bearer of residual culture into the future, an ark who preserves social memory and consciousness until such time as the plague resides, memories return and society can be reconstructed. The plague can thus be understood as a return of repressed consciousness of nature–human relations in which the crisis provoked by the plague produces a fissure in ideological certainty with the potential for the deconstruction and recomposition of established material structures and cognitive compartmentalizations.

In the 'The House of the Frankfurt Mapper', a Turkish illegal immigrant to Germany discovers an electronically projected map in a glass tower, which she has been forbidden to enter by her Bluebeardesque captor, Klaus:

> Everything was written over with a scurrying swarm of texts and symbols too dense even to make out ... Floating, ghostlike, behind the map, in the dark centre of the Pacific Ocean was the logo of Kaufmann Velocity Mapping AG.[32]

This map encapsulates the dynamics of neoliberal scientific-technological development, in which technologies of surveillance, transport, communication, data assessment and calculation have been integral to the development of 'just-in-time' production systems and the suppression of resistance.[33] The techno-sublime of Klaus's digital palimpsest figures the phantasmagoria of the disembodied, ghostly circulations of finance capital, its derivatives and sub-prime mortgage packages and futures. The story's setting wryly prefigures the dominance of Germany in EU economic policy and represents the international division of labour in neoliberal capital, in which a mobile precariat of illegal migrants fill service jobs in western European markets. On the map, Deniz sees her own country, Turkey, as a blank space, except where an oil pipeline has been sketched running from the Black Sea to Germany: it does not yet exist, but Klaus has portrayed it as already present, in order to rationalize resource extraction from Europe's eastern peripheries. His technological aim is to map the whole of nature's diversity and rationalize it within an algorithm that predicts 'the velocity of exchange' as a 'vital index for investors and policymakers', locating sectors where surpluses can be extracted (112). Klaus's rationalist cartography, whose totalizing categories regulate space in order to subject it to capital, is thus opposed to the novel's own cognitive mapping of the world-system through fabulist transformation tales.

When Deniz is sent by Klaus to work illegally in a local hotel as a maid, she encounters his uncanny twin 'Hans', who is identical in every aspect of his appearance, except for a more sinister and hungry air. She learns that he is responsible for the disappearance of women in the hotel: these wives of Bluebeard have not been murdered in passion but rather sacrificed as sex workers or as illegal organ donors. The official economy of financial speculation in which Klaus participates is thus shown to have an occult twin, the shadow economy of organized crime that manages the black-market trade in illegal labour, sex workers and bio-commodities. At the uncanny conclusion of the tale, Deniz returns to confront Klaus in his tower and sees what seems to be a swarm of pink butterflies obscuring his magic map, which she suddenly realizes are labia. These butterfly genitals, like the proliferation of disembodied limbs, orifices and wounds throughout the rest of the novel, are a return of the repressed which make visible the 'unspeakable things' in the shadow economies accompanying the rationalization of the neoliberal market: the sex trade in 'the love of women, love of men and if you were prepared to pay enough, the love of children'; the trade in biocapital, dismembered organs, body parts and human embryos: 'if you did not want whole people you could buy pieces'; and the draining of peripheral ecologies in the process of petrolic and mineral extraction (114).

Kaushik Sunder Rajan argues that contemporary biotechnologies such as genomics can only be understood in relation to the economic markets within which they emerge. 'The Billionaire's Daughter' is precisely concerned with the emergence of biotechnology companies in India. The story is set in New Delhi, and follows Rajiv, a CEO who diversifies his father's old-fashioned steel company into a 'global industrial empire' (54). Rajiv is afflicted with eternal insomnia, wandering like 'a ghost condemned to revisit a castle every night for eternity' (54). His perpetual wakefulness personifies the restless dynamism of capitalism and the neoliberal innovations in surveillance and information technology which characterize the regulation of the labour force in 'new India', whose ability to generate profit surpluses, according to Rajiv, 'will come not from any natural resource but from ... its one billion people awake while America's three hundred million sleep' (59).

Yet his own body bears witness to the trauma of the division of labour imposed between core and semi-periphery and the reorganization of the space–time sensorium enabled by combustion engines and internet technologies in the age of globalization. The disjuncture between the biological rhythms of human life and the temporalities in which capital and commodities circulate is described as a physical contradiction: 'He now carried Indian Standard Time in his guts into far-flung places, and there was an ear-splitting tectonic scraping within him as it went where it should never have been' (62). Rajiv ruthlessly extracts maximum efficiency in his hyper-efficient telecom centre, where 'every worker had to average thirty calls an hour' (56). His post-Fordist 'factory' of service workers is described as an uncanny 'insect battery', full of 'tiny vespine heads … trembling with larval energy', articulating ecophobic fears of dehumanization and swarm-like revolt (56).

However, Rajiv's own physical exhaustion incarnates the metabolic rift in neoliberalism's maximization of labour productivity. He is described as hollowed out, drained of all vitality: his body 'which had never learned to restore itself after expenditure, seemed to have shrunk correspondingly' (88). Jason Moore argues that neoliberalism's technological strategies have been primarily oriented towards driving down the costs of strategic inputs – the 'four cheaps' of labour, energy, food, resources – yet without generating a sufficient revolution in labour productivity that would address progressive ecological exhaustion and the contraction of opportunities for the commodity frontier strategy. For Moore, the global food crisis, the acceleration of 'yield suppression' for major cereal crops, looming peak oil, mounting pressures on aquifers, water scarcity, reduction in global cropland, all signal the decline of the first 'green revolution' and the exhaustion of human and biophysical natures.

Indeed, the last story of the collection, 'The Recycler of Dreams', specifically figures this food crisis and exhaustion in relation to the Argentine economic collapse of 2001, which itself prefigured the greater global crisis of 2008. The story encodes crisis through the bodily disorders affecting the main characters Gustavo and Carla, whose love affair is doomed never to be consummated because neither is able to eat. Though consumed by hunger, they violently vomit up everything they swallow, figuring the mass evacuation of capital from the Argentine economy, the hollowing out of social institutions and the collapse of the grazier monoculture. When a doctor comes to inspect Carla, he cuts her apart and inserts a beefsteak into her grotesquely opened stomach, exclaiming 'Sometimes we have to resort to extreme measures' (363). As she vomits it up again, the doctor smiles 'hollowly' and presents a bill worth more than Gustavo's life savings. The steak figures Argentina's main export, beef, returned by importers because of the deterioration of agri-industrial standards during the crisis, while the doctor's grotesque methods parody the savage austerity cuts and IMF debt inflicted even as capital drained offshore. The poor and dis-possessed were made to pay for the ineffective bailout, even as rising food prices rendered basic staples too expensive to acquire. Gustavo and Carla are reduced to a liminal, zombie-like state, unable to die, but unable to perform basic life activities: to pay rent, eat or work. As they read in the papers notices of crises in other world cities – plague in Paris, monkeys running wild in Frankfurt, all intertextual references to previous stories in the novel – Gustavo and Carla lament that 'The outside world seems to understand nothing of what has affected them' (364). The story thus offers the lived experience of macroeconomic crisis as an antidote to media representations which portray economic crisis as 'a mere blip in an abstract system, as if it were impossible to convey anything *felt* or *lived* about it'.[34] Instead, the metabolic rift pro-duced by the exhaustion of existing biological webs which had enabled profits in previous commodity regimes is figured as a somatic pathol-ogy of the 'digestive system', a condition of 'perpetual hunger and exhaustion', which figures the collapse of an ecological regime and an impending revolution in social–nature relations (364).

In 'Billionaire's Daughter', Rajiv's exhaustion and biological crisis of reproduction similarly embodies the exhaustion of an ecological regime and its inability to reproduce itself – 'his sleepless body incapa-ble of rejuvenating itself, would never produce seed' (60). His turn to 'biotechnology' as a cure for infertility parallels neoliberalism's search for new commodity frontiers in molecular components, as well as its failure to reverse the decline of productivity. The group of scientists whom he commissions to clone a child from his own genetic mate-rial is clearly driven by neoliberal market imperatives: 'to develop a patent portfolio of world-class sheep and cattle genetic material, and the techniques to exploit that material in the global agricultural mar-ketplace' (60). They successfully implant two cloned foetuses in Rajiv's wife, and she gives birth to twins: a 'shrunken misshapen' boy, Imran, and a beautiful girl named Sapna. The clone is an eerie 'manufactured animal', exemplary of artificial organic forms produced by biotechnol-ogy in the Anthropocene age – the non-genetic evolutions and food technologies that Bruce Sterling calls 'culturally-emerged nature'.[35] To

Rajiv's horrified eyes, Imran's 'outsized head' has the 'pointed shape of a cow's', a 'taurine air' that implies a monstrous intermingling of human and cattle biomaterial, a modern-day Minotaur which uncannily stages capitalism's reduction of human and extra-human life to interchangeable parts and marks the disintegration of the division between external nature and the human subject (64). Rajiv gives Imran away to a pair of adoptive parents and sets out to 'disremember' him, while lavishing all his affection on his extraordinary daughter.

However, Sapna is possessed of an uncanny fecundity. Her breath causes a 'nocturnal hypertrophy' that reverses the commodification of nature and brings *things* back to organic life: 'wherever Sapna slept, things burst into life: sheets, clothes, newspapers, antique wardrobes – all rediscovered their ability to grow' (67). This produces in Rajiv an overwhelming 'terror of vegetation', what Simon Estok would term 'ecophobia':[36]

> He would stare at the upstart plant matter that had invaded his daughter's room with the purest hatred he had ever felt. It began to take him over. He could not work for his visions of galloping, coiling roots and shoots. (67)

Sapna signifies the 'commingled, hybridized, chimeric future' of 'next nature', repudiating the myth of nature as 'a given, solid, static entity to be discovered, dissected and destroyed by human agency', and embodying nature–human relations as dynamic and mutually constitutive with capital. Fearful that she will inadvertently cause the reforestation of the entire city and seeking to protect her from the Defence Minister, who suggests militarizing her abilities in order to 'recultivate some of the desert regions', Rajiv locks her in a tall metal tower (69). Meanwhile, Imran grows 'slowly and unevenly', his disproportionate growth allegorizing combined and uneven development. After he is recruited by a toothpaste corporation to play the 'Plaque Devil', his 'much-prized deformity' becomes a commercial 'embodiment of every kind of threat to middle-class life: germs, crime, poverty, unwise consumer decisions', and he is eventually cast as the demon-king Ravana in a film of the *Ramayana*, achieving national celebrity with his 'strangely magnetic' portrayal (77). Imran's body materializes national anxieties about the reorganization of human–nature relations in neoliberal India: he is the spectre of repressed class struggle who returns to haunt Rajiv when he explodes Sapna's tower and liberates her, enacting a hybridized version of Ravana's theft of Sita, the Sleeping Beauty myth and the prince's rescue of Rapunzel.

Unaware that they are brother and sister, Sapna and Imran fall passionately in love, and Rajiv furiously re-imprisons them in an asylum. In the story's climax, the asylum explodes in a hypertrophic eruption of vegetation:

> Buds of bulging paintwork were appearing all over the walls: green shoots burst from them ... streaked through the ceiling, swelling into vast boughs of furrowed wood and ... lifting the entire asylum clean off the ground and carrying it aloft. ... The ring of trees wrenched the building in all directions; it opened like a flower, and its centre fell out and crashed to the ground. (86)

The revolt that had been prefigured in Rajiv's description of his telecom workers as insects is realized when the inmates flood into the city in an uncanny swarm: 'The asylum broke open like a wasp's nest, as white-robed pupae began to rain from it and wriggle away who knew where, ready to infiltrate the city and lay new eggs of their own in its fissures and sewers' (86). Here, the swarm is not merely an ecophobic expression of nature's revenge, but rather one of political and sexual movements that challenge the regulation of subjectivity within the neoliberal state: 'Thousands of people spread out into the dawn: they ... stripped off their clothes and jumped into a fountain where they splashed each other joyfully and clasped strangers to themselves in glee' (87). Dasgupta's ecoGothic incorporates the revolutionary energies of the diverse struggles of tribals, Maoists, peasants and women over land, food and resources in contemporary India, all of which are determined by an attempt to refashion human–nature relations and constitute what Joan Martinez-Alier has called the 'environmentalism of the poor'.[37] Just as soil exhaustion and the proliferation of peasant revolts heralded the collapse of feudalism, this outburst of revolt expresses the socio-ecological contradictions of neoliberalism, signifying the crisis and impending exhaustion of the current ecological regime, to which biotechnology cannot provide a satisfactory 'fix'.

The incestuous union of Sapna and Imran at the end of the tale parodies the artificial reconciliation of social contradictions in conventional Gothic narratives, traditionally achieved through marriage. But it could also be read as the subversive reunification of alienated spheres: the melding of the clones, the cleavage of divided classes and genders, the re-conscionization of nature–society relations. Their sexual intercourse is described as a violent rematerialization of biological interdependency: 'their groins heaved with the effort of penetrating all that separated them, as their bodies hinged extravagantly at their join' (89). The story refuses to project a return to a unifying paternal figure: instead, at the moment of their union, Rajiv is 'forced to abandon the idea of the future' and finally falls asleep for the first time in his life (89). In this story, instead of expressing the alienation of First World subjects and their delusions of plenitude, eco-monstrosity and transmutation represent how characters outside the core must somehow imagine radical transformations of themselves if they are to survive within the peripheries of the world-ecology. The monstrosity of the incestuous twins is not contained but rather celebrated, so that the real locus of horror in the story, and the novel as a whole, becomes the systemic violence of capital, not the alterity of human or extra-human nature.

Eschewing plot conclusions which re-erect acceptable forms of 'fairy-tale' reality to assuage the previous eruptions of a nightmarish Real, *Tokyo Cancelled* adopts irrealist aesthetics to stage the interplay between ideology and the conditions of real existence, where those events which seem most dream-like or surreal are those which are most real and felt. In Dasgupta's version of the ecoGothic, the resolution of social–ecological contradictions is complicated, producing ambivalent reconciliations that neither redeem the violence which has gone before nor expel the monstrous and reassert paternal authority. According to an interview with Dasgupta, the archaic plot structures of his Gothic tales bespeak an 'inadequacy' to represent the 'vast reality that is not quite their own', and the 'ancient comforts of fairytales' are deliberately represented as emerging into the twenty-first century 'somewhat mutilated and flat, displaying a wisdom that is either unclear or childishly naïve'.[38] In the ecoGothic corresponding to neoliberal capitalism, residual literary forms lose something of their force, having already been assimilated and recycled, and function as spectres of loss figuring commodified and exhausted ecologies and cultural formations. The banality of the frame narrative, with its indistinct characters and platitudinous dialogue, speaks to the difficulty of establishing a collective consciousness: unlike Chaucer's pre-capitalist pilgrims, the postmodern travellers have no sacred destination which yields meaning and closure, only the terminal 'in the Middle of Nowhere', a 'back corridor between worlds' (1). Yet the novel's form attempts to circumnavigate the paradox that surrounds the effort to describe the totality of the capitalist world-ecology, in which the more fully a writer represents a closed and terrifying system the more a reader is paralysed by feelings of the impossibility of revolt. The structure of the 'novel-in-fragments' demands a dialectical reading which correlates the parts in order to apprehend the whole, thus mirroring the systemic structures which connect peripheries and cores. Thus, the story-cycle represents the impact of abstract global processes in multiple world cities as local enchantments couched in catachrestic Gothic aesthetics that signal the limits of their ability to wholly apprehend the 'unspeakable', 'vast reality' of the world-ecology, even as they powerfully transmit its presence.

Notes

1 Max Horkheimer and Theodor Adorno, *The Dialectic of Enlightenment: Philosophical Fragments*, trans. Edmund Jephcott (Stanford, CA: Stanford University Press, 2003), p. 193.

2 Horkheimer and Adorno, *Dialectic of Enlightenment*, p. 193.

3 Adrian Ivakhiv, 'Stirring the Geopolitical Unconscious', *New Formations: Earthographies: Ecocriticism and Culture* 64 (2008): 98–109.

4 Ibid., p. 107.

5 Ibid., p. 101.

6 Ibid., p. 108.

7 Ibid., p. 99, original italics.

8 Jason Moore, 'Wall Street is a Way of Organizing Nature', *Upping the Anti: A Journal of Theory and Action* 12 (2011): 39–53, at p. 44.

9 Jason Moore, 'The End of the Road? Agricultural Revolutions in the Capitalist World-Ecology, 1450–2010', *Journal of Agrarian Change* 10/3 (2010): 389–413, at p. 405.

10 Moore, 'Wall Street is a Way of Organizing Nature', p. 46.

11 Moore, 'Wall Street is a Way of Organizing Nature', p. 44.

12 David Harvey, *The Enigma of Capital and the Crises of Capitalism* (Oxford: Oxford University Press, 2011), p. 185.

13 Karl Marx, *Capital: Volume III*, trans. David Fernbach (Harmondsworth: Penguin, 1981), p. 949.

14 See John Bellamy Foster, Brett Clark and Richard York, *The Ecological Rift* (London: Monthly Review Press, 2010).

15 Elizabeth DeLoughrey and George B. Handley, *Postcolonial Ecologies: Literatures of the Environment* (Oxford: Oxford University Press, 2011), p. 26.

16 Stephen Shapiro, 'Transvaal, Transylvania: Dracula's World-system and Gothic Periodicity', *Gothic Studies* 10/1 (2008): 24–47.

17 Stephen Shapiro, *The Culture and Commerce of the Early American Novel: Reading the Atlantic World-System* (University Park, PA: Penn State University Press, 2008), pp. 35, 303.

18 Michael Niblett, 'World-Economy, World-Ecology, World Literature', *Green Letters* 16 (2012): 15–20.

19 Rana Dasgupta, 'A New Bend in the River: The Future of the Indian Novel in English', *The National*, 26 February 2010, http://www.ranadasgupta.com/texts.asp?text_id=48 (accessed 25 June 2012).

20 Mike Davis, 'Magical Urbanism: Latinos Reinvent the US Big City', *New Left Review* I/234, (March–April 1999), http://newleftreview.org/I/234/mike-davis-magical-urbanism-latinos-reinvent-the-us-big-city (accessed 25 June 2012).

21 Fredric Jameson, *Postmodernism, or, the Cultural Logic of Late Capitalism* (Durham, NC: Duke University Press, 1991), p. 54.

22 Rana Dasgupta, 'Narrative Planes: Interview with Sarah Crown', *The Guardian*, 29 March 2005, http://www.ranadasgupta.com/notes.asp?note_id=50 (accessed 26 June 2012).

23 Dasgupta, 'Narrative Planes'.

24 Dasgupta, 'Narrative Planes'.

25 Dasgupta, 'Narrative Planes'.

26 See Michael Taussig, *The Devil and Commodity Fetishism in South America* (Chapel Hill: University of North Carolina Press, 1980).

27 See Kaushik Sunder Rajan, *Biocapital: The Constitution of Postgenomic Life*, (Durham, NC: Duke University Press, 2006).

28 See Vandana Shiva, *Biopiracy: The Plunder of Nature and Knowledge* (Boston: South End Press, 1999).

29 Moore, 'Wall Street is a Way of Organizing Nature', p. 44.

30 Paul Virilio, *Open Sky*, trans. Julie Rose (London: Verso, 1997), pp. 39–40.

31 Fred Botting, 'Aftergothic (Consumption, Machines, and Black Holes)', in Jerrold E. Hogle (ed.), *The Cambridge Companion to Gothic Fiction* (Cambridge: Cambridge University Press, 2002), pp. 277–300, p. 292.

32 Rana Dasgupta, *Tokyo Cancelled* (London: Harper Perennial, 2006), p. 112. Subsequent references are to this edition and are given in parentheses in the text.

33 Moore, 'Wall Street is a Way of Organizing Nature', p. 47.

34 Rana Dasgupta, 'Global Enchantment: Travis Elborough Talks to Rana Dasgupta', in *Tokyo Cancelled*, p. 17.

35 See Bruce Sterling, 'What is Next Nature', *Next Nature*, http://www.nextnature. net/2010/09/next-nature-intro-by-bruce-sterling/ (accessed 25 June 2012).

36 See Simon Estok, 'Theorizing in Space of Ambivalent Openness: Ecocriticism and Ecophobia', *ISLE* 16/2 (2009): 9–36.

37 See Joan Martinez-Alier, *The Environmentalism of the Poor* (Cheltenham: Edward Elgar, 2002).

38 Dasgupta, 'Global Enchantment', pp. 7–8.

Index